KATHARINE SCHERMAN

Spring
on an
Arctic Island

WITH ILLUSTRATIONS

Boston · Little, Brown and Company · *Toronto*

W

Published simultaneously in Canada
by Little, Brown & Company (Canada) Limited

PRINTED IN THE UNITED STATES OF AMERICA

Spring on an Arctic Island

The most beautiful thing one can experience is the mysterious. It is the source of all true art and science. He to whom this reaction is a stranger — who no longer can pause to wonder and stand wrapt in awe — is as good as dead, his eyes are closed.

ALBERT EINSTEIN

Foreword

THIS is the story of the unfolding of an arctic springtime, a subtle and exciting flowering which dwellers in the Temperate Zone can only fleetingly imagine — perhaps on an early morning in April. Woven through the story is the life, even less imaginable, of the Eskimo hunters in that cool northern world.

My husband and I and our friend Rosario Mazzeo organized a six weeks' scientific expedition in the summer of 1954 to Bylot Island, four hundred and fifty miles north of the Arctic Circle in the Canadian Eastern Arctic. It is a region where conditions — and possibly also man — are similar to those of the last ice age of Europe and North America.

We three are amateur ornithologists with some knowledge of wilderness camping. None of us had been in the far north, and we had a consuming curiosity about the humans and animals that can live in such inhospitable surroundings. However, one cannot build a trip to the arctic simply on curiosity. In order that our venture should be a scientific success we had to include men who knew the ways of the north and its creatures. Five of the eight members of the expedition, therefore, were trained scientists with experience in northern field work. Our journey was sponsored by the New York Zoological Society and the Arctic Institute of North America. These organizations gave every cooperation in getting our party safely and easily up to the unknown wilderness of Bylot Island.

From reports of people who had touched on Bylot Island in the course of northern journeys we had learned that this lonely and mountainous place is a favorite nesting ground for some thirty species of birds, many of which do not breed any further south. A multitude of hardy flowering plants carpet its uninviting tundra and we could expect to find insects — flies, mosquitoes, beetles, spiders, even bees and butterflies — colonizing the desolate countryside and basking in the twenty-four-hour-a-day sunshine.

The scientists, therefore, planned a combined and intensive study of the wildlife on a small area of the island's tundra barrens and coastal waters. The comparatively low number of species and the clearly visible relationships between them on this open, undisturbed land made Bylot Island an ideal choice for such a short-term ecological study. Valuable data might be collected on the relations of plants, mammals, birds and insects to one another; their adaptation to the short spring season with its permanent sunlight; their even more surprising adaptation to ice-age conditions, permanent frost underground and frequent below-freezing temperatures above.

This book is not a digest of the scientists' findings — it is a personal record. We left New York a little frightened and more than a little ignorant. We left Bylot Island six weeks later with the sense that we were leaving the happiest and most peaceful world we had ever known. We had learned the serene timelessness of the long, long day (the sun does not set for three months at that latitude), the exhilaration of hunting through the cold, pale-gold night, the low-toned beauty and myriad small life of the treeless tundra, the tense drama of travel over rotting, drifting sea ice.

Above all we got to know some Eskimos. The natives of this sparsely settled region have been exposed to small doses of white civilization for only thirty years, and the questionable influence of our mores has not penetrated very deeply. The Eskimos there are still, as they have always been, hunters of the seal, the walrus, the narwhal and, when they can find some, the caribou. Being hunter-predators, they are both cause and victim of the fluctuating balance of nature, and, as with wild animals, nature is their only government. Closely attuned to their origins, they are yet intelligent, gentle, trustful, merry: man as he should be — as perhaps he was before he started progressing.

We came at the beginning of the flowering and breeding season and we stayed until its end. The creatures of the arctic unfolded themselves to us gradually, like characters in a novel, and I have written their stories as I saw them develop — with constant, incalculable help from the scientists of the expedition, who interpreted, explained and classified as we went along. It was an adventure in ecology. But six weeks were not enough. The dry tundra, glaciers, icy coastal waters and wild black mountains of the seventy-third parallel on Baffin Bay are not only beautiful and exciting — they are nearly untouched fields of scientific research. So this account is full of question marks — for the next set of adventurers.

It must be noted that my firsthand knowledge of arctic people is restricted to the small group of Baffin Island Eskimos who visited us and traveled with us and to the seven white men who lived at Pond Inlet on Baffin Island, twenty miles south of our camp across the sea ice; and, further, that the firsthand naturalist observations here recorded can be applied with accuracy only to Bylot and northern Baffin islands.

Knowing that our five scientists would publish complete and careful analyses of the results of their observations, I have avoided technical language and detail. But I am deeply indebted to all of them, as much for their gay companionship as for their unstinting generosity with their knowledge.

The expedition members were:

Josselyn Van Tyne, of the Museum of Zoology at the University of Michigan, who studied the courting, feeding and nesting habits of the tundra-breeding birds, collected specimens of them and made up the skins for his museum.

William Drury, of the Biology Department at Harvard University, who studied the relationship of bird and plant life, the effects of frost on soil and vegetation and the mysterious geological phenomena of frost action. He also collected plants for the Gray Herbarium at Harvard University.

Richard Miller, of the Biology Department at Harvard University, who studied insect populations and collected specimens of insects for museums throughout the United States. He also collected data, with the help of Eskimo hunters and Hudson's Bay Company records, on the interdependence of mammals, including man, in this underpopulated, delicately balanced world.

Dr. Benjamin Ferris, of the School of Public Health at Harvard University, who studied the physiology of the Eskimos of northern Baffin Island. He also kept the weather chart. And, with Edward Ames, he made a week's exploratory trip into Bylot Island's uncharted mountains.

Edward Ames, senior at Harvard University, who assisted

Dr. Drury and made botanical collections, with particular attention to mosses and lichens.

Mary Drury, Dr. Drury's wife, who helped organize and manage our big household. She also kept daily records of every one of the sixty-five pairs of breeding birds whose fortunes we followed.

The nearest white settlement was Pond Inlet, and its inhabitants — two Hudson's Bay Company traders, two constables of the Royal Canadian Mounted Police and three missionaries, one Anglican and two Catholic — were ever cheerful, generous and peaceful of mind. They have our warmest gratitude for their help to the Outsiders, the newcomers to their quiet world. The one who most showed us the true and selfless and casual kindness of the arctic was Pete Murdoch, the senior factor of the Hudson's Bay Company there, who helped immeasurably in making the expedition run smoothly. From him, also, I learned most of the folklore and legends of the Baffin Island Eskimos which are here recorded, and he helped me to understand the customs and thought patterns of these gentle people whose world is so far removed from ours.

Heartfelt thanks and admiration go to those remarkable air pilots, Mr. Patterson of Arctic Wings and Mr. Allard of Mont Laurier, and their intrepid crews, who got us safely if excitingly there and back.

The Hudson's Bay Company was most helpful in arranging for the purchase and transport of much of our equipment. We owe thanks, not only to the company, but to its individual employees who aided us continually with that generous spirit of kindness peculiar to the north.

What can we say to Idlouk, the proud and gay hunter who was our guide and lived with us? He and his family taught us what it was like to be "uncivilized" — to laugh at misfortune and difficulty, to relax and let the long, slow northern peace enter the heart, to observe every facet of the unceasing, subtle life of tundra and sea ice, to be always generous, gracious and tactful. Idlouk lived in the springtime of mankind, and for a short time he took us back there with him. The best thanks we can give him is to return the unself-conscious and high-hearted friendship with which he honored us.

Axel, my husband, was my constant, kind and thoughtful companion, who calmed me down and cheered me up and always made me feel good. I wouldn't have gone to Bylot Island without him; I wouldn't have written this book without him.

Contents

List of Illustrations

Spring on an Arctic Island

1

Back to the Ice Age

IT was one of the loveliest of June days. The sky looked soft and the sun was gentle. The sentimental fragrance of white roses and honeysuckle filled the garden. Peonies drooped with their own heaviness and white petals of syringa lay on the thick green grass like snowflakes.

In a few hours my husband and I would be on a plane to Canada and within three days we would be in a land devoid of trees, covered with ice and snow. It seemed a surprising objective on this flowery day. Trailed by our two little girls, who had not any idea what "arctic" meant, we wandered once more around the garden — drinking in great drafts of trees, green grass, hot sun, and worrying about everything. The pear tree was thick with tiny pears. Soon the squirrels would be eating them. The young tomato plants were healthy, but who would water them in the inevitable July drought? There were gooseberries for at least seventy-five pies. They would fall off their bushes or be eaten by birds. The ancient white oak had a branch hanging dangerously low and heavy over our neighbor's house. Would it fall in a high wind? We filled our eyes with the big white oak. . . .

Bylot Island, the lonely land of our dreams, our plans and now, suddenly, our fears, is a squarish island about the size of Connecticut. It lies just northeast of the top of Baffin Island, on the seventy-third parallel. To its east is Baffin Bay and four hundred and fifty miles across the water is Greenland.

The island was discovered in 1616 by William Baffin and Robert Bylot. Bylot had been on the ship *Discovery*, captained by Henry Hudson on his final, fatal attempt to find a northwest sea passage, and he had participated in the brutal mutiny in which Hudson and eight others were set adrift in a small boat in arctic waters. Escaping punishment, Bylot was later made captain of the same ship, the *Discovery*, for another attempt to find a way westward through the eternal pack ice. With the capable Baffin, an able explorer and scientist, as first mate and navigator, the *Discovery* sailed up through Baffin Bay to the frozen, unknown islands of the American arctic, making her way further north than had any previous ship.

After the discoveries of this ambitious pair everyone was too busy looking for a northwest passage to pay any attention to the barren, mountainous islands on Baffin Bay's western shore. But in the eighteenth century Dutch and British whalers ventured west and found Baffin Bay a fertile ground for the enormous, gentle Greenland whale. The whalers were in and out of the Eastern Arctic Archipelago for a hundred years until they managed to bring the Greenland whale to the verge of extinction, early in the nineteenth century. For nearly another hundred years, then, the Eastern Arctic was a closed and unknown land. But the European sailors had left their blood strains among the native tribes and their bones in shallow graves all over the islands. Faint memories of them still remain in the Scottish Highlander airs, Irish jigs and English folk songs danced and sung by the primitive Baffin Island Eskimos.

At one time there were a few Eskimos living on Bylot Island. It was a land rich in game — fox, bear, goose and above all the vital, plentiful caribou. But the grassy lowlands that supported the deer were too near the shore, and hunters could get at them easily. When the Eskimos took to using repeating rifles instead of bows and arrows the caribou were doomed. Some of the herds moved to inaccessible inland grazing grounds on northern Baffin Island. The last of the remaining Bylot Island deer were exterminated in 1942, and the Eskimos deserted the island. They still lay trap lines there in the winter for white fox and ermine, but their permanent stone and wood igloos are on Baffin Island, across narrow Eclipse Sound. Depending for their livelihood almost entirely on creatures of the coastal waters — seal, walrus, narwhal and bear — they are not migratory.

Except for the coastal area, Bylot Island is unmapped and unexplored. One white man, Patrick D. Baird, crossed its southeast corner three years ago by dog sled. On the way he climbed (also by dog sled) a mountain which he believed to be Bylot Island's highest peak, Mt. Thule, about six thousand feet. From Thule he saw a multitude of inland peaks, a forbidding black and white wilderness of mountains. Air photographs, which we studied carefully, show a narrow stretch of beach, in some places disappearing entirely where sharp black cliffs come straight down to the sea. Immense glaciers pour eternally from the towering inland peaks — primeval ice seamed with ancient crevasses. Rivers from these glaciers have formed deep canyons, but at their mouths they widen into shallow deltas filled with silt. The sea beyond these deltas shows pale gray in the photographs, where the rivers are gradually carrying Bylot Island's hills down into the ocean.

5

Rolling tundra, barren and monotoned, lies over the foot-hills of the fearsome black mountains.

Our island is at the northern limit of Eskimo civilization on the North American continent. These far northern tundra bar-rens and wild mountains are too inhospitable even for Eskimos! We were likely to find ourselves completely isolated. Since we were going to a land where there were none of the ac-couterments of civilization — not a house, not a telephone, not a stick of wood for fuel, nothing to eat except what we brought with us — we were prepared for the most inclement and uncomfortable conditions.

Our equipment included about three thousand pounds of canned and dehydrated foods; twenty gallons of gasoline and ten gallons of kerosene; six small primus stoves and one two-burner Coleman stove; many tents — for sleeping in, for eat-ing in, for carrying up mountains, for housing the taxidermy shop, for pressing plants; an awesome trunkful of medical equipment; a shovel and an ax (what would we chop down with an ax? — the nearest tree was eleven hundred miles away); snowshoes, ice axes, climbing rope, willow stakes, three walky-talky radios; traps for small mammals, fishing equipment, rifles, shotguns and enough ammunition to sup-port a big-game hunting operation in the jungles of Africa; hundreds of pounds of woolen and weatherproof clothing.

I also brought along a soprano recorder, on which to pipe tunes to the unresponsive wilderness.

Maybe Eskimos couldn't live on Bylot Island. But if they cared to come calling they would find some pretty fancy camping there. . . .

Now, at last, dressed in ski pants, mountain boots and flan-nel shirts and carrying knapsacks, ice axes and snowshoes, we walked outside into the dreaming summer day and turned our faces north, toward the unknown.

We flew to Ottawa, where our chartered plane, a DC-3, of Arctic Wings, was waiting for us. We saw it first in the middle of the night. It loomed monstrous in a dark, lonesome field where the soft summer wind rippled the long grass and the moon shone dimly. Inside, by the light of a flash, we saw a hopeless tangle of baggage — crates, duffels, plane tires, gasoline drums. Along one side was a narrow, uncomfortable-looking metal bench. This flying boxcar was to be our home for the next two or three days. It was to fly us over the tundra, through the unmapped mountain wilderness of the Eastern Arctic and land us — on wheels! — on the frozen, snow-covered ocean.

All that night we flew north over Canada's deep spruce woods. There were fifteen people in the plane and in the darkness no one knew who anyone else was, though we kept tripping over one another. At intervals we tried to sleep — some curled uncomfortably on the metal bucket seats, some high up near the ceiling on the softer parts of the luggage, some on the floor. I chose the floor. The space was so narrow that I touched on both sides, baggage on one side, bucket seat on the other. Too cold and uncomfortable to sleep, I practiced recorder fingerings in my mind. My last waking thought was: my feet will be cold for seven weeks. (They were.)

I awoke in the dim dawn to see an immense figure spread-eagled above me. It was Josselyn Van Tyne, our six-foot-seven ornithologist, reaching across the baggage for a Fig Newton. I closed my eyes again, but opened them instantly, to see a large, cleated, mountain boot making directly for my face. It halted in mid-air, then went on, missing me by an inch. It

7

was morning, time to get up. Breakfast was three Fig New-tons.

We landed at Kapuskasing and stepped out of the plane into a pure and lovely dawn. The air was clear and dry, the sun dazzling in the thin northern atmosphere. In every direction stretched flat miles of forest and the air was filled with a strange, sweet smell — that of an old French church, dim, cool, soaked with centuries of incense. This nostalgic con-notation could not be reconciled with the open, vast, empty northern woods shimmering in the cold, bright air. Balsam poplar, we were told, produced the sophisticated fragrance. It was a scent to store in the memory, to take to the treeless barrens.

Gradually, as we flew north, the trees thinned out and we came to the edge of the permafrost, or tundra. This is land which is permanently frozen hundreds of feet down. Only a thin top layer has a chance to thaw during the brief summer, so only small, creeping, shallow-rooted plants can grow there, and mosses and lichens. There was not yet much of it and it showed as patches of brownish, dead-looking areas between the trees, as if the land had leprosy. We began to see drumlins — elongated hills and lakes pointing north and south, straight as rulers, where the slow-moving glacier had grooved the land — and strangmoors — wavering, stringlike peat ridges, formed by a slow, mysterious action of frost on earth.

Usually I dislike looking at scenery from an airplane, wish-ing rather to be down there in the middle of it. But this was scenery which no one would want to be in the middle of. It was dead and horrible country, ancient sea bottom, wet, for-bidding, full of mosquitoes and quaking bogs. Nobody could live there, our pilot told us, and it was not good for anything.

Its stunted spruces were too thin for logging, its soil too soggy for farming. There were no minerals to speak of and trapping was almost impossible due to the difficulty of getting around. Besides, hardly any animals lived there.

What a fearful country to be lost in. But a party of nine men had recently been lost down there, we learned. Their plane had crash-landed and for more than a month they had crept around in circles trying to find a way out of the labyrinth of mosquito-ridden marshes, living on berries and a few birds. I got a volume of Chekhov stories out of a knapsack and tried not to look at the scenery.

"Look at the rabbits," said Axel.

"What?" I shouted over the noise of the plane.

"Rabbits," he shouted back. I looked down and saw nothing except two canallike lakes with an unimpressive waterfall between them.

"Rapids," Axel repeated in my ear. Wanting so much to see a living creature in the deadness below, I had almost purposely misunderstood him.

But the earth's history was written over the bald landscape. One could almost remember the Keewatin Glacier, a mile thick, scraping heavily down the land, paring it flat, leaving its long, deep tracks. The thin black lines of the strangmoors, whose causation no one knows, many centuries old and still in the process of formation, wandered across the tawny bogs like forms on a mathematician's graph. The peat bogs and the stagnant lakes that had once been ocean slowly gave up their water to the relentless sun. The last of the trees, thin and unhappy, eked out a miserable existence in the poor, shallow soil.

The barren permafrost areas gradually ate up the landscape

9

as we moved north. The tundra was full of stagnant puddles with tawny-colored bogs along their shores: the country was soggy and arid at the same time. Since there is little air circulation over the vast, flat inland stretches of Canada's tundra the rainfall is slight — less than that of the Sahara desert. But the land is always wet. With a bed of impermeable frozen soil the water cannot sink into the earth, nor can it run off the flat surface. The weather is so cold that there is little evaporation, so all the moisture in the earth is used, and the low plant cover is comparatively lush. But if the climate should become warmer and the permafrost melt, as they say it has been doing lately, the Canadian tundra might become a vast desert, the biggest on earth.

Then there was a new sight in the misty distance — the old shore line of Hudson Bay. The water of this inland sea has receded during many centuries, and the ancient beaches rise in a series of rippled, terraced ridges. Beyond the ridges we could see a thin white line, the bay itself, still frozen. Shortly after that we circled low over Churchill, a collection of shacks and frame houses, the northern edge of the tree line, where the north truly begins.

This port, the end of the Canadian National Railways, is the oldest settlement in Canada's north. It was founded three centuries ago by the adventurous seafaring son of a Danish nobleman. Now it is an important town, the center of commerce for the Eastern Arctic. Boats laden with fur and minerals from the far north put in at its docks. Eleven million bushels of prairie wheat left it last year, bound for Europe. Other boats leave there loaded with gasoline, flour, sugar, print dresses and Bibles for the convenience and edification of the scattered arctic population. In Churchill Indian and

Eskimo meet, without friendliness. The Eskimos traditionally despise the Indians (*Irkrelret* — "Lice") and the Indians fear the barbaric little northern men (*Eskimo* is Indian for "Eaters of Raw Meat.")

Churchill was a scattered, unattractive collection of shacks built carelessly on the surface of frozen mud and pre-Cambrian rock. This hard, tired, featureless rock, two billion years old, was the substance of the earth's surface before there was any life.

Telephone poles leaned at a forty-five degree angle, held in the shallow earth by triangles of poles and networks of guy wires. Furs of wolf and bear hung, enormous, on back-yard fences. Eskimo and Indian children stared at us, expressionless, dark-faced and unhealthy-looking. The Hudson's Bay Company storeroom was hung with beautiful, shimmering furs, while in its front room the store offered the shoddy accouterments of our civilization at fantastically high prices.

Underfoot was mostly mud and the few patches of grass were dead gray. The snow had come off, we were told, only two weeks before, and nothing had started to grow yet. The bay was silent and white and the temperature was that of New York in January.

But it was clearly springtime. At ten in the evening in the light of the golden sun, low over the bay, a wealth of little birds sang and soared and scrabbled in the dead grass. Lapland longspurs, ubiquitous and tame as English sparrows at home, filled the air with their trilling song. Brilliantly black and white snow buntings sat on the tops of poles and sang their hearts out. These brave, noisy, proud-plumaged birds seemed no relation to the drab, pale snow buntings that drift in silent flocks over the winter dune grass at Jones Beach.

Early the next morning we took off again. At the edge of the airport we saw the last outpost of trees, a thin line of scraggly white spruces. Beyond them lay the arctic barrens, thousands of miles of snow, ice, rock and tundra, unsullied by a tree. For the first time, as I looked ahead over the limitless, lonely land, I had a sense of exaltation.

Now we were over Hudson Bay. The ice was an enormous, cracked expanse, gleaming like polished steel, hurting the eyes, and the whole horizon was white from reflected ice. Here and there we saw drifted snow in geometric wind patterns, looking like huge triangular footprints. Sometimes there were patches of fog below us, more brilliant and blinding white than the ice, and occasionally we passed over open water. In the sun it was of deepest, purest blue, flecked with tiny pieces of ice that looked like whitecaps.

The plane stopped briefly at Coral Harbor on Southampton Island. We half expected white beaches, coconut palms and barracuda. But it was a drear stretch of flat brown-gray tundra with snow peeling off in dirty strips. It contained a Canadian air forces and communications post with a little recreation hut labeled SOUTHAMPTON INN: GUESTS WELCOME. Around the hut drift snow was piled to the roof.

"When will summer come here?" we asked.

"This is summer," they said.

The tundra was lifeless and terrible. Where the snow had melted off there was a thin, slippery layer of mud with absolute iron hardness underneath. In a few places the sun had dried the land and there one walked in a halo of stifling dust. The twelve men who were posted there for six months to two years felt imprisoned by the dead, unmoving land. But there was a saving grace — the bay. It gave them a feeling that they could get away, or that anyway they could rest their eyes on something that could get away, something that could move.

We took off again and I looked into the distance and saw mountains. I gazed at them with ecstasy and a feeling of homecoming. But they were only cloud formations. Below us the land grew icier. No longer were there large patches of open tundra, but snow lay everywhere. We were clearly flying into the ice age. How could anything live here?

Suddenly there were really mountains — black cliffs glimpsed through drifting clouds. Excitedly we crowded to the windows, setting our cameras and calling out light-meter readings. Then dead ahead was a tremendous black wall. We were headed straight for it. We veered off at what seemed like fifteen feet and entered a deep, rocky gorge — Oliver Sound, on northern Baffin Island. We cruised between fearful crags which towered darkly above us. Axel, who had been up front with the pilot, came back to tell me that most of the mountains of northern Baffin Island were inaccurately marked on the maps. The pilot had pointed out to him a mountain on his left labeled fifteen hundred feet on the map. Then he had showed him the altimeter. It read thirty-five hundred feet, and the mountain peak soared above us.

But Pat Patterson was an extraordinarily able, practiced pilot, one of a brave breed. Depending entirely on their own observation and judgment, the Canadian pilots of the bush and tundra are among the best in the world. They have to be. Maps of this wild country are inaccurate and radio contact is infrequent and unreliable. Landing fields are rough sea ice, pocket-handkerchief lakes, marshy tundra or spruce-dotted badlands. Compasses are useless because of the proximity of the magnetic pole. Planes must therefore fly close to the land in order to keep their bearings — and this land near which we flew, almost caressing it with our wing tips, was seamed with rocky gorges and sudden mountains, and often shrouded in fog.

But Patterson had a quick eye and a cool head. He and his crew were as much at home in a plane in the unmapped wastes of the arctic mountains as I am on a bicycle on the roads around my home. Knowing this, one could watch the wild scenery with a sense of exhilaration enhanced by danger.

"Sit down!" someone called sharply, and at that moment the plane dipped with startling suddenness. We scrambled for seats and seat belts and hung on tensely, not moving, making small, nervous jokes as the plane circled over Pond Inlet. There was a glimpse of a tiny row of red-roofed houses and an infinity of rough-looking sea ice with shreds of mist flying over it.

Eskimos, we had been told, would lay out a line of blackened jute bags to mark the smoothest spot on the ice. The pilot brought the plane low, searching for the landing strip. Instantly we were enveloped in dense, cottony fog. For agonizing seconds the plane almost scraped the ice as the pilot tried to see through the cloud. Then we swooped upward suddenly and started circling again.

Three times more the plane dipped low and the ice came up to meet us sideways, frighteningly close and looking like frozen surf. The fourth time we saw some tiny black dots on the whiteness — the loveliest sight in the world — our landing strip! Again we closed in on the ice. The perspective was so strange in the absolute whiteness that it seemed we were still several hundred feet in the air when we hit. There was a series of soft bumps, and we stopped. It was not quite so smooth as Idlewild, but we were there.

I I
Pond Inlet

WE climbed out of the plane and stood quietly for a few minutes, trying to adjust from the tense drama of our landing to
the misty, silent world around us. We were enveloped in
deepest winter. Soft snow was falling, making no sound as it
blended into the soft snow underfoot. About a mile away was
Pond Inlet, a row of white frame houses, green-trimmed and
red-roofed, and a smaller line of white tents to one side. Bylot
Island towered across frozen Eclipse Sound, immensely bigger than we had expected, with wide, seamed glaciers leading
back into the grim, frowning mountains. The white world lay
in utter stillness, as if it had just been created.

Then in the distance began a strange, high, musical howling. At first there was one voice alone, rising and falling, the
very soul of loneliness. Others joined until there must have
been a hundred voices interweaving in a wailing, eerie harmony. Dogs, we supposed — but not like any dogs we had
ever heard. They sounded like the dead souls of dogs. At the
edge of Pond Inlet something dark was moving on the snow.
Slowly we began to distinguish outlines of peaked hoods,
dozens of them.

The moonlike scenery, the weird howling of dog spirits,
the little white-hooded figures approaching us slowly across

the snow did not belong in any real world. We had been whisked without ceremony into the middle of an ancient legend.

Then suddenly they were upon us in a galloping rush — a mass of huge, furry dogs, five or six sleds, several dozen Eskimos grinning happily under their white, furred hoods, two or three white men. Many children had come out to see the strange machine. They were wide-faced, red-cheeked, shy yet vivacious. Whenever we looked at them they giggled. There were young women, very small, with dark, quiet, Oriental faces. When they caught one's eye they lit up with wide, sweet smiles, but they seemed even shyer than the children. Their snowy white parkas were beautifully embroidered with many-colored wools, and babies peeped out of the voluminous hoods, their faces startlingly pale.

The little Eskimo men (hardly more than five feet tall) scurried around like elves. Laughing and shouting to one another, they had our four thousand pounds of equipment out of the plane within a few minutes. Without appearing to strain a muscle, they lifted immense crates on their shoulders and slung them easily onto the long, narrow sleds. If one of us was caught struggling awkwardly with a heavy duffel an Eskimo gently took it, with a smile, and carried it in one hand to a sled.

Dogs lay everywhere, attentive and suspicious, their long traces a dark tangle on the snow. Almost as big as timber wolves, they had a striking similarity to their wild ancestors. Their dense fur had subtle shadings of gray, amber and brown and they had wide, heavy heads with slit eyes and alert ears. Long, plumy tails curled over their backs. As they waited they sometimes howled, sometimes snarled and started to fight for no visible reason. A single sharp sound from an Eskimo and they slunk apart, tails low.

The white men sorted themselves out. Doug Moodie of the Royal Canadian Mounted Police was a big, slow-moving, graceful man dressed in a loose dark-blue parka, decorated at the hem with colorful braid, and boots of silvery sealskin with cuffs of heavy white wool, brilliantly embroidered. Pete Murdoch, the senior Hudson's Bay Company trader, was lean and young and blue-eyed, with red hair faded by sun and weather and a look of friendly eagerness. He wore a fitted jacket of sealskin, intricately pieced together, and trousers of the same shadow-patterned fur. The men of the north, beside our bedraggled, wrinkled, dun-colored party, were decidedly dandies. The third white man, dressed in a long black robe, was Father Danielo, a French Catholic missionary with sparkling eyes and a big red beard flecked with white.

A new sled arrived. Its Eskimo driver dismounted and waved his thirty-foot-long whip slowly a few times in front of the dogs, murmuring a long, low-voiced "Whoa-o-o." They watched him closely, then, unafraid but obedient, slowly lay down, ears alert. As the new arrival approached us the other Eskimos fell back in unconscious deference. This Eskimo was even smaller than the others and he was thin, frail-looking and not young. His dark face was bony and extremely Mongolian in structure. He wore glasses and carried a camera slung around his neck. His white parka, decorated with colored braid, was spotless and its hood was lined with soft red dog fur. On his breast gleamed a gold medal.

At first glance this little Eskimo was not impressive, and

the medal, camera and glasses were incongruous. But clearly written on his face were wisdom, kindness, humor and a searching intelligence.

Axel was the first to recognize him — Idlouk, the most famous Eskimo of the Northwest Territories; whose life had recently been celebrated in a movie; who had received one of the only two Coronation medals given in the arctic to Eskimos outstanding among their people; who was the star hunter and acknowledged leader of the Tunnunermiut tribe, the two hundred and twenty-seven Eskimos of the Pond Inlet area. Idlouk was to be our guide and hunter during our six weeks on Bylot Island.

Axel stepped forward immediately to greet him. Idlouk removed one sealskin mitt and shook hands formally. He gave Axel a searching look with his keen, wise eyes, but his face gleamed with happiness and pride that he had been recognized. He then shook hands all around, probing each of us with those dark, bright eyes that missed nothing. At the same time he smiled widely, showing large white teeth. He apparently knew no language but his own.

The sleds were loaded, the huge crates tied on with sealskin thongs. The dogs stood up, stretched themselves, looked around expectantly. Idlouk gave me a kind smile and motioned me to his sled. I smiled back at him and perched on the crates, which were covered by a heavy white polar-bear skin. It occurred to me that for six weeks we were probably going to converse entirely in smiles. The others climbed onto the high-laden sleds, there were some low grunts from the Eskimo drivers, brief flicks of the long whips — and the heavy sleds slid quietly over the soft snow. The dogs, about fifteen to each sled, trotted easily, their long traces hardly taut.

I looked back at our bright red and silver plane, lost and out of place in the vast, primitive whiteness. We had come to the north like a thunderbolt out of heaven on man's most modern machine. And we were immediately transferred to the most primitive of conveyances, drawn by creatures whose second cousins were wolves and guided by men of the Stone Age. The plane was clearly an anachronism.

But we, whisked so rudely back to the springtime of mankind, felt quite at ease. Even during those first few minutes of the north we felt the considerateness with which the Eskimos handled us. We had to be taken care of, they realized — we were not going to be very efficient in this world of real men. With unthinking kindness they set out to help us, to educate us, to coddle and spoil us as if we were children. Stone Age Man, we felt immediately, was a great improvement on Atomic Age Man.

Pond Inlet's white men, too, had this spontaneous kindness. We were welcomed like long-lost brothers and sisters, invited to partake of pies and fresh bread baked that afternoon especially for us, invited to stay the night and for as many days as we wished.

"But we don't want to take your beds," we said, looking around the tiny Hudson's Bay Company house.

"Oh, that's all right," said Bren Halloran, the HBC's second man, a dark-haired, gentle-faced boy of about nineteen. "I slept last night."

"We only sleep every other night," Pete explained, smiling. "And after all, we can't have ladies sleeping on the floor."

He added shyly, "You are the first white women I have seen in five years."

Mary Drury, the other girl of our party, looked at me silently and we both cringed. Mary sneaked out to the bedroom. I followed and found her before the mirror.

"If he hasn't seen a white woman in five years," she said, "the least I can do is comb my hair." But femininity, I realized ruefully, looking in the mirror, was not going to be our strong point. How can anybody look pretty in a flannel shirt, two sweaters, baggy ski pants, cleated boots and a man's eiderdown coat reaching to the knees, shapeless and unbelted. For the next weeks we were going to look like overstuffed horsehair sofas.

The HBC house was small and attractive, with deep, soft chairs and bright-flowered cretonne curtains. (But this was modest, Pete told us. At his last post he had had curtains made all of silverjar sealskins.) A cabinet was filled with soapstone and walrus-ivory carvings made by Eskimos, graceful and realistic small figures of animals and hunters. A great coal-burning stove provided a fearsome amount of heat for the whole house. We sat in the wondrously hot kitchen eating warm, newly baked bread and raisin and apple pies that Pete had made himself. Eskimos wandered in and out, staring and smiling. Pete talked to them in their own language and his clipped Scottish burr disappeared entirely when he spoke the lilting Eskimo phrases. It was a singing, softly guttural language, flowing like low music.

Under the influence of warmth and food we grew sleepy. But there was no question of going to bed. After all the day was twenty-four hours long. In fact it was four months long.

We began to have our first taste of the timelessness of the north.

Suddenly the telephone rang. What a distasteful sound! Somebody calling to ask me to sell tickets for a benefit, I thought involuntarily. But it was only the police, inviting us to their house to have some more to eat. There were only two telephones in Pond Inlet, said Pete. They connected the HBC house with the RCMP house.

Why? The two houses were about a hundred yards apart.

"So that I can call up and ask Doug, 'How's your fire?' and he can say, 'Fine, come on over and have some coffee.'"

"That is the only good use for a telephone," I said.

We did as we were told, and talked and ate and drank for another hour with the constables. At midnight we went outside to say good-by to Pat Patterson. Our remarkable pilot was about to take off, after only a few hours' rest, for the long, weary trip south.

But nothing happened. The plane remained deserted out on the ice and we stood in a loose knot on the snow-covered beach, sleepy and cold. It had stopped snowing but the low, fog-shrouded sun gave no heat. Eskimos stared at us, curious but friendly. We stared back at them, also curious and friendly. Children whispered and giggled. I saw a woman sitting on the roof of a shack, surrounded by five little children. She was chewing a sealskin. I thought it was an odd thing to do at midnight and took a picture of her. She posed self-consciously and gave me one of the loveliest smiles I had ever seen. She was Kidla, I was told, Idlouk's wife.

Two young white men wandered down the beach and we were introduced to them — pleasant government geologists looking for minerals. I hoped secretly that they would not find any.

At one o'clock the plane was still there and looked as if it were going to put down roots. So we tramped tiredly back to the HBC house and had sandwiches and coffee. Pete felt like talking. The Eskimos were much interested in us, he said, as they saw few strangers from Outside. Only six planes had ever landed at Pond Inlet and many of the natives had never seen a plane before ours landed.

The ways of Outsiders appeared to them peculiar and off-balance. To look at small birds — that was a strange way to spend one's time. And why bother to take a picture of a woman sitting on a roof chewing sealskin? All Eskimo wives always chewed sealskin. If one were lucky enough to have a roof to sit on and the sun was bright at midnight, why not get a little work done in the fresh air?

But they were eager to help us, he continued, even if they thought we were a little crazy. They wanted to know more about us and the work we planned to do. They had even begun to give us Eskimo names. With the simplicity and directness of children Eskimos give everyone descriptive appellations. Sometimes these are sly insults or mockery, sometimes they are merely physical descriptions. They did not know us yet, so our new names only pointed out salient physical features. Josselyn Van Tyne, the very tall ornithologist, was Eveeshago, a long, slender fish. This description of the wise and gentle professor was to stick to him for the whole six weeks. Ben Ferris, the doctor, was Shoologali, Long Feather, on account of the impudently big feather he wore in his broad-brimmed black felt hat. I did not yet have a name. I was simply "Idlouk's woman," because I had come to Pond Inlet on his sled. Mary, by the same token, was "Kudlu's woman."

I looked out the window as Pete talked. Though it was two o'clock in the morning the sun was still above the mountainous Bylot horizon. It shone, low and pale, through a thin mist. How delightful to have daylight all night long! I was full of sleepy exaltation at the pure, light air, the shadowed mountains across the inlet, the changing gold of the sea ice. Pete noticed my silent gaze. It was a view he never tired of, he told me, though he had watched it now through five years of winter darkness and summer light. For a few white men, evidently, the bleak, inclement north was full of beauty.

The talk slowed, grew sleepier, stopped altogether, then started again, murmuring. They did not want us to go to bed. They had so little company, these kind and lonely men of the far north, that they wanted to keep us with them forever. But we gradually drifted off, unable to stay awake any longer. I laid out my sleeping bag in the airless storeroom, which was also Pete's photographic darkroom. Axel lay down in the middle of the living room and slept amid the murmur of conversation. Bill and Mary Drury had Pete's room. The others found sofas, chairs, floor space. There were many more people than beds in Pond Inlet that night.

Surrounded by films, enlarger, hypo bottles, stacks of pilot biscuits, cans of orange marmalade and an impressive array of spices and herbs, I slowly fell asleep. Dimly I heard the roar of the plane as it took off, down to another world.

Four or five hours later I was awakened from a heavy sleep

by the insistent ringing of a church bell. Hundreds of dog voices joined, mocking it, entwined in mysterious, primitive harmony.

I had not the faintest idea what I was doing lying on the floor in a sleeping bag. Level with my eyes were a dozen boxes of Shredded Wheat. Why were they in my room? Or in the plane, I suddenly thought, beginning to remember. With difficulty I figured backwards, trying to learn what day this was.

"This is the twelfth of June," I told myself sternly. "The day we are moving over to our island." I got out my ever-handy little notebook and wrote it down. I am not so absent-minded as this sounds. We were already learning how difficult it was to distinguish night from day and one day from the next in this timeless, relaxed world, and we clung almost desperately to clocks and calendars. Later on we wouldn't care.

A leisurely breakfast was going on in the overheated kitchen. After an hour or so of burned toast and strong coffee we walked out into a warm, sunny morning. We had planned to get an early start. But it did not look as if anyone had any intention of ever going anywhere. All the Eskimos were apparently still asleep, the wooden doors of their white tents tightly shut. Hundreds of dogs lay chained, some asleep, some quietly scratching. The long, narrow wooden sleds were abandoned at the edge of the sea, where the tides had pushed the sea into wild, wrecked ridges. Our mountainous baggage was piled every which way in an empty Hudson's Bay Company storehouse.

Snow buntings sang passionately on the radio aerials in the still air. Lapland longspurs, as in Churchill, scrabbled in the dirt, singing sweetly and absent-mindedly as they fed. Glaucous gulls, huge, white and ghostly, floated like bird spirits over the settlement, looking for garbage. On the bare hillside above the town the snow was melting visibly, and the earliest spring flower, deep-pink saxifrage, was already blooming on the muddy brown earth.

Pond Inlet, on a low ledge above the beach, was a single row of white frame houses, small, neat and as white as if newly painted. The houses were joined by a gravel path lined with whitewashed stones. Beyond the living quarters and storerooms of the settlement was an untidy row of Eskimo tents on the stony beach. The tents were temporary, we learned. Eskimos had come from outlying camps to trade furs and buy staples. Soon they would be gone, back to their camps or off on hunting trips. Wash lines were hung with shining furs of arctic fox and polar bear, interspersed with shapeless, monotoned Eskimo garments. Beyond the tents was a small cluster of dirty shacks, mere wooden boxes precariously held together with one or two rusty nails and patched with bits of tar paper. Here lived the few Eskimo "poor," the shiftless slum dwellers. Beyond shantytown was rolling tundra, brown and white and empty. On a steeply rising hill back of the settlement were the letters POND INLET spelled out in whitewashed stones, bravely proclaiming themselves to the inhuman and eternal wilderness.

We wandered into a Hudson's Bay Company warehouse. There were piles of silverjar skins (the three- or four-month-old ringed seal) and fuzzy white baby sealskins, some of them made into rugs, mittens and slippers by the ever-busy Eskimo women. Hanging from the ceiling were white fox furs and precious ermine (the white winter coat of the weasel), which lit the dark room with soft radiance. In one corner loomed the enormous white head of a polar bear. The warehouse had a penetrating odor, the oily smell of sealskins. It was to become so intimately a part of our lives that forever after we would associate it with the north.

In the Hudson's Bay Company store, next door, the shelves were nearly bare. The supply ship came in once a year and its arrival was only eight weeks off. Tobacco, tea and ammunition were the most important Eskimo staples, with the accent on the first. The tobacco supply was now dangerously low. Eskimos smoked long before traders came to this part of the arctic, and they were the most passionate and persistent smokers we had ever known. We never saw an Eskimo over the age of seventeen without a stubby, blackened pipe in his mouth, or an untidy, lumpy, hand-rolled cigarette. Before the Hudson's Bay Company began bringing in endless streams of tobacco the Eskimos got their tobacco from Siberia via Russian traders. Tobacco, native originally only to North America, was taken by the Spanish to Mexico, thence to the Philippines, to North China, to the Amur tribes, to the Russians, who grew it in Siberia — and so, wrapped in reindeer skin, by ship, dogsled and snowshoes, back to the continent of its origin.

Other staples were sugar, flour, powdered milk, Pablum, chocolate and dried fruits. There were few luxuries. Idlouk and his family were going to have a gastronomic holiday over at Bylot Island on our chile sauce, nuts, sardines, candy and canned Boston brown bread.

We met the other white men and began to learn something of their life. Pond Inlet had been founded in 1921 as a Hudson's Bay Company post and at the same time the police had arrived to make known to the Eskimos that they were citizens of Canada. In 1930 missionaries had come to preach and teach. Now there were seven white men living in easy amicability in a cozy and civilized little village on the edge of the vast tundra barrens. Their well-insulated houses were heated by large coal ranges. The coal came from a small surface vein a few miles inland, mined by Pond Inlet Eskimos for a few weeks every spring. The natives were paid by the HBC, which used the coal for cooking and heat. Recently mined, the coal was now piled on the beach in sacks, where dogs dozed on it. Every house had electricity from gasoline-powered generators (gasoline came all the way from Montreal on the yearly government ship and cost $1.50 a gallon — without tax). They had indoor bathrooms whose plumbing consisted of large cans. The "plumbers" were hired native helpers who not only emptied the cans but supplied blocks of ice for the big water barrels which stood on the kitchen porch of each house, brought in wood and coal for the stoves, painted and repaired the houses, kept the gravel walks neat, hunted seals to feed the official dogs and guided the white men on visiting trips and patrols. Each house also had its native "maid," a little Eskimo girl, usually not more than seventeen, who managed the housekeeping in her own unsystematic way, undisturbed by discipline of any kind.

The native helpers, we were told, were essential to the life of Pond Inlet. Sometimes they disappeared on a hunt or a visit for a week or two. Then civilization at the settlement began to show its seamy side as stove fires went out, cans overflowed, drinking water became low and brackish, dishes piled up in the sink and dust gathered on the neat cretonne curtains. The white men were good cooks and could upholster furniture, repair motors, hunt seals and drive dog teams almost as well as the Eskimos. But they were not housekeepers, and allowed themselves to be spoiled by the kindly, willing natives.

For entertainment the white men depended on each other's conversation, on books and on the radio. In the Hudson's Bay Company house were hundreds of books ranging from *The Origin of Species* to *Kiss Me Deadly*. In the winter, Pete said, he read two books a day. He would even read the dictionary for fun, or a London newspaper dated six months earlier. Especially he loved nineteenth century English poetry. Byron's graceful, sentimental love poetry and Shelley's lush lines breathing the air of the soft English countryside must indeed have been appealing in the long, bitter, arctic night.

The radio in the HBC house was on all day and most of the night. We never noticed anyone listening to it, but the men apparently absorbed it through their pores. They knew every word of every American popular song and could converse learnedly on bands, singers and disk jockeys. Radio Thule, Station KOLD, broadcast from the American air base in Greenland, provided the most constant entertainment. It carried good, varied programs of jazz, classical music and news, interspersed with noisy military band music. Occasionally the Voice of America or Radio Moscow was heard over short wave. The Voice of America, they said, was sometimes excellent but usually irritating. There would be a little music followed by a long, unintelligible speech in Polish or Chinese, which might be cooking recipes or a lecture on political science. Radio Moscow was always in English and consisted of unpleasant news items clipped pettishly out of context from British and American newspapers.

Pond Inlet's white men did not appear to be bored or sullen in their years-long isolation. They loved company but they got along all right when they had no one but one another. Their manner was relaxed, cheerful and hospitable. They were all completely at ease with the Eskimos, who came and went informally in their houses, ate with them and traveled with them. There appeared to be no distinction of class or race. After all why should there be? It was the Eskimos' world, not theirs. If a white man was contemptuous, we were told, the natives sensed it immediately and they had subtle methods of revenge for the occasional unfriendly foreigner. But most Outsiders soon came to love and trust the Eskimos — kind, honest, gay and clever people in whose hearts there was no room for pride or scorn.

At the moment these reflections got no further than conversation. The relaxed world of the Eskimos had not caught any of us strangers yet. As we saw them emerge sleepily, one by one, from their tents we gathered nervously in the storeroom to sort our baggage. The natives were in no hurry, but we were busy and harassed. We ordered one another around and distracted Pete and Bren with conflicting lists, instructions and questions. The storeroom was a wilderness of confusion and irritation.

Unused as we were to slow, peaceful, arctic ways, unable to converse with the Eskimos and bewildered by the formidable problems of setting up an extensive base camp on a deserted island, we needed someone with a steady hand. This was Pete. Quietly and modestly the twenty-three-year-old trader took the loading operations out of our nervous hands. He set up a charge account for us with the Hudson's Bay Company and promised to take care of all our accounts. He took orders from us for clothing to be made by Eskimo women; worked out, with Idlouk, the best camping spot for our ecological research; called in several of the more knowledgeable Eskimos to ask them about birds; translated the English names of birds, insects, mammals and plants into Eskimo for us; went over maps with us to show us what trips we should take and arranged for Eskimos to guide us. No problem was too slight or too complicated for him to give it his patient and careful attention. His favorite phrase was "No trouble a-tall," always accompanied by a winning smile. The easygoing, friendly, capable young Newfoundlander with the Scottish accent was our steady anchor. Without him our expedition would surely have foundered that first day.

We were uneasy with Idlouk. His English was almost non-existent and we were afraid he would not understand our peculiar scientific requirements. It would not take long for us to discover how extraordinarily observant, responsive and understanding he was. But at the moment he was shy and we were baffled. So Pete decided to travel to Bylot Island with us and stay until we were settled.

Suddenly the sleds were all loaded and the dogs harnessed. The drivers grunted their unintelligible, low-throated syllables and the willing dogs set out at a fast trot, ears eagerly forward. Pete, on Idlouk's sled, already several yards from the shore, called urgently to Axel and me. We leaped for the moving sled and clung precariously as it bounced over the debris of tumbled pressure ice at the shore's edge. This was a land of sudden changes. Hours might be spent in preparation for leaving or simply in doing nothing. But when the Eskimos were ready to go they went — without any warning. The unwary novice was often left behind sprawling helplessly in the snow while the Eskimo driver laughed merrily and the dogs leaped over the lumpy ice.

I I I
Across the Sea Ice

THE sled swayed and whispered over the snow like a little boat. Ahead of us was a dim white desert on which nothing moved, and Bylot Island's dark, enormous mountains were like mysterious castles at the end of the journey. Sheathed in mist, they seemed to recede as we advanced. I lay down on a polar-bear skin and stared up at the white sky. Seven snow geese flew low over us, gleaming white with black wing tips — seven enchanted princes.

From the front of the sled came Idlouk's low, hoarse voice grunting at his dogs. Every now and then one of them gave a perfunctory, comic howl. Idlouk's syllables gradually became distinguishable. *Ei-ei-ei-ei* was quick and sharp, *Woy-woy* long and slow with an upward inflection at the end, *Oonh-eh* emphatic and deep in the throat, *Hut-hut-hut* urgent and hurried. All these were vowel sounds from the bottom of the throat, not translatable into our alphabet. The most frequently recurring word was *Bakshu!* Whenever Idlouk said, "Bakshu," one of those short, silly howls followed. Sometimes there was the sharp crack of the whip, but not often. Idlouk evidently depended more on his voice than his whip for obedience.

Pete explained the Eskimo syllables. *Ei* meant go to the left, *Woy* meant go to the right, *Oonh-eh* just meant keep going, *Hut-hut-hut* meant go fast.

33

"What does 'Bakshu' mean?"

Pete laughed. "See that lazy dog at the side with his trace loose?" he said. At that moment Idlouk shouted, "Bakshu!" again, and whipped the snow just beside the dog. The lazy animal gave one of his little barking howls and leaped ahead, tightening his trace momentarily.

"That's Bakshu," said Pete. Idlouk turned around, said something and laughed.

"He says that his team is not very good," Pete explained. "Five of the dogs are puppies and just being trained. He says that Bakshu is the worst puppy."

Bakshu was big and beautiful, his heavy fur yellowish brown with subtle touches of red on the legs — but he had an unfinished, adolescent look. Continually running back and forth among the other dogs and tangling his trace, he did not seem to be very sure of himself. He was apparently unaware that his function was to pull. Idlouk told us, through Pete, that Bakshu was just nine months old.

At eight or nine months the dogs started their training. First they ran beside the team, unharnessed. Later harnesses of sealskin were put on their backs, but they were not fastened to the sled. When the dogs got used to the leather they were put on a short trace, close to the sled, where they didn't have to pull very hard and could receive the constant attention of the driver. The dogs in this part of the north, where the country was open and treeless and most travel was on sea ice, were harnessed in a rough fan shape. One of the cleverer, older dogs was made lead dog, but they were interchangeable. Idlouk's usual lead dog, Oogliaksheea, a small black and white female, had been off hunting when Idlouk harnessed his dogs this day. It was unusual to keep female dogs, because they did not work well in a team. But Oogliak-sheea, calm, tough and hard-working, was one of the best dogs in the district, though she had a deep-seated prejudice against going to the right. Today Idlouk had put a big, handsome, brownish male in her place. He went wherever he was told, but he didn't appear to be much interested.

The whole system looked hopelessly informal. The dogs crossed back and forth until their traces were an inextricable tangle. The fan shape was a myth — it was a shapeless conglomeration of dogs.

"The Eskimos know how to get around us," Pete said when we commented on the disorderly traces. "A white man usually insists on keeping going at a fast pace. 'Let's get there,' he says. But an Eskimo likes to stop for tea from time to time. Without saying anything he whips up the dogs and gets them running. The faster the dogs go the more the traces get tangled. Then the Eskimo says he has to stop and untangle them. Might as well get the primus stove started at the same time and have a little tea to keep warm."

As if he had prophesied we saw that the three sleds ahead of us had stopped. Our dogs suddenly broke into a wild gallop and nearly piled us on top of the halted sleds. Idlouk grunted a word deep in his throat, leaped off the sled and waved his whip. Instantly the dogs lay down. A good driver, Pete said, can with a single word make his dogs stop and lie down in their traces. Sometimes that word is simply "Tea!"

Someone had shot a seal. The dogs had heard the report though we, our ears still unattuned, had not noticed it. Knowing what the sound of a shot meant, the dogs had hurried to see if they could steal a free lunch. There was blood all over the snow around the dead seal. It was an awfully dead seal. Its eyes were oozing pools of blood and its body was a fat, limp sack. It did not look as if it had ever been alive.

The primus stoves were out and snow had been piled into black kettles. While we waited for tea the Eskimos played games. Three of them lay face down on the snow and hopped forward on their fists and the tips of their toes, in a race. They looked like seals; and perhaps it was the seal, hopping awkwardly over the ice on its flippers, which had inspired this game. Some of us tried it. We couldn't even manage one hop but fell ignominiously on our faces in the snow. Two Eskimos faced each other, crouching low, and did a leg-throwing dance like a Russian *pezotska*. Was that a dim memory of their Central Asian ancestry? More likely it had come with Russian whalers and explorers and made its slow way across the continent to the Eastern Arctic. They did it very well. One man placed a tin can on the snow and four others flicked at it from twenty-five feet away with their long sealhide whips. They did not miss. Within a few minutes the can was twisted and broken. They used the whips with easy grace to flick mitts and berets out of one another's hands. They tested their strength with arm-to-arm wrestling. They jumped over the high-piled sleds with both feet together. Through it all they laughed and joked continuously.

I picked up a whip, walked far away by myself and tried to crack it. Instantly the heavy wet whip curled itself around me in a hideous tangle and I felt as if I had been embraced by a python. I hoped no one had seen. But of course they had — they never missed anything. Idlouk laughed as I untangled myself.

Tea was hot, black as soot and full of tea leaves and caribou hairs. We filled cups of it with copious spoonfuls of mixed sugar and powdered milk and drank it gratefully.

It was an hour before we were ready to start again. The sun had disappeared some time ago and snow was falling. Mist had closed in before and behind us. Pond Inlet had vanished and Bylot's black cliffs were a dim grayness off to one side. Our five sleds, widely separated, seemed brave and small in the lost, lonely land.

The dead seal was left behind on the ice, to be picked up later on the way back. A lone dog, not a member of any of the teams, sat with ears cocked, waiting for us to be gone. As we pulled off he trotted casually to the seal and started working on it.

There wasn't going to be much left of that seal, we remarked. Pete answered that many of the Eskimos were shiftless about seals. They left them lying on the ice or cached them in shallow drifts where polar bears and foxes found them. The Hudson's Bay Company, interested in skins, was concerned over the waste of seals.

One of the sleds ahead had stopped and its driver was adjusting the sealskin thong that held the baggage on. We passed it, going at a fast trot. Idlouk muttered something almost in a whisper. Instantly the dogs of the halted sled set off at a gallop. The sled lurched over the rough snow, baggage falling off in every direction, while the Eskimo driver ran and shouted far behind. Idlouk went off into peals of laughter. So did Pete — and so did the running Eskimo. We laughed too, though we didn't quite know what we were supposed to be laughing at. This was apparently the favorite form of Eskimo humor. The victim of the joke appeared to be just as happy about it as the perpetrator.

For a long time there was peace and we grew very cold. It became evident that Eskimo jokes and games, however rude, served a practical purpose on the long, slow, freezing journeys.

"There's a seal," said Pete suddenly, looking off into the foggy whiteness. Axel and I strained our eyes but could see nothing. Pete pointed. "Over there, about a quarter of a mile away," he said. Under his influence we found a dozen black spots. They all resolved themselves, through the binoculars, into bits of rough pressure ice — humps and ridges pushed up by the surging tides of the narrow inlet.

"How do you know it's a seal?"

"You get so you can see them. You're so anxious to see something alive. Up here, this time of year, before the birds come and the sea ice breaks up, everything is so still that you keep looking for something that moves. When I came here my eyes were terrible. Now I can see as well as the Eskimos. They don't have very good eyes, but they never miss anything — you'll find out."

Idlouk stopped his dogs, took a telescope out of a white canvas case and watched the seal for about five minutes. Then he got out another canvas bag and carefully unfolded from it a square piece of immaculate white cloth. This he stretched over two crossed pieces of wood about three feet long, making a shield. He took his rifle out of its fur-lined caribou-hide case and set out slowly across the snow, almost tiptoeing.

By this time we had spotted the seal and watched it through binoculars. It lay flat on the ice, but about every thirty seconds its head went up. Each time this occurred Idlouk dropped on his knees, hiding behind the white shield. Slowly he crept across the ice, making several wide detours and bobbing up and down every few seconds in rhythm with the nervous seal. When he was within about a hundred yards of it he stopped. For a long time he hid behind the shield, while the seal's head went up and down. Once it raised itself far up on its flippers. Then a shot rang out and the seal's head dropped forever.

The stalking had taken three quarters of an hour. During all this time the dogs lay unmoving on the ice, their ears pricked forward, their eyes glued on the distant figure of their master. At the sound of the shot they instantly started galloping. We grabbed cameras, binoculars and other belongings and leaped for the sled, landing every which way, trying to hold on. The sled dashed full speed over the ice and came to a sudden halt inches away from the seal.

It was neatly killed with a shot in the eye. The technique was explained. The seal lies right beside its *agloo*, or breathing hole. It is half asleep, but it keeps looking around, almost unconsciously surveying the landscape. It is alert to smells, sights and sounds. The hunter must make a long detour to come in upwind; he walks in cold puddles of melted snow so the seal won't hear his feet on the crackling ice; he crouches behind his white shield when the animal's head goes up. The seal is supposed to think he is only a piece of snow.

When he gets within range he whistles softly. This makes the seal curious. It raises its head and shoulders high to see what made the sound — and gets shot in the eye. It has to be shot dead instantly. If only wounded it slides into its hole and sinks. Eskimos say the seal likes to be killed. It is like a little drop of cool water falling on its head.

Idlouk took from his sled a knife with a blade eighteen inches long, of a wicked sharpness. He touched the seal's belly with its point, and almost of its own weight the knife made a long, easy slit deep into the flesh, guts spilling out behind it. He reached in and pulled out the big, dark liver, detached the gall bladder from it (so the seal's insides would not be contaminated by bile) and put the liver back in. Separating the thick layer of fat from the skin, he made several small slits in the skin along the edges of the cut. Neatly he sewed the gash together, lacing a length of slippery gut in and out of the little slits he had made. It was a small, quick masterpiece of surgery, dreadfully bloody. Idlouk's hands were dark red and slippery with blood. He washed them thoroughly in the snow and wiped them on a rag, *not* on his clothing. Eskimos appeared to be fastidious about their persons.

Idlouk's seal was only three or four months old. The adolescent ringed seal, from one to four months old, called silver-jar, is preferred because its hide brings three dollars at the trading post. Adult seals bring only twenty-five cents to a dollar, depending on the condition of the skin. Newborn seals, creamy white and fuzzy, bring one to three dollars.

The ringed seal, *Phoca hispida*, is the common seal of these far northern bays and inlets. Apparently this most northerly of seals has no urge either to congregate or to migrate, and it seldom ventures into the open ocean. The young are born in very early spring, March or April. To prepare for the coming of her single pup the mother digs a hollow between the sea ice and the snow which lies on it. This has no entrance from above, but a passageway under the snow leads to her breathing hole so that the mother seal can come and go in the water without disclosing her den. The pup is born with white fluffy fur subtly tinged with yellow. The creamy color is caused by the baby's drinking the amniotic fluid in the womb, mixed with its own urine. Seals, unlike most mammals, whose waste is carried away by the mother's blood stream, urinate directly before they are born — an evidence of the fact that they must be prepared at a very early age to be self-sufficient. At birth the pup weighs four to six pounds. But for the first weeks of its life it lives entirely on the richest milk in the world, and by the time it is ready to feed itself, at about four weeks, it is three feet long and its fat takes up nearly two-fifths of its weight. By this time it has lost its baby fur and acquired coarse-textured silvery hair (its name, *hispida*, means rough-haired) patterned with shadowy rings. At this stage the mother takes her baby into the water, teaching it to swim and by example showing it the food that seals eat. Soon afterward she leaves her pup. Ringed seals do not ordinarily gather in colonies. But the young, frightened at being left alone, sometimes draw together in small groups for a while, living off their own fat, and complaining. Soon, however, they discover that shrimps are easy to catch and later they realize that tomcod and sculpin taste quite as good as milk and that the sharp cusps on their tricuspid molars are supposed to be used for holding fish. Then they no longer need one another's company, and the bays and inlets become as lonesome and empty as Eclipse Sound this day.

The history of the ringed seal and man shows little change in their relationship throughout the years. Early whalers found the Eskimos using the seals, as they do now, for nearly every household purpose — the hide for clothing and leather, the flesh for men and dogs, the blubber for fuel oil, the gut casing for windows. The Europeans looked curiously but not covetously on these small sea mammals dotted over the

ice of straits and bays, far from the storms and predators of
open ocean, and called them "ice rats" because of their small
size (adult males do not exceed six feet). The hide was considered worthless by explorers and traders. In any case, since
the seals did not colonize, hunting them was a slow, difficult
procedure, largely a matter of stealth and patience. In the
dark, bitter winter the Eskimo hunter had to stand for hours
over an *agloo*, while others of his family, down to the littlest
children, guarded other breathing holes. If the seal showed
its nose it was driven down until eventually, sometimes after
a whole day's waiting, it might come up in the hole where
the hunter's harpoon was poised. In early spring seals were
stalked behind a skin shield over the ice, as we had seen, and
in late spring and summer they could be harpooned occasionally in open-water leads.

Now the Eskimos have guns, and seal has a small commer-
cial value. But the natives are not money-minded, ammunition
is scarce and it is a lot of work for the women to cure the
skins and the men to bring them in from their far camps to
trade. Long before the white man came the Eskimo was lazy.
Now, with the incentive of white men's luxuries, he is only
slightly more ambitious. As in the old days he hunts seals
for his household uses only, content to let the extra dollars
go. A good trader (like Pete) can occasionally, by winning
the respect and confidence of the natives, get them to bring
in skins. But in general the Hudson's Bay Company is dis-
tressed at the waste of skins.

Thus, since the human population is small and greed has
no place in its economy, there is little danger of extermination
of the ringed seal by man. Besides man the seal has few enemies. The infrequent polar bear stalks it silently over the

winter ice and the arctic fox occasionally takes a pup in early
spring. In summer tribes of killer whales sometimes come in
from the open ocean, killing everything in sight. (The stomach of one killer whale was found to contain thirteen porpoises and fourteen seals — though the animal was less than
twenty feet long! Another had twenty-four seals inside it
and had choked while trying to eat the twenty-fifth.) The
little seals scatter before these voracious killers, sometimes,
in their terror, climbing up on land and even into an Eskimo
village. A seal has been known to dive between a man's legs
and stay there, trembling, while the killer whales cavorted
in the water. But the killers seldom come into straits and
bays, and even when they come they cannot destroy the
ringed seal en masse, since the animals do not colonize.

So, scattered and solitary, the ringed seal has led for many
centuries a well-balanced life in its frigid, quiet waters, disturbed only by the few hunters of the far north.

Idlouk tied his seal on the back of a sled. "*He* doesn't leave
his seals behind," said Pete. Idlouk indeed seemed almost old-
maidish, with his zippered cloth bags and his fur-lined gun
case. In contrast to many Eskimos Idlouk was careful and
thrifty. Anything that was ruined by weather was gone forever. Guns could not easily be replaced, nor telescopes. The
ship came only once a year, and if an Eskimo were not careful of his belongings he found himself going hungry long
before ship time. But not Idlouk.

For several hours our dogs padded along with their noses
glued to the end of the sled in front, where Idlouk's seal was
fastened with a sealskin thong. The fat seal lay on its back,
reclining gracefully. Its little flippers were folded demurely

over its breast, the head had fallen back, the tail drooped languorously in the snow. From its eye came a continuous trickle of blood. It was very inviting. Even Bakshu was alert.

We neared the shore of Bylot Island. The sheer tumbled cliffs of Castle Gables, dark and dangerous, met the sea, and behind them rose the smooth black and white cone of Mt. Thule, a feather of mist crowning its six-thousand-foot peak. We passed a wide river mouth, still solidly frozen. From the aerial photographs we recognized that this was the Aktineq River, which flowed from the broad Aktineq Glacier ten miles inland. Just beyond the river delta the land rose gently from the sea in a series of level terraces. Another half mile beyond this spot were wild gray sandstone cliffs falling abruptly to the sea. Our camp was to be made between the river and the cliffs, on the snow-covered tundra.

As we touched land, at eight o'clock in the evening after six hours of travel, the clouds parted above Bylot Island's mountains and the low sun shone suddenly. Far away on Baffin Island the icy hills gleamed golden under heavy black clouds, and the sea ice was full of shadows.

To the ancient Greeks Thule was the northern end of the habitable world, and it appeared that we had come to that place.

I V
White Spring

THE southern shore of Bylot Island, where we made our camp, was on Eclipse Sound, protected from the storms and winds of the open ocean. Rolling tundra stretched inland from the sea in rising plateaus to the Aktineq Glacier and the tall, jagged peaks of the interior. The tundra back of our camp was traversed by ravines and rivulets and dotted with small, stagnant lakes; it was said by the Eskimos to be favorite nesting grounds for snow geese, old-squaw ducks and many shore birds and song birds. (Although the natives never killed small birds, as it was not worth their while to waste precious ammunition on such meager pickings, we were to find that they were extraordinarily observant of the appearance and habits of every small tundra creature from a beetle to an American pipit.) The climate of the southern shore, gentler than that of the ocean side, favored the growth of flowering plants and insects. We were within easy dog-sledding distance of Pond Inlet. And the mountains — for those who fancied climbing six-thousand-foot peaks through waist-deep snow — were less than a day's travel inland.

When we arrived the beach and much of the tundra above it were still snow-covered. But there was a narrow, level strip a few yards above the beach where the snow had partly melted off. It was a tattered graveyard of stones and bones.

Strewn over the land were caribou horns, rotten and green with moss, hundreds of small white seal bones, an occasional dog skull, two gigantic vertebrae of the Greenland whale and the titanic skull of the same creature (the Greenland whale is sixty feet long and its head is nearly a third of that). Large stones, forming rough rings, had clearly held down many generations of Eskimo tents. Idlouk had chosen this spot for us, knowing that it was a favorite camping place for Eskimos hunting and trapping on Bylot Island. That meant that there should be snow geese, foxes and other edible or salable creatures in plenty. Our scientists would not have to go far to find specimens. It also meant that there was good water nearby and that the spot was probably as sheltered as any we could find along the open beach or the unprotected inland tundra.

There were some difficulties in setting up the tents. The ground was frozen a few inches beneath the surface, and trying to put tent stakes in it was like hammering them into concrete. So the shallow-planted stakes were held in place with picturesque piles of stones and caribou horns, and reinforced with ice axes.

Another hazard was presented by the dogs — the dozens of them who had brought us, and who now slept peacefully and immovably all over our narrow strip. If an Eskimo wanted a dog out of the way he picked him up bodily by his harness and threw him. If we wanted a dog out of the way we approached gingerly, stopped three feet from him and said, "Go away." The dog did not even open his eyes. A tentative touch with the foot and he did open his eyes but made no further gesture. The next step was to call Idlouk.

Slowly, as the tents rose, our little village took shape in a homelike arrangement above the beach. For cooking, eating and social life there was a tall, handsome eight-by-ten-foot tent with zippered, mosquito-netted window flaps across the width of two sides. One window opened on a glorious view of the sound and the low white mountains of Baffin Island, and from the other we could see the rising tundra and the broad Aktineq Glacier. Bill Drury, botanist and biologist, had, with his wife Mary, a roomy eight-by-eight tent big enough for his plant-pressing activities. Axel and I had a similar one, where I could clatter away on my typewriter without bothering anyone. A wrinkled, tepeelike affair which had COLOSSAL ENTERPRISES painted across its front in big red letters belonged to Ben Ferris, the doctor and mountaineer. These four tents surrounded a sort of central plaza, adorned with whale vertebrae and caribou horns like grotesque modern statuary. A little distance away, in what came to be known as "Outer Suburbia," were two low white mountain tents belonging to Rick Miller, entomologist and mammalogist, and Ned Ames, young mountaineer and student botanist. There also Josselyn Van Tyne, the tall ornithologist, had a pointed, shaky mountain tent just a few inches longer than he and barely high enough for him to kneel in. When he crawled into it the whole tent rippled and bulged like an active volcano. At the end of the little row Idlouk's tent would rise as soon as he had fetched his family from Pond Inlet. Above Outer Suburbia ("But please, not too near Elm Street," begged Rick) a shallow latrine hole was dug on a cold, windy, muddy ledge.

Our water came from a shallow fresh-water lagoon on the stony beach. It was supplied by a brook which ran silently, under a heavy snow cover, down a small ravine. In the tundra barrens there are no springs — even the most determined spring could not force its way through the iron-hard permafrost. The big rivers come directly from glaciers in the mountains, and their water is so heavy with gray glacial silt that it is undrinkable. Our river's name, "Aktineq," means to spew forth rocks, pebbles or dirt, and when the river ice melted later in the spring we could see why the Eskimos had so named it. Pools and lakes on the tundra are of melted snow, and unless they are kept supplied by run-off rivulets they quickly become stagnant and dark with algae. The annual rainfall on Bylot and northern Baffin islands is about eleven inches. In late summer, when all the snow has melted and the little puddles and brooks have been eaten up by the sun, the land, for a few weeks, becomes a desert. The beach lagoons last the longest, being on low land, and we hoped that ours would stay with us.

Our lagoon looked pure, blue and sparkling in the evening sun. But it was the favorite feeding and sleeping quarters of snow geese and glaucous gulls as well as the habitat of numerous visible small water creatures and heaven only knew how many millions of invisible ones. Its water was not only teeming with life but had an unpleasant yellow tinge in a cup. We closed our eyes, and drank it.

Supper was nuts, chocolate and Triscuits. Although we had been nibbling incessantly all day we had not had a full meal for forty-eight hours. After this unsatisfactory dinner we separated to find and unpack our personal baggage, strewn indiscriminately among sleeping dogs. We all felt tired, nervous, headachy and dangerously undernourished.

Idlouk, who did not miss the smallest nuance, quietly got two primus stoves from the sleds, rummaged in the food boxes until he found some bacon and two frying pans and sent one of the Eskimos for the seal liver, still tied neatly inside the seal he had killed that afternoon. Within a few minutes an almost unbearably delicious smell floated through the chill evening air. We left our belongings spilling out of knapsacks and duffel bags, rapidly gathered in front of the cook tent and hung over Idlouk like a flock of starved vultures. We all had our knives out, ready to spear the liver almost before it was heated through.

The half-cooked liver was the most delectable food I had ever eaten. Fresh, tender and sweet, it had no relation at all to the gamy elderly calf's liver one buys in butcher shops at home. Under its influence we began to smile at each other and to look around appreciatively at a suddenly friendly arctic. The mountains opposite, on Baffin Island, took on an extra gleam in the low night sun. The sea ice was shadowed, but a tall iceberg locked in the frozen sea reflected the sun with cold fire. Snow geese honked overhead and snow buntings sang on the tundra. Silvery pussy willow and low purple-pink saxifrage bloomed sweetly at our feet.

About midnight Pete, Idlouk and the other Eskimos harnessed their dogs and set out for Pond Inlet. We watched them until they were only black specks on the immense frozen sound. We were alone on our deserted island, but we had no sense of loneliness. Warmed by seal liver and glowing with optimism, we retired to our tents and sleeping bags, to be sung to sleep by snow buntings in the light, lovely night.

When Axel and I looked out of our tent the next morning the first sight that caught our eyes was the iceberg. It had broken off from some distant arctic glacier, gone tearing and grinding down the land to the ocean and sailed through storms and sun and fog, to come to rest finally in the quiet, ice-locked harbor of Eclipse Sound. Its long journey had scarred it. One part was an overturned galley, its keel high in the air, the other a mass of twisted turrets like a nightmare castle. It lay about a mile offshore — or maybe five. Distances were deceiving in the all-pervading flat whiteness.

We had never seen an iceberg before. Yet it was of all phenomena the essential symbol of the arctic. We thought we would like to go closer to it. Ned Ames, the enthusiastic young mountaineer, had an even better thought. "Let's climb it," he said.

Soon, carrying lunch, crampons, ropes and ice axes, we were trekking lightheartedly over the sun-bright sea ice. In small cracks the water shone intensely blue-green. We leaped them easily. Not knowing the ways of sea ice, we roped up at the larger cracks and jumped one at a time, leaving wide margins on both sides.

The iceberg loomed tremendous over us as we neared. It was much bigger than we had realized, dangerously steep and seamed with broad dark-green cracks. It gave off a chill breath and even in the hot sun we shivered. When we were within a hundred yards the monster suddenly thundered at us from deep inside.

"Go away," it said clearly. We stopped instantly. But nothing happened, so we went nearer, setting our feet down as gingerly as if we were walking on china. The iceberg was surrounded by a deep moat of melted ice. The only way to get on it was over a narrow snow bridge, visibly melting in the sun.

We sat down on the snow to eat lunch and think it over. At

our backs was the cold breath of the unfriendly ice monster.
But the sun was brilliant, the sky was deep blue and the snow
gleamed. We felt adventurous, so we put on our crampons
and roped up. Ned, as an experienced glacier climber, went
first. The soft snow bridge held him, and he tried to cut steps
in the sheer wall of the iceberg. The ice chipped off in small
flat flakes and the steps were no more than shallow depressions.
Pared down and hardened by fierce winter winds, our iceberg was solid as oak. Ned managed to scrape his way up to
an easier slope on its lower lip, and we scrambled up after him.
We found ourselves on a ledge fifteen feet above the sea.
Over us leaned a slim, graceful tower of glare ice fifty feet
high, shaped by wind and sleet into beautiful curves and
carved with delicate ridges. Architecturally it was a very elegant iceberg, but absolutely unassailable. We walked around
our little promontory. On all sides it sloped precipitously into
dark open water.

At such close quarters with the sea giant we were stricken
with awed respect and a sudden fear. It seemed a tremendous
live force beneath us and above us. We could feel the titanic
power that had torn it from its moorings and tumbled it into
the sea.

"Wouldn't it be funny," said Ned in a small voice, "if this
thing gave a sigh and slowly rolled over." We laughed uncomfortably and immediately started to get off it.

Axel and I descended first, groping for footholds and slipping on the ice. Ned decided to make it easier for himself and
hacked at the top steps with his ice ax. As he gave the third
stroke there was a terrible roar from right underneath him. We
stood absolutely still for a moment, shocked into immobility.
Ned's light words seemed suddenly to be written across the

sky. Then Ned slid rapidly down the wall and we retreated as fast as we dared, not looking behind us.

You can sometimes knock over those tall, narrow icebergs with one well-placed bullet from a thirty-thirty, Pete Murdoch told us later, casually. Then he laughed. He knew, as we did, that we had been in no real danger. Eskimos often climb frozen-in icebergs to reconnoiter for seals. Eight ninths of an iceberg is under water, and ours was safely locked in unmoving bay ice.

However, we had known the fear that an immense physical force inspires. Safe our iceberg might be — but we were humble before it.

For the next few days, firmly earthbound, we explored the tundra within a few miles of our camp and began to learn its eccentricities.

Being devoid of trees, the tundra at first looked depressingly barren. But the steady rhythm of freeze and thaw on the earth's surface over a bed of iron-hard permafrost had twisted and shaped and carved the land, and as the tundra emerged from its thin snow cover it began to look as if a gang of construction workers had been there. On the level bogs frost, working over centuries, had forced the earth into regular polygon patterns, thrown up earthworks along their sides and created ruler-straight ditches around them. On dry plateaus small rocks had been pushed to the surface and thrown outward in circular patterns. Mud had oozed down the sides of hills over the eternally frozen lower soil, pushing immense rocks upright in its slow flow and leaving crowns of bare stones on the hilltops. Flat meadows swelled with regularly spaced rounded cones like the mounds of prehistoric villages. It was a peculiarly geometric land.

On the deep sea winter still held. But on the tundra it was very early spring, about like March in New England. In some places snow was still hard-packed, in others, where it was undermined by invisible rivulets, our feet broke through a thin crust and we sank to our thighs in slush and mud. On exposed hillsides and plateaus it had melted off, and there the tundra was springy and felt alive under our feet. There also bloomed the first small life of springtime. Last year's grass, dry and yellow, lay in low clumps. This year's saxifrage, brilliantly pink, blossomed where there had been snow only a few hours before. Arctic willow crept over the ground, covered with pussy willows and tight-rolled, fat pale-green leaves. By what right, we wondered, was this little crawly plant, seldom more than five inches high, classified as a tree? But examining it with a clear eye, we could see tree characteristics. Its roots were long and gnarled and tough. Its minute branches were clothed in unmistakable bark. The arctic willow, puny as it looks, can live about eighty years.

Mosses and lichens carpeted the earth with many colors and patterns, from pale gray-green delicately lacy *Stereocaulon* to heavy black filigree of *Parmelia sorediata* (these lowly plants are known only by Latin names). The most striking was *Caloplaca*, a flat brilliant-orange lichen which we found on lookout rocks of snowy owls, hawks and jaegers. The birds' droppings on the rocks provided the nutrient layer necessary for the growth of the lichens, and they were probably transported from place to place on the birds' feet.

Once, surprisingly, we found a large, flimsy mushroom on

the unblooming earth, where snow had just come off. It looked like a stray from a cool August night in a Maine pine forest. As I carried it home it became increasingly sagging and flabby. The botanists could not identify it but assumed it was last summer's, which had frozen and stayed intact under the winter snow. In a few hours it had shriveled to a little brown pile like an unwrapped mummy.

On the tops of the low rolling hills, where rocks were exposed, we found pellets of the snowy owl, gray and fragile with age. This owl, like most others, partly digests its food in the front part of its stomach and disgorges whatever won't go any further down, usually fur and bones. The pellets looked like long-dead mice — and that was just about what they were. The snowy owl prefers lemmings. There were no new pellets, or owls.

Everywhere there were lemming holes, the homes of thousands of the tiny, brown, furry, arctic rodents. Most of the holes were choked with dead vegetation and were obviously not new. We saw no lemmings. We found some droppings of the arctic hare and, rarely, the dainty tracks of the arctic fox crossed and recrossed each other over the snow.

Live creatures were few. Although it was the middle of June we had beaten most of the birds to Bylot Island. The first few days the only birds we saw in any quantity were snow geese. (This variety was the greater snow goose, which does not breed any further south.) They were big white birds with black wing tips, their heads and throats red-orange from dabbling in the iron-filled marshes of the Chesapeake Bay region, their winter home. They waddled around the edges of snow-covered inland pools, sometimes as many as sixty in one place. Apparently they were courting, but they did not seem to mind one another's company in their romantic pursuits. However, it was impossible for humans to approach within eighty yards of them even with the most careful stalking. They had enemies on the tundra, and they were careful. Once Axel approached close to ten geese, crawling on the ground to keep a small ridge between him and them, and holding his camera cocked, with telephoto lens attached. Cautiously he raised his head, covered with a parka hood as dun-colored as the tundra, over the top of the ridge. But they must have seen his bright-red sunburned nose — we were all painfully sunburned those first days. There was a hysterical honking and the geese spread their immense wings (they have a five-foot wingspread), stretched their long necks and flew easily out over the sea. The birds had looked ungainly on the ground, like farmyard geese; but in the air they were proud and beautiful.

Old-squaw ducks began to arrive within a few days. These diving ducks occupied our water-supply lagoon since nothing else was free of ice, and set up an interminable, complaining conversation day and night — *Anh-angh-ya* — like old-fash-ioned automobile horns. The males were decorative, with sharply contrasting black and white plumage and long slender tails which curved like black daggers out of the water. However, they lost a great deal of their flashy dignity when they tried to dive in the too-shallow lagoon and found themselves upended, rumps in the air like puddle ducks. The females were drab and unpretentious but very popular. There were many more males than females and sometimes one little brown girl would have seven handsome suitors at a time, all shouting "*Anh-angh-ya!*" at her and swimming in eager circles. The Eskimos, we learned later from Idlouk, used this high-pitched, querulous call as the bird's name. His children would answer the birds with accurate mimicry and try to hit them with slingshots, giggling constantly. The ducks didn't seem to mind. They just said, "*Anh-angh-ya,*" and swam slowly and deliberately out of range.

All around our camp, even in the central plaza, were Lapland longspurs. These northern sparrows were tundra-colored — red, brown and gray — and almost invisible when they stood still, which they never did. The snow buntings, small finches, also wore protective coloring. In their black and white plumage (brown and white in the female) they looked like little patches of half-melted snow unaccountably walking around. Hoyt's larks, a subspecies of the horned lark, and American pipits, larklike birds that sing on the wing, began to arrive about four days after we did. And on our second day we saw the first golden plover, one of the most beautiful birds of the tundra, velvet-black on its belly and all the way up its throat, vivid white on its head, intricately patterned in gold and black on its back. Baird's and white-rumped sandpipers, small shore birds with indeterminate mottled brownish plumage, fed silently and almost invisibly on the shore and at the edges of inland pools.

These songbirds and shore birds did not seem to mind us in the least. They hopped unconcerned at our feet as we walked, too intent on finding food, mates and nesting sites to worry about unknown monsters. Yet in their southern winter homes most of them were shy and fearful. Apparently their psychology changed with the change in locale. Here on the tundra they had few enemies, and they knew it. Also time was short for them. Having to court, nest, raise their brood and fly south with the young ones all within five to eight weeks, they had no leisure to worry or fuss.

Axel and I spent most of the first week just walking, for hours every day, over the wet, snowy tundra, to learn what the land looked like and what lived on it. On one of our long walks inland we came across a rock ptarmigan, a chubby, chickenlike bird which fluttered up a foot in front of us. It was speckled brown and white, its plumage just changing from winter white to summer brown. This bird changes its plumage almost feather by feather to accord with the changing color of the tundra in spring and summer. The ptarmigan walked a few steps away, stopped — and vanished. We couldn't believe it. We walked to the place where it had disappeared, and found it still there, crouched low on the ground in absolute stillness. It had melted itself into the tundra and wouldn't move until we almost kicked it. We took color pictures of it. Later, when they were developed, we saw merely pictures of tundra, with no bird in them. We knew the ptarmigan was there, but it was hard to convince anyone else.

It had puzzled us before we went north that small birds could nest successfully on bare land with no grass or bush cover, open to the searching gaze of predatory birds and pathetically accessible to the keen noses of weasels and foxes. We began to understand — all they had to do was sit still. Further, there was a notable absence of the creatures that eat small birds. During our whole stay we were to find regularly feeding near our camp, of the common arctic raptorial birds, only one pair of long-tailed jaegers, one pair of ravens and one (or possibly two — they were never seen together) duck hawk. Only once, on a trip away from camp, did we see a snowy owl. And we found no gyrfalcons at any time. There were very few signs of weasels and foxes. These birds and mammals feed mainly on lemmings, turning to birds only when the lemmings disappear. An acute shortage of lemmings during the winter months, when there are no nesting birds, will cause most of the meat-eating birds and mammals to move elsewhere, die of starvation or take trap bait. We had apparently happened on one of the lean years, and it was possible that a lemmingless winter and spring would result in an increase of the population of small birds. The balance of nature, we began to see, depended to a large extent on the lowly lemming.

After we had seen the ptarmigan we continued inland, climbing from ridge to ridge, each one a little higher than the one before, toward the talus of the Aktineq Glacier. The land leveled off as we walked, though it continued to rise slowly. Ahead of us was the glacier, an enormous, dangerous, sloping highway leading into the mountains, gleaming white and seamed with great crevasses. Behind us the sound was hidden by the high ridge just above the shore. As we climbed higher we saw fewer birds and winter still lay heavy on the land. Where snow had melted the tundra was dry, pebbly and bare of grass. The birds apparently preferred the comparatively lusher vegetation and better water supply of the lowlands.

The last bird we saw was a long-tailed jaeger, a large gull-like bird with gray wings, a white breast and a black mask across its eyes. It sat silent, baleful and beautiful on a high rock. It wasn't hungry and it wasn't sleepy and it had nothing to do — but it was not going to miss anything. Its black mask made it look like an old-fashioned robber, which it was. The jaeger, when it can't find lemmings, robs nests of eggs and newly hatched young, and snatches food out of the mouths of terns and gulls. One pair of jaegers can make the life of a tern colony so miserable in a mouseless year that the birds cannot even begin to nest.

This one was not in the least afraid of us. In fact it was not even interested. Axel got within three feet of it and took camera portaits, while the bird nonchalantly looked the other way. Finally it flew, silent, powerful and streamlined, its long, slender wings beating the air slowly, its deeply forked tail opening and closing like thin-bladed scissors.

The mist slowly closed in as we walked, and the endlessly rolling hills began to disappear. We grew tired and a little frightened — every step was an effort in the soft snow or brown bog, and we had no idea where we were. We rested for a while on a hilltop in the frozen stillness. Nothing grew where we were, and nothing moved. Were we still on the earth, in the twentieth century? And then suddenly we heard a bumblebee buzzing as cozily as if it were fussing around the honeysuckle in our garden. It was impertinent and funny in this lost world.

It was dangerous to try to reach the Aktineq Glacier that day, as we had intended. The snow was too deep and the fog too dense. Besides we no longer knew where it was. So we started home through the drifting mist. We thought it was impossible to get lost, even in heavy fog. One had only to keep going down or to follow a ravine which must eventually lead to the river. But there were no reliable landmarks on the tundra. Every hill looked like every other, and the few big rocks took on strange, changeable shapes in the fog. A snow-drift which had been a landmark yesterday was today an open blue lake. A big triangular rock which had looked like a sure thing on the way up turned out to be another rock on a similar hill. Ravines led not to the river but into marshes, where we floundered in mud and slush for half an hour at a time, looking for dry land or reliable snow. We kept going down — then suddenly we found ourselves unaccountably going up. We followed fox tracks and walked in mazes.

At one point a strange, homely sight loomed through the mist — a rock cairn. Who put it there, where did it lead to? On the tundra there was nothing in the nature of a trail, as no one in the far north except crazy American scientists ever took walks. The cairn was as out of place as the cozy bumblebee. Then it occurred to us — cairns would mark the Eskimos' winter trap lines. It was consoling that human beings had been there, even if six months before.

Eventually, we found the shore of the Aktineq River and followed it home along a steep snow cliff. In many places the snow near the river had caved in, eaten away by the relentless silent water below the ice. We saw immense overhangs curtained with icicles, and deep blue-green caves.

In mid-June three years before we had walked high in the Swiss Alps, and the land was as white and frozen and pristine as this. But in Switzerland we always knew that if we walked far enough we would come to a village or an inn with hot chocolate and featherbeds. Here the best we could look forward to was a damp tent and a Coleman stove. We didn't mind. We walked in loneliness and peace over the foggy, snowy tundra, and there was a pervading sense of being back at the world's beginning.

Near camp we dug out several flat, long-rooted plants which Pete had told us were a favorite Eskimo delicacy, one of their few "vegetables." (They don't need fruits and vegetables — they get more than enough vitamins and minerals from seal liver and similar meat foods.) *Irok* the natives call this plant, and its Latin name is *Oxytropis maydelliana*. It possesses no common name, like many of the arctic plants unknown in the Temperate Zones. The roots were long and tough, and had twined themselves around rocks and earth with the tenacity of boa constrictors. We got back to camp with snaky roots sticking out of us in all directions, and our pockets bulging with small wilted plants for Bill Drury to identify.

We peeled and cut up the tenderer parts of the roots, then hacked off a piece of flesh from Idlouk's seal, rendered it in a frying pan and dropped in our little pile of crooked sticks. They rapidly turned black and a strange, delicious smell filled the tent — seal oil. It was not strong or fishy as one might expect, but warm and delicate. For supper that night we had our burned Eskimo sticks, which had a faint taste, a little like almonds, through the sweet flavor of seal oil. We were also treated to one snow bunting and one golden plover, fried in seal oil. Josselyn had taken the birds, made up the skins and handed over the interiors to the kitchen. I got the snow bunting, which was one small mouthful of strong-tasting dark red-brown meat. But we didn't depend on living off the land. We had dehydrated beets, Minute Rice, canned corned beef and brilliantly green Jello. Probably somewhere in the mixed feast we got our vitamins — and somehow the cold tent seemed more like home than home did.

We ate by candlelight. It seemed absurd that in a land of

61

continuous daylight we should have to grope for our food in the dark, trip over one another's feet and mistake the soup for the Jello. But the cook tent was dark green and had an aspect of permanent twilight. On cold windy evenings we couldn't open the window flaps to let the light in. Even as it was we had to eat with our mittens on, and foggy dampness seeped inexorably into the tent as soon as the stove was put out.

During those first days we all went to bed very early. The thermometer hovered around freezing, and we were not yet well enough adapted to the cold weather to be able to sit still for long without getting painfully cold feet and shivering uncontrollably. I usually tried to write after supper. But typing was a misery. After ten minutes at the typewriter my fingers were numb. The Bylot Island Secretarial Service, Ben Ferris had named me, seeing me one evening hard at work, sitting in my tent on a pile of bedding, with a case of Ry-Krisp for a table. But who ever heard of a secretary who typed with mittens on?

The only way to be warm was to get into our sleeping bags and pull them up over our heads. So by ten o'clock we were all tucked in, our bags piled high with clothing until the tents looked like pack rats' nests. My night costume was heavy wool socks, long wool underwear, a cashmere sweater and a scarf. I toyed with the idea of wearing a hat but didn't have one comfortable enough. I wrapped a blanket around me, crawled into my sleeping bag, zipped it up to the top and burrowed inside like a lemming in its tunnel. It could be darkest winter night. Outside it was snowing — *patter-patter* on the tent side — hard, tiny snowflakes that sounded like tin. Inside the sleeping bag it was stuffy, but if I put my nose out it froze. Better to be stuffy.

In the night I awoke and peered briefly out of my warm, dark hole. A brilliant ray of golden sunshine came through the tiny slit of our closed tent window. Sunlight at three o'clock in the morning! I never got used to the long day. Whenever I was aware of it delight flooded over me.

Every place in the world gets the same amount of daylight during the three hundred and sixty-five days of the year. But I will take mine all at once.

V
Kukukulik

THE arrival of Idlouk and his family took place about eleven o'clock in the evening of the second day we were there. Why is it, I wondered sleepily as I heard the howling of what sounded like five hundred dogs, that Eskimos do everything at night. The howling went on for a long time, then changed to snarling and growling, finally stopped altogether around midnight. Axel, who had gone out to greet our guide and his family, came back to say that the dogs had been fed and that was the reason for the howling and snarling. Their way of saying, "Please pass the butter."

Eskimos apparently always traveled in caravans. One hardly ever saw fewer than three sleds set out on a trip, each one loaded with children, mothers with babies in their hoods and several grown men. This time there were three sledfuls. Idlouk's friends had ostensibly come along to help him raise his tent. But the real reason was that they just wanted to go visiting. The next morning we saw that a heavy white canvas tent had gone up during the night at one end of our camp. Out of it came by degrees, very late in the morning, at least fifteen Eskimos of all sizes and ages. The tent was no bigger than Axel's and mine.

The guests stayed two days, all living in the same tent. On the evening they departed they fed the dogs once more.

Eskimo dogs had a meal only two or three times a week — this was not a matter of policy but simply because the natives couldn't catch enough seals. Hunting for the dogs is a serious problem to the Eskimos. In the old, simple days, before trading and trapping became a major part of his life, a hunter needed no more than three or four dogs. Now he needs twelve to fifteen to carry his long sled and his heavy load, and these indispensable animals take most of his hunting time.

Two men cut up two seals. First they laid the seals open at the belly with their long sharp knives. One knife was apparently not quite sharp enough and the Eskimo sharpened it nonchalantly on his companion's sleeve. Then they sliced the skin off neatly and cut the animals' flesh into pieces each weighing about a pound. Idlouk gathered up the flippers and threw them far out on the ice (because he didn't want the dogs to waste time chewing on flippers, which are almost entirely bone and sinew). The skins, rich with nutritious fat, were left for the dogs. Apparently these skins were not worth trading, because Idlouk never wasted anything.

The butchering took five minutes. While it went on one man stood before the crowd of hungry dogs, nearly fifty of them, waving his long whip and shouting gutturally. The dogs sat in a half circle around him and when he wasn't looking those on the outer edges crept forward on their bellies. The center ones, meanwhile, sat upright, good as gold, their ears pricked forward. The Eskimo turned and flicked the reprobates with his massive whip and they retreated with a few perfunctory howls. But in the meantime the center dogs were creeping forward. It was like the children's game of Red Light.

Finally the ordeal was over and the dogs rushed on the meat in one solid, furry mass. The Eskimos retreated hurriedly, leaping over the backs of the furiously hungry creatures. But Idlouk immediately waded in among them. He picked up a few choice bits of meat and fed them to Bakshu. The young dog could not hold his own in the tangled melee of bodies and teeth. Bakshu, it seemed, wasn't very efficient about anything. But Idlouk had an obvious liking for his bumbling puppy.

In a minute and a half there was no meat left. But the dogs were still hungry. They started fighting over the bones. A large dog would set on a smaller one who had a bloody bone in his mouth. Instantly the weaker dog dropped the bone and rolled over on his back, whimpering, his paws in the air. The big dog hung over him, his teeth bared in a fearsome snarl. But as long as one dog remained helpless the other would not attack. Gradually the stronger one withdrew, his fur still raised angrily along his back, picked up the abandoned bone and trotted off with it.

It was a striking demonstration of the predators' code of honor. These dogs, half wild, are one of the few breeds whose ancestors were bred with wolves. (Chows, Malemutes and Samoyeds are others which have some wolf characteristics.) Wolves, in common with other dangerous predators, will seldom fight to the death. The weaker fighter, when he finds he is outmaneuvered, will expose his most vulnerable parts and the victorious animal is prevented by an instinct stronger than his will from killing his opponent. Hackles raised and teeth bared he hangs over the coward, willing him to get up and fight. Slowly he moves away, still growling but unable to attack. It is a valuable instinct for the survival of the race.

These animals are so strong and so vicious that if it were not for their strange code of honor they would quickly exterminate themselves.

After ten minutes there was nothing left but two tattered skins, a few bits of white bone and a wide circle of blood on the white snow. The dogs were harnessed, still growling and unsatisfied. But we noticed that they never attacked an Eskimo no matter how roughly they were handled. When the leather was on their backs they stopped grumbling and soon they trotted off equably into the golden sunset.

Part of our arrangement with Idlouk was that he could take all his meals with us. Though he was amused by our company and found our strange food delectable (dehydrated carrots, mashed potatoes and tapioca pudding were evidently gourmet's delights to him) he found our strict meal hours a sore trial. He hated to get up in the morning. The Eskimo system of life did not include regular bedtime hours and Idlouk was quite likely to hunt seal on the sea ice all night long. Coming home at four or five in the morning, he would drop on his sleeping platform and be dead to the world until the alarm clock went off at eight. More than sleep, it seemed, he wanted Wheatena, canned bacon and dehydrated eggs. He never missed a meal, but he was never on time for one either.

When he came into the cook tent, however late, he smiled with dignified friendliness at everyone in turn. But he did not speak. Eskimos do not say hello. When they meet they smile to show they are friendly, then they wait until they have come together in feeling and thought before they begin to talk. Idlouk was by nature a voluble and expressive talker. If another Eskimo was in the tent he would talk sometimes for fifteen minutes without stopping, his hoarse voice alive with feeling and drama. In fact all the Eskimos we saw talked a great deal. A rule of Eskimo life is that a man must not keep any thought to himself — for if he does so he will go mad. Idlouk also talked constantly with us, partly in English, mostly in Eskimo, using gestures and facial expressions plentifully. But he never spoke during his first few minutes in the tent.

Our guide, who was thirty-nine years old, had nine chil- dren, of whom two were married and lived in their own tents at his camp on Baffin Island. The other seven, ranging in age from two months to seventeen years, lived in the little white tent at the edge of our camp with Idlouk and his wife Kidla, thirty-eight. It was an unusually large family for that part of the arctic. The Eskimos love children, long for large families and eagerly adopt orphans. But the average Eskimo family in the district had only two or three children. There is a com- paratively small infant mortality in the Eastern Arctic — children just don't get born. A mysterious, benevolent nature apparently prevents frequent pregnancies. The high northern tundra barrens cannot support a large population. And even if they could it would be almost impossible for most natives to get food to feed a large number of children, since hunting is difficult, strenuous and often unrewarding. Even Idlouk, a wise and energetic hunter, had a hard time feeding his big family. But he was openly proud of his nine children as well as tenderly affectionate with them.

At first we saw the children only from a distance. They played behind his tent, and from that section of the camp came a continuous joyful shrieking and giggling. Though they were lively their voices were never overexcited or shrill, and there were no tantrums. Even at their wildest they sounded gentle, and the soft Eskimo syllables shaped by little children's tongues were especially enchanting.

Living so intimately close to their parents they followed everything the adults did and learned without realizing it skills which would later be their own livelihood. Their games, like those of wild animals, were a form of practice. They shot stones out of inefficient little slings aiming at the chained dogs, who appeared to be used to it. They picked up old bits of rope and used them as whips, driving one another in makeshift harness across the tundra, calling, "*Hut-hut-hut, woy-woy!*" Sometimes they ventured out on the sea ice, testing it carefully with their little sealskin-booted feet as they had seen their father do. But a single word from Kidla or Idlouk brought them back to safety.

With us they were very shy and at first they ran away when we approached. But when we were all inside the cook tent they would sometimes venture near, and we heard soft laughter outside. One day we saw little faces peering around the tent flap, but we could not entice them in. Finally three of them broke the spell of shyness. They were Pauloosee, Moseesee and Nua (translated into Bible English these are Paul, Moses and Noah). We had seen the three little boys marching over the tundra with their arms around one another's shoulders, their sizes ranging from about two to three and a half feet high. Dressed in identical red-checked shirts and heavy black wool pants tucked into little sealskin boots, they looked like a half-pint vaudeville act.

One afternoon they moved from just outside the tent flap to just inside it. They stood there, grinning widely but not uttering a word. Someone asked, "Do you want some chocolate?" and held out three pieces. Three little pairs of eyebrows went up and they took the candy eagerly. Eyebrows up, apparently, meant, "Yes, thank you." The little boys were bottomless pits. They ate steadily for half an hour, ruining their pretty white teeth on chocolate, nuts and jam. Finally there came a time when, in answer to the question, "Do you want some chocolate?" three little noses wrinkled. Since Eskimo children have almost no nose the nose wrinkling was a dainty, almost invisible gesture. It obviously meant, "No, thank you." After this they murmured in unison, "*Kuayana-mik*" (thank you) and "*Tabaoshi*" (good-by), and departed, zipping the tent flap up and down a few times with gusto as they went.

A tiny, chubby girl about two years old always trailed behind them. Rootay (Ruthie) had thin black hair falling across her wide red-cheeked face and she wore a little suit of soft gray caribou skin with fringes on the sleeves and legs and a convenient flap down the back which opened when she squatted and stayed closed when she stood upright. When we tried to lure her into the tent she stared solemnly and the corners of her mouth went down and down until they nearly touched her chin. Tears were very close — but so was laughter. She ran away like a wild animal and a little later we heard shrieks and giggles as she jumped on her trio of brothers and they all went down in a squirming heap.

Her reluctance to enter the tent was finally overcome by the zipper on the front flap. She discovered it one day and from then on she would not be parted from it. Up and down it went, while Rootay shouted with laughter. Her shyness departed magically and she consented to devour huge quantities of unhealthy food.

Idlouk's children were full of curiosity and merriment — everything about us entertained them. This was apparently their summer holiday. We learned later that the winter is also their winter holiday. There are no schools, no bedtimes, no chores, no music lessons, no doctors or dentists. We never saw a stern or nagging parent and we never heard an Eskimo say a harsh word to a child or strike one. Children in the north country seemed to have a perennial good time.

With all their enviable freedom, however, they learned politeness and obedience from their first breath. "Honor thy father and thy mother" was an unquestioned axiom, a necessity of survival. The Eskimos were strict disciplinarians and there was always dignity in the adult's relation with the child. But discipline was accomplished with gentleness, love, relaxation and humor. A single quiet, smiling word from Kidla and a small child would instantly stop playing with his father's rifle.

There was no planned system of education, but neither was there tenseness in the atmosphere — perhaps one follows the other. Idlouk's children were the best brought-up youngsters I had ever seen. They smiled and laughed constantly; they did as they were told; they ate what was given to them; and they always said thank you.

One day Nua, Moseesee and Pauloosee brought us a present, pride and happiness shining on their faces. The present was two goose eggs. But we were without words to thank them. The day before Bill and Mary Drury had discovered the first bird's nest, that of a snow goose. It was in a small ravine near the beach, close to our camp. With pointing and gestures we learned that the children's present came from that nest.

We did not want to hurt their feelings and took the eggs with gratitude. But Bill called Idlouk and a strange conversation ensued in which Bill tried to explain to our guide that our purpose in being on Bylot Island was not to eat eggs but to watch them. Idlouk understood some English although he found it difficult to pronounce — his consonants could not find their way from the bottom of his bronchial tube to the palate, where English consonants belong. As he listened to the slow, careful sentences his brown face screwed up in the effort to understand. After a question he would look off into the distance for a long moment. Then his face would clear, he would smile and say with definiteness, "Yes. No." It was a little while before we realized that "Yes" meant that he had understood the question and that the answer to it was "No." At the end of the lecture he said, "Yes. Yes," with deliberateness. Idlouk was a careful man who abided by the laws of the white man. He was also, we knew, opposed to waste or senseless destruction of animals. He obviously took in the meaning of the little speech. On the other hand, birds' eggs are a great delicacy for the Eskimos, whose diet is, to say the least, uninteresting.

Afterwards he talked to his children for a long time, very expressively. He was not cross with them, but he was voluble. He was probably saying, "These people are rather foolish and they don't know much yet. But they are nice and they give you chocolate. So lay off their birds' nests. You can find others back in the hills if you are really hungry."

The geese deserted the nest. That was the first and last live goose nest we found.

We asked Idlouk to commission his eager trio of small sons to find lemmings for us, as we had been asked to collect some live specimens for the Bronx Zoo in New York City. One day they found an inhabited burrow and they set to work with as much bustling activity as the lemming itself, digging from different directions with their hands to unearth the little rodent from its network of tunnels. They brought it to us in a tin can, their brown faces alive with smiles. The little creature cowered hopelessly in the bottom of the can, a soft brown ball with shining eyes. We made it a bed of shredded newspaper and gave it oatmeal to eat, and still it did not move. It seemed to be in a state of deep shock. But the next morning the oatmeal was gone and so was the lemming. The little boys found no more.

The evening after the lemming was caught we made our first radio broadcast to Pond Inlet. We had brought with us three lightweight walky-talky hand sets which looked like toys and turned out to be no more useful. Pete had taken one of them back to the mainland and we were to try to establish contact three times a week at eight in the evening. We all, including Idlouk, climbed to the top of a hill behind the camp. Bren or Pete, we knew, would be on the tall hill back of Pond Inlet (we had twenty miles of the earth's curve to overcome).

Ned turned on his set and got a sound like a storm at sea. He shouted several times, "Bylot Island to Pond Inlet. Can you read me?" After a while, to his surprise, he received a faint, buzzy answer. He immediately turned the set over to Idlouk, who had never seen this gadget before and was almost jumping with excited curiosity. Idlouk chattered over the instrument for a long time with an unknown friend at the other end. There was a great deal of incontinent laughter and we were sure that they were telling unprintable Eskimo jokes.

(We found out later that he was telling Pond Inlet about our new lemming pet and its escape.) After ten minutes the reception grew weak, and finally died out altogether.

Idlouk was delighted with the toy and laughed all the way down the hill. He had an idea, he told us. Talking with motions, facial expressions and an occasional word here and there, Idlouk was fairly easy to understand. One hunter, we gathered, would go out on the ice with his rifle and a radio, while another sat on a high hill with a telescope and another radio. The watcher on the hill would tell his friend on the sea ice, over the radio, where the seals were lying. We were given to understand that this would revolutionize seal hunting. Anyway it would be fun. How much do these things cost, he asked.

"Three hundred and sixty dollars each," Ned replied.

Idlouk's face fell. He wrinkled his nose and said, "*Aka!*" with vehemence. His expressiveness left no doubt of the meaning of the word. "*Aka!*" meant "No."

Shortly after Idlouk's family arrived we began to have Eskimo visitors. Sometimes these were travelers from the mainland, willing to take a forty-mile detour on the way from Pond Inlet to their home camps in order to see the strange scientists who looked at birds ten feet away through glasses, picked up insects with their bare hands and put them in bottles and had unlimited supplies of candy and jam. Sometimes the visitors came from Iglookishak, a temporary Eskimo camp about three miles from us on the other side of the Aktineq River. It was said to be a slipshod camp, a kind of arctic Tobacco Road. Idlouk wrinkled his nose whenever it was mentioned.

The visits from Iglookishak started after a walk Axel and
I took during our first week. We decided to go to the neighboring camp one afternoon, but we ran into trouble almost
immediately. The river delta was about a mile across and in
many places the churning water had ripped the ice apart,
leaving undercut ledges on either side of the fast-flowing
shallow streams. It took us more than an hour to cross, and
we got our feet wet — a constant danger in the arctic, where,
even in summer, toes can freeze before one notices it. But as
long as we kept walking the water sloshing inside our rubber
boots stayed warm. On the other side of the river the hills
were sharp; the foothills of the coastal mountains began immediately beyond the Aktineq delta. Plunging up and down
steep hills through knee-deep snow, with the high sun burning
through our clothing and the brilliant reflection scorching
our faces, we quickly grew tired. Now we knew why Eskimos
always traveled at night, when the snow was hard and the
sun low. We did not reach Iglookishak, though we saw many
Eskimo tracks. Late in the afternoon we turned back.

The next morning there was an untidy old man sitting in
front of Idlouk's tent, whittling aimlessly at a piece of soapstone. Idlouk called Axel over and the grizzled Eskimo stood
up, fumbled in the depths of his ragged clothing and pulled
out a pair of Eskimo sun goggles carved of wood, with narrow slits for the eyes. It was made for an Eskimo face, wide-
cheeked and flat-nosed, and was smooth as silk from long
use. Idlouk made Axel understand that some Iglookishak people had seen us yesterday although we hadn't seen them.
They had felt sorry for Axel because he had no sun goggles
(he had taken them off for a few minutes while we rested
before returning home). And so the old man had come over

75

at two o'clock in the morning to bring him something with which to protect his eyes. We were touched by this direct kindness. The old man apparently wanted nothing from us. He smiled all over his dark, wrinkled face, shook hands and trudged away across the snowy tundra toward his home.

After this Iglookishak sent delegates from time to time. Although curious and friendly they never appeared to want anything, and they never stayed more than a few hours. Idlouk apparently discouraged them. He did not approve of Iglookishak.

I remembered Kidla, the roof sitter in Pond Inlet with the beautiful smile, and wanted to make friends with her. But I had already discovered that Eskimo women were very shy and I did not wish to frighten her. One morning she came out of her tent and walked back over the tundra, bouncing as she walked, to rock the baby in her hood. As she tripped along she hummed a little tune.

Ah, native Eskimo music! I was washing socks in front of my tent in the sunshine, but left them full of soap and dived in to get my recorder. After listening to her a few minutes longer I played the beginning of the tune on the little flute. She turned around, smiled her glistening smile and beckoned me to come. There, outside her tent, I played again, while the children gathered and watched me with wide grins. I got Kidla to understand that I wanted to learn the rest of the tune. She sang it and I played each phrase after her. It began to sound familiar. Suddenly I realized — I was playing an Anglican hymn. Native music indeed!

But Kidla had got the idea and now she sang hymn after

hymn, which, perforce, I repeated on the recorder. She was delighted and her beautiful calm face was alight with smiles. Her daughter Leah, about fourteen, came out of the tent and approached tentatively, almost walking sideways in her shyness. Pete had told us that Leah understood English but was afraid to speak it. She had been Outside for a year when she was eight, with tuberculosis. Eskimos in hospitals Outside are miserable. They cannot communicate, they don't know what is being done to them or why, and they feel lost. Leah had been treated gently; she had acquired some English and an inexplicable taste for white women's clothes. She admired, even adored white people — but it had been a strange world and it had frightened her badly.

I played a scale several times very slowly, then handed the flute to Leah. She blew into it and produced a breathy squeak. The other children went off into peals of laughter and Leah giggled, looking at me sideways with her lids half down over her shining dark eyes. Immediately she tried it again. She looked like a Japanese painting as she sat straight-backed and intent, holding the flute in her small, delicate-boned hands.

Within a few minutes she had mastered the first octave. But the recorder requires complicated cross-fingering and is difficult to play. So I got from my duffel bag a little tin fife and gave that to her. In ten minutes she had learned "Hot Cross Buns," a simple two-phrase melody. I tried to harmonize with her on the recorder. My instrument was a quarter tone lower than the tin fife and the result was hideous. But the children were openly delighted and hung over me as I played, almost touching my fingers with their flat little noses. I played some songs for them. When I started "On Top of Old Smoky"

Leah smiled and sang with me, in Eskimo. Then I played "Oh! Susanna" which she also repeated in Eskimo. I wrote down the words. It goes:

Aglaktee shevook took tu
Nuanga nualamik
Ilninga tubak tuak tu
Tubak tua vinamik.

It means, "Aglaktee smokes a pipe with a curved stem. If he had a son his son would chew tobacco." Eskimo "native music" was apparently restricted to Stephen Foster and Burl Ives, with a veneer of Eskimo wittiness. Probably the natives, several generations before, had heard whalers singing these songs. Not understanding English they made up words to suit themselves, usually humorous.

After a while Kidla reached back into her hood and pulled out the sleepy baby, a two-month-old girl named Susanna. Kidla motioned me to play the flute for Susanna. I played "Rockaby, Baby." Susanna screeched horribly and everybody laughed. Kidla, still laughing, took the baby, uncovered a large, luscious breast, and in a moment Susanna was happy again.

After the music lesson I rose to leave. Kidla said, "*Tabaotik,*" in her slow, courteous manner. "*Tabaoshi,*" she made me say. By her gestures I understood that she was saying good-by to one person and I was saying good-by to several people. Our Eskimo family was not going to be difficult to communicate with.

As I sat in my tent, about a hundred yards from Idlouk's tent, the strains of "Hot Cross Buns" floated to me, repeated over and over. It occurred to me that we were probably going to hear "Hot Cross Buns" once too often. After a while the music stopped and Leah appeared at my tent door. She stood there silently, timidly, until I invited her in. Without a word she handed me a book. It was the *Golden Book of Christmas Carols.* I opened it to the first carol and we sang it together. We went through the whole book, Leah singing all the songs in English, apparently reading the words. What did she make of such words as "th'almighty"?

When she got up to go she said, *"Tabaotik, Kukukulik,"* in her soft voice.

"What is *Kukukulik?*" I asked. Leah couldn't tell me but suddenly became shy again, and fled. Much later I learned that it was my new name — "the one who plays the flute."

V I

The Rhythm of the Tundra

THE days sparkled with sunlight, hour by hour the snow melted and the tundra teemed with busy, ever-changing springtime life. Spots of brightness appeared on the brown hills as the new, tiny flowers of early spring bloomed. They were so little and inconspicuous that at first we did not appreciate them. But once we got over thinking about the roses and honeysuckle of home we saw that the flowers of the tundra were beautiful. Most of the blossoms looked delicate and frail. We could not understand how they withstood the frequent below-freezing temperatures and the snow and freezing rain and the bitter east wind or how they had managed to find homes at all in a land which was half desert, half bog.

The soil, we learned, was originally prepared for them by lichens. These lowly, primitive plants are usually the first to appear on barren land. A lichen, flat and rootless, can exist on a naked rock. Acid-producing fungus in the lichen gradually disintegrates the rock. As the plant propagates and spreads, the rock becomes more crumbly — and then, one day, it is soil, ready for a buttercup or a willow.

But tundra soil does not favor deep-rooted plants. Either it is too soggy, so that a few inches below the surface roots cannot get air, or too sandy, so that they cannot get water. Most of the tundra plants, therefore, had wide-spreading, shallow roots. Their leaves were thick, small and often hairy, and their stems were furry, to protect them against the cold. They grew close to the ground, where the temperature was nearly constant and the wind could not disturb them.

The arctic flowers, blooms of cold and treeless barrens, were closely related to those we had found in other Junes on the high rocks of Switzerland and Italy, far above tree line. Mountain mustard, with delicate, spidery, white petals, has cousins dwelling in misty crevices of the Italian Dolomites. Cinquefoil, yellow as sunlight on gray, desertlike sandstone slopes, brightens also the high meadows of the Alps. *Astragalus alpinus*, a convoluted lavender blossom, is first cousin to lupine. Woolly lousewort (formerly reputed to bring vermin to grazing sheep) was red-pink and fat, with white cotton puffing out between its small blossoms. *Erysimum pallasii* was a perfectly round pink cluster smelling dusty-sweet and sending long roots across dry sand. We saw an occasional buttercup in a moist valley, unexpected reminder of home.

Bees buzzed and fussed around the new blossoms, to the horror of the Eskimos, who were afraid of them. Once, while I watched Kidla scraping a sealskin, she suddenly shrieked, jumped up and ran into her tent. A bee had landed on a blossom beside her. She peeked out a moment later, gave me an embarrassed look and laughed her hoarse, blithe laugh. But she would not come out until the inoffensive bee had disappeared. Eskimos, who do not fear death, are afraid of all insects. They run when they see the harmless spiders and beetles of the tundra, and a bee sends them into a panic.

I, on the other hand, was on friendly terms with at least one bee. It lived in a lemming hole right outside our tent flap. I spent much time there on sunny days, typing and doing laundry, while two feet from me the bee went busily in and out of its hole.

These bees, actually bumblebees familiar to temperate climates, are almost the only and certainly the most numerous *Hymenoptera* in the arctic. (*Hymenoptera* include all the insects with a highly organized social life.) In the spring, as soon as the sun melts the snow and warms the frozen earth, the queen bee, warm and secure underground, usually in an old lemming hole — bless the useful lemming — begins to produce worker bees. Later in the spring she gives birth to males, and in midsummer a new queen is produced and the old one dies. The bees are active in June, July and August diligently pollinating the flowers and building a new nest for their queen. At the end of summer they die. Only the queen is left, now fertilized, sheltered in a nest lined with moss and grasses. There she exists, half alive, in a temperature just about at freezing point, until the thawing of the earth warms her to life and the new cycle of reproduction.

Bees were not the only insects we saw those first days. The tundra was busy with small crawling or flying creatures — springtails, beetles, spiders, an occasional butterfly. Rick Miller, our entomologist, was off on a trip, so we caught a few, put them in bottles and laid them in rows, like glass coffins, in his little tent.

There were no worms. The weather was too inclement for them even in summer, and they could not dig deep enough into the damp, airless soil to escape the winter freeze. The function of worms in kinder climates was taken over on the tundra to some extent by soil mites and springtails in larval form. But the chief influence on the soil was the lemming. With their myriad crisscrossing tunnels the little rodents broke up the earth and aerated it so that plant roots had a chance to take hold. Vegetable matter, passing through their bodies, enriched the soil. Soft, moist mosses were attracted to the edges of their holes; these held the moisture near the surface, encouraging the growth of grasses and other plants. The extra moisture also resulted in frost erosion, which broke up the soil still further. On the other side of the picture the lemmings, in years of high population density, destroyed the land cover by eating both the tops and roots of plants.

Here was yet another example of the supreme importance of the humble lemming. Simply by being the most multitudinous animal of the tundra it was the central core of the interdependence of arctic life. Both by its presence and by its absence it influenced the lives of all other tundra creatures, including man.

The lemming population is in a continual state of wild fluctuation, as is that of most small rodents. In its northern home, where predators are few, the small rodent breeds very fast (one pair of breeding mice, unchecked, can have seven hundred and thirty-eight descendants in one four-month breeding season), reaches a peak of population about every four years and destroys its own feeding grounds in the frantic effort to get enough to eat. Then it dies of disease or starvation, or migrates, leaving the land a wasted, ugly desert behind it.

The population fluctuations of this maladjusted animal leave a trail which spreads like the ripples of a wake over the whole of the delicately balanced tundra world. Snowy owls, ravens, jaegers and hawks depend on the lemming for food. When the lemmings disappear these birds are in serious difficulty. Many of them subsist thinly on the eggs and nestlings of songbirds and terns. Often these large, hungry birds do not breed in a lean lemming year. (But in peak years, it has been noted, owls and hawks lay more eggs than usual.)

If the lemming crash occurs in the winter the predatory birds must migrate or starve. Ravens, which are generally not migratory, will eat bear leavings. Sometimes a surprised trapper finds a raven in his fox trap, devouring the bait. Snowy owls, which also prefer to stay in the arctic through the winter, will usually migrate far to the south in a lemmingless season. The winter before our expedition reached Bylot Island there had been a large influx of snowy owls in the northern United States. In the treeless prairies and rolling fields and open beaches of the Temperate Zone these great white predators see land similar to their native tundra. There they settle, to be quickly decimated by eager hunters and irate farmers. Hardly a single owl survives to make the return flight to the lonely, safe northland.

One creature influenced in a different way by lemmings is the caribou. It has been noted that when the lemmings are at their most numerous the caribou herds move away. Probably the raveled moss, tattered ruined grass and ubiquitous mouse droppings offend the sensitive noses of the deer. This is a disastrous occurrence for many inland Eskimos and most northern Indians, who depend on the deer for food and clothing.

Foxes and weasels depend almost entirely on lemmings. If the lemming fails in the summer the foxes can subsist on the eggs and young of birds, mostly ducks and geese. If starvation comes in fall or winter the foxes will follow polar bears, devouring their leavings. The bears feed on seals and go south on the pack ice, following seal migrations of many hundreds of miles. Why the seals go south is not entirely clear. But in the late summer, before the pack ice starts moving south, fish caught in polar waters are found to be emaciated almost to skeletons and the seals probably move southward to find food. One begins to see the striking interrelationship between life on land and sea in a food chain which leads from a failure of fish around the North Pole to the ultimate fate of an arctic fox (which has occasionally been trapped as far south as Nova Scotia, at least a thousand miles from its native tundra).

The foxes that remain in a starvation winter are further reduced by the activities of weasels. These wiry animals, intelligent and capable, can follow lemmings right into their burrows. Having nothing else to eat and being unable to migrate, the weasels feed on most of the remaining lemmings before the foxes can get them.

The unfortunate fox is left with the only alternative of taking trap bait. In winters of severe fox famine the hunters take record numbers of foxes in their traps, even though the actual fox population may be relatively small. Next winter, Idlouk told us, would be a very big fox year. Most of the remaining lemmings would have been destroyed and there would be no edible winter birds except the elusive ptarmigan (whose numbers the hungry foxes had probably already reduced during the past year). However, the winter after next there would be almost no fur game, and many Eskimos would exceed their credit at the Hudson's Bay Company store and go hungry. Lemming — ptarmigan — fox — man. It is like a slow game of ninepins.

Somehow a few lemmings survive, to propagate and start a new chain. The revival of foxes, weasels and raptorial birds lags well behind that of the lemmings, since there are fewer of them and they are much slower breeders. So the little rodent has a chance to revive its race before its hunters catch up with it. This convenient arrangement of birth rates, typical of almost all predator-victim chains, keeps the world going in a constantly oscillating balance. "No predator," it has been remarked, "can afford to be too efficient."

In other lands man has proved to be a predator too efficient. But in the undisturbed world of the arctic the rodent cycle was allowed to have its full effect, unhampered by man-made experiments in rodent control, destruction or encouragement of mouse-eaters, or creation of artificial environments such as cultivated fields and pruned woodlands. Man, in this case, was a victim, not a cause, of the natural fluctuation of the lemming population. And, along with man, almost every creature of the tundra, even down to the grasses and mosses and the insects that lived in them. And even below that, to the condition of the soil. The lemming is the god of the arctic — the helpless, maladjusted, nervous, frightened, persecuted deity, to which all life on the tundra must bow.

Bird life changed every day. We had been greeted by hundreds of snow geese, feeding and courting all around our camp. Now they were beginning to disappear, and within five days of our arrival we could find only an occasional courting pair. They still flew overhead in large flocks, on feeding expeditions. But most of them had finished courting and retired to inaccessible ravines to establish their households.

New birds were coming in. One morning, in a brown puddle high above our camp, we came across six red phalaropes just in from their five- or six-thousand-mile migration from the South Atlantic. These are slim, long-beaked wading and swimming birds, red-brown in front, mottled gray-brown on the back. Like most of the birds which nest in the arctic the phalaropes could melt into the tundra just by standing still. But these birds were whirling in nervous circles as they dipped their beaks into the swampy puddle, and they didn't seem to know we were there. The purpose of this neurotic-looking behavior was to stir up delicacies — plankton and algae — from the muddy bottom so they could eat without getting their faces wet. Within three or four days the phalaropes had gone, presumably to inland nesting grounds to set up their reverse housekeeping. The phalarope is one of the few birds species in which the female is larger and handsomer than the male. She courts him, and when the time comes he takes complete charge of brooding the nest and feeding the young — does everything but lay the eggs.

After their departure golden and black-bellied plovers began to arrive in numbers, sleek and elegant as if they had just stepped out of a *couturier's* shop, although many of them had flown some three thousand miles from South America. These birds, very close cousins, have never been known to nest side by side. But on Bylot Island they did so. They were not pleasant about it — black-bellied plovers frequently invaded the territories of goldens only, apparently, to annoy them.

One morning we watched a pair of black-bellied plovers courting. By our standards it was a dull procedure. First the male fluffed up the feathers of his back, stretched his neck and lowered his head until he looked like a hunchback. The female stood ten feet away, watching stolidly. He kept his unattractive stance until she pattered casually past him, looking straight ahead. Ten feet beyond she paused and started to feed furiously (an instinctive nervous reaction). After about fifteen minutes he walked past her and assumed the hunchback pose again, while the female looked the other way. For an interminable time they stood stock still, facing in opposite directions. Then the female walked past again and ate another large meal. Probably she had not eaten that much since the same time last year. The procedure was repeated for about an hour, then we gave up. At this rate they wouldn't even be on a first-name basis by the time the mating season was over. We went back the next morning to see if they had got any more verve into it, but they weren't there any more. Either they were on their honeymoon or the thing had got too long and boring even for them.

The courting of the Baird's sandpipers was much more spirited. The male, standing still, slowly lifted one long, slender wing straight up into the air, pointing at the sky. He did the same with the other wing. Then he spread both wings wide, fanned his tail and hurtled across the ground towards his beloved. She ran away. He stopped, practiced the wing exercise, then threw himself at her again. Again she ran away and he flew off, apparently discouraged. It was a short romance — about five minutes. But not long afterward we found a nest near there, a shallow depression in the ground near a clump of yellow grass, with an almost invisible tundra-colored egg in it. A mother sandpiper cried distressfully and dragged her wings on the ground nearby, trying to distract our attention.

The little Lapland longspurs were laying out their territories, and although they were not yet nesting they protected vehemently what they considered their boundaries. The territories seemed unconscionably large. They couldn't possibly need that much to eat (but we learned that it is also a method of birth control — the larger the individual territories the fewer birds will be able to make nests in any given locality). When a longspur feels belligerent he flies directly upward, high in the air, then floats to the ground on outspread wings, warbling a long sweet song. It is a lovely way of being angry. On landing he approaches the intruder with a warlike air, fluffing out his black neck feathers in a pretty ruff. The two warriors circle each other until one of them gives up. Sometimes they fight — a real knock-down, drag-out fight.

Many of the other small birds also soared and sang, and when we walked the air was full of the enchanting warble of a multitude of angry little floating birds. This is typical open-country activity. All songbirds proclaim their ownership of land and express their displeasure with an intruder by singing. Most of the birds we know perch on a prominent tree branch, where they can be seen, to talk back to their neighbors. The small birds which nest where there are no trees have to get up in the air somehow to display their male plumage while they sing — so they have developed the soaring procedure.

The tundra birds, we noticed, were well adapted to an open-country life, and far more generalized than birds which can live only in tropical or temperate zones. As one moves northward the brilliant-plumaged birds and those with fussy tastes — fancy nest builders, worm-eaters, tree dwellers — drop out. On the tundra we found only birds which could live on almost any kind of insect or vegetation, which didn't need to build complicated nests, which could crouch on open ground and disappear by sitting still, which could defend boundaries and protect eggs and young by simple devices of attack or lure.

We often walked down the beach, a narrow strip still mostly snow-covered, with immense cliffs of sandstone towering above it. The soft stone of the cliffs was eroded and carved by wind and snow into monolithic shapes, enormous figures of hooded, armless men, like half-realized sculpture. Once we came across a perfect small column, smooth as marble and broken off at one end as if had been part of a building. We had been told there were prehistoric relics in the Eastern Arctic. This piece of pillar looked man-made, and we thought we might find the remains of an ancient pre-Eskimo settlement at the top of the cliff. But, like "native music," this new theory was short-lived. We scrambled up the crumbling cliffside, clinging to handholds only to have them turn to dust in our hands, pulling out grass clumps by the roots in our efforts to keep from slipping backwards. We arrived at the top sneezing and coughing and gray from head to foot with sandstone dust. Bare tundra greeted us, pure and empty as the day it was created. A snow bunting sang at us derisively, flew down the cliff and vanished halfway.

Well, at least we might find a snow bunting nest. We slid down a narrow chutelike ravine, clouds of dust flying around us. Digging our legs into soft dust up to the knees, we managed to stop near where we had seen the bird disappear. One by one we crawled carefully over the edge of our chute and spread-eagled on the crumbling rock. Sure enough, there was a hole. Deep inside it we could glimpse an untidy nest of feathers and grass, and one small egg. We slid down the rest of the way, sat on a sofa-shaped piece of pressure ice on the beach and watched the hole. A pair of snow buntings hovered anxiously near. We remained absolutely still and soon they apparently decided we were rocks. The female landed on the ridge and hopped into the hole without disturbing a grain of dust. After a while a bee went in too, and Mama hopped out again angrily. This was definitely not their day.

We left them and walked on, the sandstone cliffs above us becoming taller and wilder. Two ravens rose heavily from the beach and flapped up a steep ravine. These birds, more than any others, are associated with desolate regions of rock and desert and mountain, and the ragged, forbidding cliffs were a fitting home.

About a mile from camp, on the top of a jutting cliff that looked like Prometheus's Rock, a duck hawk was perched — a fierce and noble predator similar to the European peregrine falcon. We had often seen it fly, straight as a bullet, over our camp, and Josselyn had tried in vain to shoot it. Since a hunting duck hawk has been clocked with a stop watch (by airplane) at one hundred sixty-five to one hundred eighty miles an hour, Josselyn's failure was understandable. This was the first time any of us had found its perch. There appeared to be only one bird, but perhaps there was a nest. Again we scrambled up the sandstone. The hawk watched us fixedly as we approached from the back, turning its head as if it were on a swivel. Before we could reach its perch it flew, made a few wide circles and disappeared into the white sky. Its rock was a narrow, crumbling overhang over which we walked gingerly, looking through eroded holes down to the beach several hundred feet below. Though the rock was covered with droppings there was no sign of a nest.

We wandered home along the beach. A light mist rose off the melting snow and the sun shone behind us through thin clouds. We were each ringed by a small bright rainbow. As we walked, clothed in rainbows, we picked up shells — mussels, small clams and delicately tinted coquinas, a tiny shellfish usually found on the shores of the Gulf of Mexico and the Caribbean Sea. We came across several more of those prehistoric pillars. Some of them were part of the sandstone cliff, and we realized that the hands that had carved them into such smooth perfection were wind, snow and erosion.

This strange land of carved sandstone and personal rainbows seemed quite unreal. We walked in a dream.

While Axel and I were learning the life of the tundra from the outside, strolling, observing and collecting in our unsystematic way, the scientists were busy digging into its inner life. In one case this was a literal fact. Bill Drury spent hour after hour with a shovel, making holes in the thin top layer of thawed earth in order to study the frost forms beneath. Ned joined him and even Idlouk, the proud hunter, was occasionally seen trudging across the heaths with a shovel over his shoulder, looking like a gnome between two tall scientists, his dun-colored parka melting into the pale-brown tundra.

What, Bill wondered, made the tundra so astonishingly geometric? Even the smallest bits of frozen earth or rock were angular and regular in form, as if shaped by a chisel. If one picked up a pebble one found it was a microcosm of the tundra, a tiny, perfect example of the geometric effects of rhythmical freezing and thawing.

He studied the peat-ridge polygons, crooked checkerboard patterns over the flat bogs, where the earth had been broken apart by some unknown function of frost action. These flat, raised earth shapes were lined by dikes, and ditches about a foot deep ran absolutely straight along their sides, cut sharp and neat as if by peat diggers' knives. The ditches, it was discovered, ran both parallel and at right angles to the direction of the flow of water on the earth. Standing on top of the sandstone cliffs, Bill noted the pattern of the cracking sea ice — and with an excited sense of wonder and discovery he saw that it was the same as that of the peat ridges. The cracks ran parallel and at right angles to the shore line, creating straight-edged ice polygons. It reminded him of the breaking of a pane of glass, which will similarly crack in straight lines under pressure. Glass, ice, frozen earth — in some way they were bound by the same physical laws.

This land had once been under glacier. Under its centuries-long frozen bondage the earth had become hard and brittle as glass. Three or four thousand years ago the glacier had retreated. The earth rose after the heavy load had been removed and pressures were set up which broke its surface. Having the consistency of glass or ice, the soil broke in the same patterns. The formation of these earth patterns had taken thousands of years — yet it was essentially the same as the breaking of a windowpane.

All over the tundra were bubbles of earth two or more feet in diameter. Digging into them, Bill found frozen soil very near the surface. A clump of flowers or a hummock of grass or a willow had probably gathered moisture around its roots. The water had attracted fine sand or silt, which adhered in a wet hump around the plant; the earth had then frozen and the moisture-laden silt expanded, pushing the land upward in a bubble. Each year more of the coarser soils and pebbles were cast out with frost expansion, and more silt collected, and the bubble became bigger.

Another kind of patterned ground that Bill examined were the pebble circles that looked like little tent rings. The centers of these circles consisted of fine sand and silt. Adhering with moisture, like the earth bubbles, the finer earth had frozen and pushed the coarser soil and pebbles outward in a rough ring. With each thaw and each freeze the circle grew larger and more regular, as more fine soil accumulated and more rocks were thrown outward.

Interested in the effects of snow and frost on vegetation, Bill had defined the outlines of snow patches with white stakes, to discover whether the plants which grew in the late-snow areas were different from those which grew where the snow melted earlier. During our six weeks' stay he discovered a decided variation, not so much in the kind, as in the abundance and density of various plants at different times and places. This depended on three factors — the time of the snow melt, the exposure to wind and sun and the amount of moisture preservation. The exposed ridges were the first to be free of snow, and there grew the pale-green lichen *Stereocaulon*, the hardy saxifrage and the tough arctic willow — plants which can stand cold and wind and dryness but love the sun. In the hollows and under mud banks, where the snow came off next, we were to find heavy concentrations of arctic bell heather, a plant which likes moisture and protection. Then came a general melting of snow in all kinds of areas,

n impressive crucifix dominated Pond Inlet and bravely addressed itself to the
arren scene.

The housekeeping routine took a large part of every morning.

Idlouk watched a wary seal far across the rotting sea ice, while I took a rare re
on his komatik.

Idlouk shot a silverjar
ringed seal, after stalking
it behind his shield for
nearly an hour.

and all the spring flowers bloomed in sudden profusion, as in the high Alps in June. The stubbornest snow finally gave itself up to the hot, dry wind of early summer, and there grew another willow, *Salix herbacea*, the last-blooming plant of the short season. This tiny shrub, producing only two leaves and an infinitesimal fruit, can stand a long period of wet, cold snow, but it is apparently too meager to compete with the lusher plants of spring. From a distance the healthy fields of *Salix herbacea*, after everything else had turned brown, looked like golf greens.

Rick Miller had gone back to Pond Inlet with one of Idlouk's friends to gather information from Eskimos and traders on mammal populations and fluctuations. Having permission to study Hudson's Bay Company records for the thirty-two years they had been kept at Pond Inlet, he was making notes on the seasons and numbers of animals caught — seal, walrus, narwhal, white whale, bear, fox and weasel. He found no significant evidence of cycles in any animals except foxes. Pond Inlet was apparently rich in game and the small Eskimo population hardly made a dent in it. But the arctic fox, Rick discovered, had lean and peak years, independent of the number or industry of the hunters — and its cycle averaged out to exactly four years, coinciding roughly with the lemming cycle.

Ben Ferris, the doctor, was also at Pond Inlet, with his trunkful of medicines, to study the condition of the Eskimos who came to the post to trade. He found some tuberculosis, many colds and occasional crippling arthritis. Bad eyes were common — there is not much ventilation in the Eskimos' smoky winter igloos, and out of doors eyes are alternately seared and frozen by sun, snow reflection and bitter winter gales. On the whole, however, the Tunnunermiut, the Pond Inlet Eskimos, were a healthy lot. They were also comparatively rich, most of them owning outboard motors, rifles and telescopes. (Idlouk even owned a twenty-seven-hundred-dollar motor launch for which he had paid with many winters of successful fox trapping.) Pond Inlet was considered to be the best Eskimo colony in the Northwest Territories and its inhabitants were proud of their reputation as hunters. The reasons for their superiority were not far to seek — there were few hunters and much game. But since the coming of white men, Ben found, the population in this district had been on the rise at the startling rate of two and three tenths per cent a year. Living is much softer than it used to be.

Josselyn Van Tyne was unceasingly active with his binoculars, his camera and his gun, and hardly a day passed that we did not have several small birds in the soup or the frying pan. Part of his mission was to take specimens of Bylot Island birds in order to discover minute differences in closely related species, overlapping with slightly more southerly birds, accidental wanderers and rare breeding plumages. He made up the skins on the spot, for his museum, which has one of the largest university birdskin collections in the world. Josselyn was a mild, quiet man who did not have a hunter's instinct. The Canadian Government had issued him an unlimited license, but he never shot for fun, never killed a bird which he knew was brooding, did not take more than the absolute minimum of specimens — and almost never missed. His birds usually dropped dead at the first shot. Examining them, one could hardly find a drop of blood, though we occasionally bumped our teeth against tiny lead pellets in the soup.

The Eskimos, superior hunters, were amazed and delighted

at Josselyn's prowess with a shotgun or rifle. Idlouk took an immediate liking to the gentle professor. They never became close friends, partly because of the language barrier and partly because of the natural reserve of both. But there was an affinity born of mutual respect between the kind small native and the kind tall scientist. One of my favorite memories is the sight of the two coming back to camp together, each carrying a large dead bird. Idlouk looked like part of the tundra, a sprite of the arctic, in his dun-colored, peaked-hooded anorak, with his gun, in its furred, caribou-skin case, slung across his back. His head reached only to the middle of Josselyn's upper arm. Josselyn, tall, stooped, long-faced, every inch the careful scientist and professor, walked with a deliberate, slow stride, holding his gun loosely, with seeming awkwardness, under one arm. He did not look like any part of the tundra. But on the two faces, the Oriental brown one and the Middle Western pale one, there was the same expression — the beginning of a slow smile and a half-embarrassed look of modesty and pride.

One morning we were awakened by the tremendous roar of a shotgun. It sounded as if it had taken the top off our tent. An angry and desperate honking followed. Josselyn had shot a snow goose, one of my enchanted princes. Its bereaved mate flew low, crying and searching. Some varieties of geese mate for life, and their feeling of responsibility towards each other is so strong that if a bird is wounded its mate will stay with it even though the rest of the flock is in migration. The European greylag goose is even faithful after death, never mating again after the death of the spouse.

But sentimental digressions were out of place. Josselyn skinned the goose immediately, while I swallowed my thoughts and watched him. Those overlong, awkward-looking fingers worked on the bird with a surgeon's precision. First he made an incision in the lower part of the belly, cutting only the skin, not the flesh. He separated skin from flesh with a small scalpel and slowly peeled the skin off, inside out, like a tight glove. He used cornstarch to mop up wetness and blood as he worked the skin back, then covered the entire inside of the skin with borax, a mild curative, to prevent deterioration. When he came to the legs he pulled them back from the inside-out skin, severed them from the rest of the skeleton, parted the muscle tendons from the leg bones and snipped them off neatly. He did the same with the wings. When the skin was peeled back to the head the creature lay naked, surprisingly thin and small. With the head in the middle and a shapeless, ruined body on each side, it did not look as if it had ever been a bird or ever would be again. Josselyn cut off the carcass at the base of the skull and carefully cleaned out the inside of the head. The brain of a bird, astonishingly large and soft, has, he told me, almost exactly the same consistency as that of a man. I don't know what this means; it has nothing to do with intelligence. He popped out each eye with a deft motion of his small knife. The eyes must come out whole, otherwise the eye socket and facial feathers will be damaged. Then he filled the skull with cotton, drawing some of it through the eye sockets in neat, bulbous projections. Slowly he worked the skin back right side out. It began to look like a bird again, but it lay flat and limp, its feathers mussed, its red-brown legs hopelessly awry.

"Are you going to stuff it?"

"Don't use that word," Josselyn said with mock professorial sternness. "We don't *stuff* a bird, we 'make up a skin.'"

But I couldn't cope with the sentence structure. "Are you going to s-t-u-f-f it?" I repeated carefully. He replied that he would put cotton in the small interstices and pack the rest of the body thinly with newspaper, just enough to keep the insides of the skin from touching. The big birds would be too hard to transport if they were made up in their natural size. The little ones he would fill with a natural-shaped body of cotton rolled on a long toothpick. Now he took a few pages of the May 2 New York *Times*, worked them into the interior of the goose and arranged them in a flat, compact mass. Then he sewed the belly incision so carefully that not a stitch showed and covered the scar with feathers. He needled formaldehyde (the juice that undertakers pump into corpses) into the legs to keep them from decomposing, tied the feet together, folded the wings into position and brushed every feather into place with a toothbrush. There lay an intact snow goose, very thin, with staring eyes of cotton. My enchanted prince (this one was a princess) would need a formidable magic to awaken it from this spell.

We had snow goose for supper, boiled with dehydrated onions, dehydrated potatoes and celery salt. We also had two snow goose eggs — interior ones, without shells, unattractive, dark red and gelatinous. Mary poached them and they were passed around the tent rapidly, like hot potatoes. Each of us hastily slid them on to the next, murmuring politely that there were not enough to go around, until they came to Idlouk. He ate them both with relish.

The snow goose is a thin, muscly bird. It takes a lot of cooking and even then it does not taste very good. We preferred fried snow buntings.

VII
The Timeless Life

It's hot today," I said, coming into the cook tent one morning. Everybody laughed.

"One of those hot, breathless days," commented Josselyn solemnly. "It's not the heat, it's the humidity."

"Now we can go to bed without our mittens on," added Bill.

The temperature was forty degrees — and the date was June 20. But for two days there had been a strong, cold wind from the east. The tent walls had billowed and flapped ceaselessly and the wind had blown under the tent floors so we felt as if we were walking on balloons. We had all suffered, not so much from the cold as from the noise. Today, however, the air was mild and the sun was warm. Axel and Rick and I were to set out on a long dog-sled expedition and the April-like weather was pleasing. Idlouk was going to take us over the sea ice to Button Point, on the southeastern tip of Bylot Island. There we would see the thousands of birds which nested on the wild cliffs of the oceanside. And on the floe edge, where the solid ice of the inlet met the open ocean, we would watch the natives hunting walrus and narwhal. We would cross to Pond Inlet first to pick up Ben and Ned. (There was a constant coming and going between our camp and the mainland, and one or more of us was usually at the settlement.) The expedition was supposed to last five days. Actually, what with the slowness of travel and the extraordinarily relaxed attitude of the Eskimos toward time, it turned out to be eleven days.

Before we could leave we took part, as usual, in the housekeeping routine, which always took a large part of every morning. We considered this routine, far stricter than that of most ordinary households, indispensable to our well-being and self-respect. We were soon to learn how delightfully easy it was to live without it.

Breakfast was a four-course meal, and left the dishwasher (we took turns) with an unconscionable number of sticky, greasy pots. But he had two pans of near-boiling water and every dishwashing luxury. His helper dried the dishes, put them away each in its absolutely proper place, then cleaned and swept the tent. The damp, lumpy canvas floor was always unaccountably dirty. We painstakingly brushed our feet before entering the tent, a long iritating process which must have eaten up, altogether, at least an hour of each day. But still, somehow, mud and dry grass crept in and hid in the corners. Sweeping was a backbreaking operation accomplished with a dainty hand brush of bright-blue nylon bristles. One swept out all the dark corners, then brushed an astonishingly large pile of dirt carefully, almost a grain of dust at a time, toward the closed tent flap. One lifted the flap an inch and rapidly tried to get the pile outside. But the dust instantly flew back in one's face and settled again in the corners. It was the labor of Sisyphus.

Then there was the water detail, too arduous for the women. Twice a day one of the men fetched water, ten gallons at a time. To get to the beach lagoon he had to cross a snow-filled ravine and descend a steep little hill. He usually sank up to his thighs in the rotting snow or slipped on the muddy hill. But it was a popular detail because he could stop to watch birds or collect plants on the way. Sometimes it was an hour before the water carrier got back.

The men also had to dig ditches in the morning to lure away the large puddles which had collected behind the tents the day before. Though the tents were on dry ground there was a gently sloping marsh behind them, and water seeped inexorably under the flooring as the frozen earth melted. A faint odor of mildew hung permanently about us. Never, in the whole six weeks, were we quite dry. Idlouk's tent had a raised sleeping platform and no flooring except pebbles. It was always dry and warm. Even in such small matters we were learning how the natives had made themselves a life of comfort in a land of hardship.

After the general housekeeping we straightened our home tents. The sleeping bags were turned inside out and flung over the ridge pole, the tumbled piles of clothing that kept us warm at night were brushed, aired and folded, and a hopeless attempt was made to get the wet floor clean. Then the tents flaps were opened wide to the brilliant morning sun.

I liked our tent. On each side was a low, lightweight folding cot. At the foot of our cots were our duffelbags and at the head were small grocery cartons for articles we used constantly. A heavy carton served as a table for my typewriter. Over our heads, on the back pole, a picture of the children was fastened with Scotch Tape — two little mermaids sitting on a rock at the edge of the Hudson River. In bed, at night, we could reach anything we needed without even unzipping our sleeping bags. It was a handy little house.

We did not bathe often because it was complicated and very cold. We did not feel specially dirty, but I suppose we were. The men, however, shaved with fair regularity. None of them liked beards — said they were scratchy. Besides, they felt that the beardedness of explorers had been overdone. This morning we felt we ought to have sponge baths before we started on our journey. It would be many days before we would be clean again. A sponge bath was literally that — a sponge, a shallow basin with a little hot water in it and a piece of soap. The secret, we found, was not to use much soap, otherwise one got sticky. Still, after a bath, one felt quite clean. Just the smell of soap made one seem cleaner, at least to oneself.

It was half past three in the afternoon before we had finished the complicated routine, collected food and packed duffels and boxes. But we felt no sense of pressure. It made no difference to anyone at Pond Inlet whether we arrived there at nine in the evening or five in the morning. We were not even sure they knew we were coming, as our toy radio had ceased receiving altogether.

As I jumped on the end of Idlouk's sled and we bounced over the rough shore ice I had the same feeling of adventurous elation that had filled me the first time I rode on a komatik, the Eskimo dog sled. But the ice was unpleasant. The powerful Aktineq River was eating away the ice from underneath and the broad delta was ugly with wide black cracks and brown slush. The dogs halted at the cracks, tails down, looked back unhappily at their master, then leaped. Usually several dogs were pushed or dragged into the water amid the leaping, clawing tangle of bodies. They thrashed frantically in the water, enmeshed in their traces, until Idlouk could pull them out. Then they gave themselves a quick shake and resumed their brisk, efficient trot, plumy tails waving, ears alert. Idlouk's dogs were no sissies.

Beyond the river delta the cracks were narrower and less frequent, but we rode through deep slush covered with a thin icy crust. I lay on the polar-bear skin, dreamily watching the wake of the sled over the slit belly of a dead seal. Now, if I close my eyes, I am there again. The deep tracks of the sled runners, about two feet apart, are bluish gray from the watery slush. On one side of them is the thin, wavering track of the whip, on the other the path of the dead seal's head, with blood in it. All around these tracks is an uneven spattering of dogs' prints. Some of these are bloody — the frozen crust splinters like glass and cuts the dogs' pads. Directly behind our sled are the wolflike, slit-eyed faces of the following team. The right-hand front dog always catches up to Idlouk's dead seal and chews briefly at its face before the whip gets him. The seal's head grows bloodier. The rough cords cut into the seal's fatness; the dark-red slit in its belly is sewed together with its own gut. But I am getting used to seeing the insides of things — seal's stomachs, inside-out birds, un-born eggs.

Beside me, trailing on the ice, is the tip of the whip, which flicks the snow lightly like the tail of a snake. Every now and then Idlouk calls, "Bakshu!" Instantly there is a little howl — the well-taught puppy knows what is coming. On the heels of the howl the whip leaps from the snow and there is a momentary lurch of speed. Sometimes a dog's trace gets caught on a snowy protuberance. The dog is dragged behind the sled, howling miserably, until Idlouk frees him. It is again

Bakshu — but it is his own fault. He trots far out to the side, only pretending to pull, and his loose line catches on every hump. Idlouk laughs, half impatiently, whenever his inefficient, gold-bricking puppy gets into trouble.

On the komakik behind us ride Rick and his Eskimo companion, Kudlu. Rick has taken over the driver's place. He cracks the long heavy whip and shouts the deep-throated Eskimo syllables with a clear California accent. Kudlu, meanwhile, reclines behind him on a polar-bear skin, taking his ease like an Oriental prince. He puffs black clouds of smoke from a stubby pipe and laughs at Rick. Everything is funny to him, particularly when Rick catches the whip on the end of the sled or wraps it around himself. "Kooka!" shouts Kudlu with a burst of laughter. Kooka is the Eskimos' name for Rick. From his first day in the north Rick had made himself at home with them, and they liked him better than any of us, took care of him, made fun of him. *Kooka* is an Eskimo nonsense word which has no meaning but always sends the Eskimos off into helpless laughter.

Kudlu is a strikingly handsome Eskimo. His face is dark red (the usual color of the adult Eskimo is sallow brown), his eyes are bright brown and his nose is jutting and high-bridged. He looks more like an American Indian than an Eskimo. Though he is no taller than the other natives he has a better physique, heavier and stronger. His father was a French trader.

The sun is bright silver through the fog. Beyond it are layers of cloud, gray on gray. Even Bylot's grim black cliffs are softened by the mist. The whole landscape is silver and gray and white. We cannot see the shore of Baffin Island, we are riding into an eternity of mist. I marvel at the primordial loneliness of this icy world — meanwhile I eat cashews out of a Planter's can.

We stopped for tea four times on the six-hour trip. We couldn't find our cups so we took turns drinking out of the Planter's can. I had thrown it away, but Idhouk had thriftily run back and picked it up.

As the only woman I had a recurring problem on dog-sled trips. What do you do on an absolutely flat expanse of white ice? Nearby, at one tea stop, was a little floe to hide behind, but it frightened me. The snow was soft and deep around it and I was afraid of vanishing into a crevasse. One could carry modesty too far. Finally I decided just to walk a little way from the sled and not to care, like the Eskimo women — that was not merely the simplest but the only solution.

At 9:30 in the evening we reached Pond Inlet and were greeted with warm enthusiasm by the Hudson's Bay Company and the Royal Canadian Mounted Police, as well as our companions Ben, the doctor, and Ned, the iceberg climber.

"Well, has the big town changed any since you last saw it?" Ben asked.

"Yes. Now it looks like civilization; a week ago it did not." Actually the evidence of Ben's pale, tired face and Ned's drooping eyelids made Pond Inlet appear almost decadent. For eight days we had lived on Bylot Island a superhealthy, well-regimented life, outdoors all day long, ten hours in the sack. Here, apparently, no one went outdoors except to get to another house for another cup of coffee, and no one went to bed at all.

We were fed raisin bread and coffee. When did they eat in the arctic? The home of real men, one would imagine, would be the home of real eating. But our menus since leaving Bylot Island would have shamed a ladies' tea party. Lunch was Ry-Krisp, cheese and tea. Tea was tea. Supper was raisin bread and midnight snack was cookies. In between we nibbled at apricots, nuts and chocolate. The Eskimos also appeared to exist on this dainty fare. Where were the "Eaters of Raw Meat," the heroic chewers of blubber? The dogs were the only creatures who got real meals — and they were fed only twice a week, or three times if they were lucky.

At midnight, after the cooky snack, Axel and I walked with Pete down to the edge of the sea. The sun had come out again, low over the mountainous horizon, and the sky was lined with clouds, gold and silver, almost too bright to look at. I took a photograph across the brilliant, tumbled ice — a picture of the sun at midnight on the longest day of the year.

Back in the hot HBC house we sat in the kitchen while the eternal coffee bubbled on the coal range and the eternal radio blared forth cowboy songs in the living room. In there Constable Doug Moodie sat on the sofa, his head back, fast asleep. Weary as we were we talked and drank for another hour, unwilling to let go. There was a warmth of spirit, a sense of peace and timelessness, that overcame our fatigue. Pete started telling Eskimo legends.

"There was a woman," he said, "who was afraid of her husband because he beat her and was always angry. She went out to a place with new-fallen snow, bowed her head in her arms and said, 'O moon up there, come and get me.' She heard a sound like a sled on hard snow, and a voice spoke. It told her to get on the sled and to keep her eyes closed. For a while she heard the snow, and then not any more. When she opened her eyes they were on the moon. There were many wolves. Takerk Anutinga (the Man of the Moon) told her to enter his house but not to look on the porch on the right. That was where his sister, the sun, lived. The woman glanced and was almost burned. The Man of the Moon took her to wife and she became pregnant. He called her over to the end of the lamp platform and told her to look down. She could see her husband and children. He told her to spit. The children looked up and said, 'There is a shooting star.' ["Star spit" in Eskimo.]

"When the woman's time came close he took her back to her husband. After the child had been born, one day she heard a thump on the ground. Going outside she found a hind quarter of deer meat which had been dropped from the moon for her. She got all her food this way. When there was no oil in the lamp she shook it and it filled up. She had to shout when it was full, otherwise it would overflow. Her husband asked her what she ate and she said, 'Deer meat.' He tried to persuade her to eat seal meat and fearing to displease him she ate some. And so she died."

The tale seemed to end in the middle. Pete told it in exactly the clipped, ungarnished sentences that I have recorded.

"That is the way an old woman tells these stories," he said. "No matter how many times she tells a story she always uses the same words. Another old woman, in an entirely different part of the arctic, will tell the same story, and again use the same words."

Very few Eskimos in this part of the north, Pete said, told these stories now. Missionaries had persuaded them that the stories were naughty, and most Eskimos didn't dare to tell them for fear of going to hell. Now only old women knew them and they didn't tell the little children. Soon all their stories would be forgotten. Pete was writing down all he could collect, hoping to publish them in Eskimo syllabic writing and distribute them to the people from whom they came, so they could learn again their own folklore. Knowing the language perfectly, he would sit in an Eskimo tent for hours or days, chatting and gossiping and telling stories. He told them tales about Robin Hood, King Arthur, Columbus. The Eskimos delighted to hear of the foolishness of white men. Wars and duels especially amazed them as Eskimos have no sense of competition. They laughed over the stupid people who thought the earth was flat and that they might fall off the edge of it. Pete also told them our fairy tales and Bible stories. "Listen," he would say, "the Bible is full of magic, just like your stories." And the old women, after a while, would respond and tell him their stories. He wanted to piece together the curious, primitive native legends of the creation. It was like a great crazy quilt, torn and patched and full of holes. The stories wandered on endlessly, changing personnel every few minutes — or else they ended with senseless abruptness like the one we had just heard.

He told us part of the classic Sun and Moon story. "There was a young boy who lived with his sister and grandmother. They lived on the shore. The boy was blind. One day, in the tent, the boy said, 'I think I hear a bear.' The old woman said, 'Yes.' The boy said, 'I will take my bow and arrow and you tell me when I have aimed at it.' When he aimed straight the old woman told him to shoot. He said, 'Did I hit it?' She said, 'No, the arrow went into the side of the wall and did not strike the bear.' But he had struck the bear. The old woman went out and skinned it and took the meat. She made a small tent for the boy outside and he lived there and ate old seal meat while the grandmother and his sister ate bear meat. But secretly the girl gave her brother some of the bear meat.

"The sister built cairns so that the boy could go fishing in the lake. One day, coming back, he felt the bearskin drying outside and knew the old woman had deceived him. He said nothing, but remembered. Every day he went up to the lake. One day he heard a noise. A loon came up in a kayak. It said, 'Get in my kayak and lie down.' He did so and the kayak went under the water. When it came up again the bird asked if he could see. He said, 'No,' so they submerged again, until the boy's lungs nearly burst. When they came up he could see dimly. The third time they stayed under until he nearly died. When they came up he could see blades of grass on the other side of the lake. It was a very big lake. The bird brought him back to shore and he went home, but he did not let his people know he could see. One day the three went out whale hunting at the floe edge. The old woman said, 'Throw your harpoon into a small whale and I will help you draw it in.' The boy pretended to throw his harpoon into a small whale, but it was really a large walrus. [The walrus though smaller, is aggressive and much more dangerous than the narwhal.] The old woman was pulled into the water. She came up several times, singing, 'Oh, my dear son, why do you treat me so badly when I was so good to you?' He sang to her, 'You are a nasty old woman.' The woman drowned.

"Then the brother and sister decided to find some Eskimos to live with. They had to make a long journey overland to find people. On the way they had many adventures. They came to a land of *kukilikgakjuak*, evil spirits with long fingernails and long teeth. The boy said he wanted a drink of water. The girl called out for it and an old man inside the tent said, 'Come and get it.' The boy said, 'Don't go in.' But his sister went in anyway, because she loved her brother. The door was very small and she had to go in backwards. As she came in they tore pieces out of her back and ate them. She called her brother and he went in with a bone club and started killing the creatures. The old man laughed and the boy killed him too.

"They came to another land where the women had no sex organs. Whenever a woman had a child she had to be cut open with knives. The brother and sister each married one of these people. The girl became pregnant. When it was time for the child the mother-in-law was ready to cut her open. Her brother said, 'No, wait.' And his sister had the child by herself. The old woman sang a song, 'At last I have a little daughter, and I did not have to cut her open.' The other women took knives and cut themselves, so that they could have children that way too. Some cut in the right place, others killed themselves.

"After many more adventures they came to real people. There was feasting and dancing. Every night a man came to sleep with the girl. It was always dark in the snow house and she could not see him. One night she took soot off the lamp and rubbed it on his forehead. When she went to the dancing the next day she found it was her brother. She was ashamed and angry and decided to run away. But first she tore off her breasts and threw them in front of him. 'I am according to your taste — here! Taste this too.' Then she picked up a torch made of a bone, with moss on the end of it. Her brother knew she was ashamed, but he did not want her to go. He picked up another torch and chased her around the house and up into the sky. Sometimes he fell, and his light went out, and he had to light it again.

"She became the sun, Sekengik, and he became the moon, Takerk. His blindness is a symbol of night." Pete was silent. Our heads rang with the eerie, wandering tale, and outside the pale sun glimmered across the rotting sea ice from the black mountain rim.

"Tell us another story," I begged.

Pete laughed. "Be careful," he said. "Once there was a little girl living with her grandmother. The little girl teased her, 'Oh, Grandma, tell me another story.' The old woman said, 'I have no more stories to tell you.' The little girl teased some more, and the old woman said, 'Once there was a great big lemming, and he was hiding under the tent flap — Ee, there he is now!' The child was so startled that she flew away and became a snow bunting. The old woman cried and her eyes turned red. She flew away to look for the little girl, and became a ptarmigan."

The stories sang in my mind all night, along with thoughts of the people to whom they were still real — people who had only been Christians since 1930. We could not possibly understand them. They were still living in a world that had not changed for over a thousand years, and our civilization had barely touched them.

It was a twelve- to fifteen-hour trip from Pond Inlet to Button Point, and we were to have started the next morning before eleven. But no one made any move to go. An old woman, Ootuokak, had come to Pond Inlet the night before, Pete said, and she wanted to dance for us. At eleven o'clock she was still asleep. Gradually the Eskimos gathered on the beach and finally the woman herself appeared, rubbing her eyes and hitching up her clothes. She was dressed in a robe of caribou hide, wrinkled and dark with age and dirt. Below its fringed hem a faded Mother Hubbard hung untidily. She had no teeth and her thin black hair hung in witchlike wisps around her raddled face.

Pete brought a wooden platform down to the beach and Makpa, his seventeen-year-old maid of all work, struck up a tune on a concertina. Makpa sat still and sad, like a painting on Chinese silk, drooped gracefully over her instrument. Her playing was spiritless and devoid of style — but it was exceedingly fast. She played sea chanteys and Irish jigs and Highlanders' flings, learned from whalers and passed from generation to generation by people with no talent for music. Ootuokak shuffled her feet and soon she stepped up on the platform and began dancing. At first she seemed to be improvising. The dance looked like a combination of a hornpipe and a rhumba, with a rich overlay of lewdness. She flirted, rolled her eyes, worked her mobile face into loose grimaces, shook her hips and made lascivious gestures with her hands and body. After two or three short dances, however, we realized that, while she was neither graceful nor beautiful, she was a real dancer and a first-rate showman. And the dances appeared to have some ancient ritual significance. Ootuokak was obviously telling stories with her grotesque contortions of head, arms and body. What the stories were no one knew. The Eskimos of northern Baffin Island, faithful to their puritanical Anglican pastors, seldom performed their dances, even among themselves. So they had forgotten the legends that went with the dance motions.

But Ootuokak lived in a distant, inaccessible ravine, far from missionary influence. Besides she was a careless old woman with no inhibitions.

Eskimos, about twenty of them, sat in a circle around her, laughing uproariously. They loved the show but they were also making fun of Ootuokak. They considered her mad, and had given her a very lewd name.

When the performance was over Ootuokak took her adopted baby from her husband, a kind-faced, middle-aged man with a beard (a rare sight, as Eskimos have little hair on their faces). She slung the baby into her wide hood, turned her head towards it, her loose-lipped ugly face suddenly sweet, and cooed a little Eskimo chant, a baby poem. Then she shook the baby down into the bottom of the hood, gave a guttural laugh and lit a stubby black pipe from which she blew clouds of malodorous smoke.

Still there was no sign of leaving. Idlouk and Kudlu took up their harpoons and had a harpoon-throwing contest on the beach. They aimed at, and seldom missed, a tin can about fifty feet away. Pete joined them, and the slender young trader had the same prowess and strength as the sturdy little Eskimos. Near them, not looking, sat two pretty girls, both seemingly about fourteen years old, with babies in their hoods. The girls were sewing in the bright sun on ancient Singer sewing machines with hand wheels. Their faces showed no expression.

After lunch we waited for the radio schedules, and then there was an hour in which nothing happened whatsoever. About six in the evening the komatiks suddenly started over the sea ice. As usual I was unprepared. I jumped for a sled, my arms full of cameras, binoculars, hat, scarf, blanket, coat.

I missed, and landed on my face in the snow, my belongings flying in every direction. The driver, a fat, dimpled seventeen-year-old named Kaunuk, stopped his dogs and giggled while I collected myself. I couldn't do anything but laugh too.

We traveled, thirteen gay and carefree people, in a caravan of four sleds. There were five of us Bylot Islanders — Ben, Rick, Ned, Axel and I. Pete came along because he wanted to get out of his hot house and do some hunting. Seven Eskimos accompanied us, just for the ride. Two of them were girls, twelve-year-old Marta, a beautiful, gay, red-cheeked child, and Makpa, the HBC maid, who was not so much the maid as part of the household. She loved visiting and she accompanied Pete on most of his trips, bringing her own tent. Idlouk was the cheeriest of all of us. His pride and happiness lay in hunting and this was hunting time on the floe edge — walrus, narwhal and seal. We five Bylot Islanders were ostensibly out for birds. What did we really want, we wondered to each other. A holiday on the beach by the sea, we decided. We felt as lighthearted as the Eskimos.

Axel and I were on the police sled, pulled by the dog team which had won the Pond Inlet sweepstakes a month before. The twelve dogs did not trot, they galloped. Our driver, full of team spirit, ran more than he rode, cajoling, shouting and brandishing his whip. We sped over the bumpy snow, hanging on precariously, with little leisure to look at the glorious golden sunset, the mountains of brilliantly lit cumulus clouds or the dramatic black gorge of the inlet ahead of us. On our sled a tiny, thin Eskimo boy of about eleven curled up on a caribou skin and immediately went to sleep, snoring loudly, while the sled pitched and tossed and Kaunuk energetically shouted at his dogs.

A sled appeared, black against the brilliant ice. It was a small sled, with one native and five dogs. We stopped and waited for it to approach. Its driver took off one mitt and shook hands formally with each of us. He was a stocky man with a cheerful round face, a big mustache and straight black bangs over his forehead. Somehow he looked Russian. Was it the furred parka? Or the heavy black hair and mustache? Suddenly I knew why — he looked like Stalin. He spoke a few words to Kaunuk, then without warning we were on our way again before the man even had a chance to say good-by. Kaunuk had spotted the other sleds coming up behind and he had to keep his lead, for the pride of the team.

About every two hours we stopped for tea. At these times we ran around, danced and played games like children. At ten o'clock Axel and I did a polka. At midnight there were wrestling, broad-jumping and whip-cracking contests. At two o'clock we jumped rope. It was faintly surprising to find oneself skipping rope on sea ice at two in the morning. A running fire of practical jokes of the most primitive variety went on throughout the night. To an Eskimo the funniest thing in the world was to tie a dangling shoelace to a sled runner while the owner (Ned) was not looking. The Eskimo doubled himself up with silent laughter and pointed until he was sure we were all watching. When Ned got up to walk away he fell flat on his face. We thought it was pretty funny too.

Our tea stops were marked, when we left, by biscuit boxes, chocolate wrappers, tea bags, bits of dead seal. I suffered a faint distaste, an old-fashioned feeling that we were desecrating the landscape. But it was foolish. This was the cleanest land in the world. Whatever could not be eaten by men and dogs was devoured by gulls, jaegers, foxes and weasels. Once we saw a dead dog on the ice. Its fur and skin were intact, but its insides were entirely gone, consumed by birds, and its bare backbone arched grotesquely out of the hide. What the birds and animals couldn't eat would sink into the sea when the ice melted.

The Eskimos themselves wasted nothing, we discovered after a few days with them. Anything that could possibly be used was saved — tin cans, boxes, bits of string, paper. If a man killed birds he ate the meat, tossed the bones to the dogs and gave the feathers to his wife to line clothing. Nearly every square inch of a seal was used. The north had no garbage problem.

We rode thirteen hours, sometimes in fog, sometimes in the pale-gold sunset which lasted all night as the sun moved along the horizon from northwest to northeast. We entered the narrow inlet in a thin mist, through which we could see the tops of Bylot's cliffs, while close on our right, on Baffin Island, a tall, menacing black mountain called Hérodier rose straight out of the sea. The Eskimos seldom named mountains. If you asked an Eskimo the name of a mountain he would say "*Kingak*," which means "mountain." They had no need to label them, for the mountains did not interest them — there was no hunting back in those forlorn, frozen wastes of glacier and rock where nothing could live. Hérodier was named only because it was a landmark for travelers on the sea. It was called after Kudlu's father, the French trader.

I tried to sleep but found the weather too cold and the sled too narrow and lumpy. As I wriggled and tossed, trying to find room for various parts of me, a small brown hand,

Kaunuk's, suddenly appeared and pushed a folded parka under my uncomfortable head. The fat young Eskimo had been so busy keeping up the morale of the prize team that I didn't think he even knew I was on the sled. He laughed at my surprise, then tucked my blanket neatly around my feet. Not to be outdone the little boy jumped off the sled and tucked me in from behind. I was pleased at their concern and they were even more pleased by my pleasure. I relaxed and went into a half-dreaming state, too cold to sleep but entirely at peace.

At four in the morning we passed some tents on a grassy plateau above the sea ice. "If you lived here," said Axel, "you'd be home now." By then I was too tired and cold to laugh. We were driving into a cottony fog. Everything was swathed in mist; our blankets were frosty, our noses were wet, our hair was rimed.

At seven o'clock in the morning we came to another grassy plateau. This turned out to be home. It was covered with dog dirt — and dogs. Three white tents of Eskimo hunters were at the far end. It seemed impossible that so many dogs could belong to only three tents. But we supposed, rightly, that there were nearly a dozen Eskimos in each tent. Beyond the tents was the white ice of a little harbor which ended abruptly about a mile from shore in a line of black water. We had reached the open ocean, Baffin Bay. Four hundred and fifty miles straight east was Greenland.

We all trailed after Pete into one of the tents, where a large family of Eskimos was sleeping. Pete had a low-voiced conversation with one of them, a middle-aged, cheerful man named Panipookoochoo. The rest of the family slept soundly while the men talked, and we took off our mittens and rubbed our frozen hands in the steamy warmth of the tent.

We carried our gear to the other end of the small plateau, pushed dogs out of the way (by this time we knew how) and raised our tents — a big white canvas tent for Rick, Ben and Ned, a small mountain tent for Axel and me, and Makpa's tent for herself, Pete, Idlouk, Kudlu and an indeterminate number of others. During the waking hours there were never fewer than fifteen people in Makpa's tent, and it was impossible to distinguish which were its legitimate inhabitants and which were guests.

We ate a mountainous breakfast (supper?) of cereal, bacon and cocoa, and at eight o'clock we sank, exhausted, onto our air mattresses. Six hours later we were up again, ready for an immense supper (breakfast?) of canned chicken, rice and coffee.

We had already misplaced the date, as well as the time of day, or night. But there was no nostalgia for the uncounted minutes, hours and days. The timeless, gypsy life of the hunting Eskimos had caught us entirely.

V I I I
Seal Hunt

Bᴇɴ and I sat in the white tent, writing. The little primus stove was going with a friendly, hissing sound, giving the illusion of warmth. It had not been off all afternoon. As soon as we had finished our nameless, timeless meal snow was put in a kettle to melt for tea, then for dishwashing. Washing dishes was simple since we ate and drank all our food out of one cup (each). Each of us had one spoon and a pocket knife or hunting knife. After every meal I washed these items in boiling water, without soap, brush or dishcloth, using a spoon as a pot scraper. Now new snow was steaming on the little stove for cocoa. We found it kept us warmer to eat all the time. Besides there wasn't much else to do. Outside fog lay deep on land and sea and a drizzly rain touched the tent lightly.

We sat in the midst of a comfortable disarray. The back half of the tent was given over to a great pile of bedding, caribou skins, clothing, duffel bags, air mattresses, rifles, binoculars. The front half, or kitchen, contained, besides two primus stoves, a large wooden box of food, two dead birds for Josselyn, their beaks stuffed with cotton, a dripping pile of cups, spoons and cooking pots and a neat mountain of trash, to be transferred later to that convenient Disposall, the frozen sea. There had been a lemming in here too, living in a box, but it got out and bit Ned three times so we let it go. The floor was a cold carpet of wet, dead grass. Above us, on the ridge-pole, hung a grimy row of socks and handkerchiefs trying to get dry.

Peace surrounded us. It seeped in through the tent walls and dropped slowly over us like a mountain mist. As we wrote we paused from time to time for conversation — about a sailing trip in the Caribbean, about meals in the French provinces, about Swiss mountain huts with featherbeds and indoor plumbing. I laughed at our choice of subjects and Ben remarked that he would not exchange any one of those places for the sloppy, cold tent where we now sat.

We heard Eskimo voices in Makpa's tent a few yards away. There appeared to be a party in there. Rick's laughter rose above the voices, followed by Idlouk's hoarse chuckle and Kudlu's shout of merriment. Pete poked his head through our tent flap. "Want some tea?" he asked.

"Want some cocoa?" we returned. He did, and in a short time we had nine or ten Eskimos and five white men in our tent. The Eskimos laughed in astonishment at our beautiful pastel plastic cups, each decorated with a strip of adhesive tape on which a name was printed in indelible ink, relics of our neat base camp. Names on cups — suddenly we realized it was absurdly fastidious. We started ripping them off. While Kudlu was looking the other way Rick pasted "Kathy" on the middle of his back. Idlouk saw it, shouted with laughter and pointed it out to everyone else. Kudlu twisted and turned and made exaggerated faces, trying to reach the unreachable spot, while the other Eskimos (and we too) were convulsed with laughter. This joke was to last a long time and have end-less variations. The adhesive strips grew grimy and blurred, but in all the days we stayed at Button Point the joke did not lose its savor. I still have a rubber boot with "Ned" stuck on it.

After an hour or so we moved back to Makpa's tent. She took up her concertina and softly played her tuneless Irish jigs while the rest of us chatted, drank tea and chewed on hard, dry pilot biscuits dripping with strawberry jam. We had brought along a tasty selection of canned goods from our home camp, and Pete's contribution to the larder was forty pounds of pilot biscuits. Our food had been carefully selected, counted and measured to feed six people for a week. But Mary, who had taken such pains over our balanced diet, had not foreseen that we would eat without stopping for five or six hours at a stretch and that, besides, we would be feeding about ten Eskimos. Our larder was quickly depleted and we fell back on Pete's pilot biscuits. By the end of five days we felt we had eaten more pilot biscuits than was strictly necessary. We never wanted to see one again.

The tea, as usual, was flavored with caribou hairs and other unidentifiable foreign matter. In the bottom of the cup, after one had drunk, was a sticky residue of tea leaves, sugar and lumps of undissolved powdered milk. The Eskimos were not as clean as we. Their method of washing dishes was to pour some cold tea into one cup, slosh it around a few times, then dump the entire contents into the next cup. The "dishwater" passed from cup to cup until it came to the last one, from which an almost solid mass of garbage was dumped just outside the tent flap, to be devoured instantly by waiting dogs.

After we had sat there about two hours Axel began glancing at me. "When is something going to happen?" he asked silently. We decided to go for a walk, stepped carefully over a dozen pair of legs and arms and waded through the hordes of dogs waiting patiently outside the tent for garbage. In a few minutes the dogs, the tents and the shore line had vanished into the heavy mist behind us.

The tundra here was carpeted with heavy, soft, deep moss into which our feet sank almost to the ankles. We picked our way around patches of rotten snow and treaded cautiously on the straight peat dikes that patterned the oily brown bogs. (When we had first noticed oil on the marshy places we had been surprised and excited. But the two government geologists at Pond Inlet had told us that it was vegetable oil from rotten plants. It was all right with us. The last place one wanted to see oil derricks was on lonely Bylot Island.)

We started climbing and soon were out of the marshy, mossy area and walking through a wilderness of stones. I remembered the impious lines that Pete had quoted to us back in the tent:

"In five days God created the heavens and earth and every creature that lives therein. On the sixth day he created the Northwest Territories. And on the seventh day he sat back and threw rocks at it." Above its boggy lowlands Bylot Island was a desert of stones, partly debris from the mountains, partly the result of frost action. When the earth freezes the soil compresses, pushing any large hard objects out of itself, and every year new stones are forced to the surface.

The frozen earth had pushed out something besides stones. Before us, in the misty grayness, gleamed white human bones. An oval of large stones marked a narrow grave and within it lay, in separate pieces but each bone in its proper place, an almost complete skeleton. The bones were large, and we thought of the European whalers who had lost their lives on these frozen shores in the frenzied, uncontrolled hunt for the mild-mannered Greenland whale. In this silent, foggy, lonely place Kipling's lines came to mind:

> *The end of the fight is a tombstone white*
> *With the name of the late deceased,*
> *And the epitaph drear: "A Fool lies here*
> *Who tried to hustle the East."*

One could picture the nervous irritation of efficient Europeans when they tried to get some action out of the easy-going Noble Savage of the Canadian Arctic. The Eskimo is hardy, courageous, alert and clever, but he is never in a hurry. Before going to the north we had had a mental picture of a life in which primitive man had to work and struggle constantly in order to keep himself barely alive, a life in which little children were killed because they could not be fed, in which old people were left behind to starve and freeze to death because they could no longer hunt. We had no idea of the slow, lazy hours of gaiety, peace and laughter in the tents; of the close, affectionate and tender family life; of the sporadic, dramatic hunting in which a wily hunter might catch in a few hours enough meat to keep him for two weeks; of the timelessness of the long, long day.

We photographed the grave, marked it with a tall cairn and made our way back to the shore. When we told Pete about the bones he said, "I'll get the Eskimos to show you the one that has hair growing out of the skull." We set off again, followed by two small, frightened Eskimo children. When we got to the stony place we motioned them to lead us. But they hung back, and suddenly turned and fled, disappearing into the mist. Eskimo children were shy but not usually that shy. We asked Pete what was the matter with them.

"They didn't like your cameras," he said. "The Eskimos are afraid to have bones photographed or even looked at. They think the corpse will sit up." So we never saw the unlikely skull with hair growing out of it. Too bad. I should have liked to see it sit up.

It was midnight, time for more tea and more pilot biscuits. In the middle of his tea Pete suddenly jumped up and said, "Who wants to go seal hunting?" There had been no change in the weather, or in the peaceful spirit of the tent. Pete was as bad as an Eskimo.

Axel and I had been up for ten hours and nothing had happened to us except the discovery of some old bones. We emphatically wanted to go seal hunting. Rick and Ben and Ned preferred to go to bed. So we set out over the fog-shrouded sea ice in two komatiks, with Pete, Kudlu, Idlouk and the two girls, Makpa and Marta. On one of the sleds was a rowboat in which Idlouk thoughtfully spread a caribou skin for me. Caribou skin is not as soft as polar bear, but it is far warmer because each hair is hollow and the air inside retains the heat.

But I couldn't sit in the boat. I was so happy to be out on a trip again that I ran alongside with Pete. We raced the dogs all the way across the little harbor to the edge of the black water. It turned out to be, not open ocean, but a wide lead about fifty feet across. Beyond it, invisible, was Baffin Bay. We all felt extraordinarily lighthearted and elated. Maybe it was an overdose of caffein — or perhaps sheer pleasure at the feel of the crisp snow under our feet and the thin chill air and the drama of a hunt.

Neither Axel nor I had ever hunted and we did not want to start now. Seals were too important to Idlouk to be wounded and lost by a couple of novices. So we watched. But watching did not mean sitting quietly on a komatik waiting for something to happen. The seals were active. This seemed to be the night that they wanted to be killed. One after another they popped their dark heads out of the water, stared at us and disappeared. The three hunters raced back and forth along the edge of the lead, shuffling their feet on the thin ice and whistling to make the seals raise their inquisitive heads further out of the water.

When a seal was sighted the nearest hunter dropped on one knee and aimed. Usually, before he could sight it properly, the seal went up and down tantalizingly two or three times. Then the shot rang out. We were all tense and excited. Had he missed? Or would the seal, wounded, exhale and dive, to vanish forever? Or, wonderful sight, would it roll over slowly as its dead body came to the surface?

These good hunters did not miss many. Within two hours they had got five seals. When the seal was shot they quickly launched the boat. One man, standing in the bow, paddled out to the dead animal, caught its nose with a heavy iron gaff and dragged it into the boat.

Axel and I trailed indefatigably after the hunters with cameras cocked. We found it worthwhile to stay close to Idlouk. Somehow he always managed to be where the seal came up — and he did not miss. Idlouk's name means "unborn seal" and it is given to children in the hope that they will grow into wise seal hunters. Once, a long time ago, a man decided he would live in the bodies of all the animals in turn to see which he liked best. He tried caribou, wolf, fox, jaeger, weasel and seal. When he came home he said that it was best being a seal. He was named Idlouk and he became the greatest seal hunter of his people. At some time our Idlouk must have lived in a seal. He had an uncanny knowledge of what they would do next.

Kudlu was also an expert hunter, though he was younger and not so wise. Through Pete he told us, with the faintest trace of irritation, that he was good because he lived in Idlouk's camp. If you lived with Idlouk you couldn't help being a good hunter. The Eskimos have no government, but live in autonomous camps. There are three or four families in each, mostly in-laws, and their members subject themselves voluntarily to the counsels of the wisest hunter among them. Idlouk was the leader of his camp by natural selection, and he brooked no shiftlessness. When he said go out and hunt, his young men went out and hunted, even though they would far rather have stayed home in their tents making cats' cradles. Idlouk, we began to see, was not entirely popular with his easygoing compatriots.

Pete was nearly as good a hunter as the Eskimos, and Idlouk watched him ceaselessly, took care of him and advised him with courtesy and tact. He loved Pete like a brother, he had told him, and treated him like a son. The young trader was high-spirited and bubbling with infectious eagerness on the hunt. He seemed far happier with natives than with whites, and he was at his best when he was out on the sea ice with them.

But the drama of the seal hunt began to lessen as the hours passed and few seals appeared. I decided to explore Bylot's oceanside shore, and walked by myself back to the dark-red rocks that rose dimly from the sea ice. The land climbed sharply and I scrambled up from rock to rock through the wet mist. After a half-hour I came to a small cliff with an overhang. Negotiating a little chimney, I found myself on a windy, grassy plateau, entirely enveloped in cloud. I could not hear the hunters or see the ice. The world was gone, I was on another planet and there were no people in my land. At my feet were little flowers, daisy fleabane and saxifrage, pure and miraculous. Above loomed a dark tower of rock, disappearing into the heavy fog.

Then Axel called and I descended. Though I hadn't been able to see Bylot's ocean shore I had felt it. It was not tundra, it was crumbling, dangerous rock falling straight into the sea.

The hunters had taken the sleds while I had been climbing and had gone further out along the lead. We followed their tracks, walking cautiously on the ice, which got thinner, grayer and mushier as we moved away from the land. It made whispering noises under us and sank perceptibly as we stepped on weak places. We expected to disappear into a watery hole at any moment. Then ahead of us a white-hooded figure appeared, looking at first like a creation of mist. Idlouk — wonderful, kind Idlouk — had come back to look for us and guide us over the treacherous ice. He carried his harpoon and tested each step as he walked. His feet, in their soft sealskin boots, knew the ice; his sympathetic mind had told him we would be frightened of it. We watched him carefully as we followed. Brownish or dark ice, it appeared, was dangerous. Blue ice was all right even if it was covered with water and looked like a bottomless pond.

Tea was boiling on two primus stoves. Nothing like a cup of tea at four in the morning, I remarked, burning my tongue on the black sweet brew. After tea Kudlu and Idlouk cut up two seals to feed the dogs, while the rest of us amused ourselves by throwing bits of blubber into the air and watching kittiwakes dive for them. These northern gulls, scavengers like all gulls, were small, neat and dainty, and swooped after the food with the grace of dancers. They almost touched the water before they came out of the dive and darted straight upwards, hardly moving a wing. In the air they rested on still wings, wheeling in wide circles.

The seals had apparently stopped wanting to be killed. The hunters went back to the shore with the komatiks and climbed over the little rocky promontory at the end of the harbor to see what they could find on the other side. Beyond the rocks was another small harbor with an open lake in the middle of it. The lake was filled with birds, swimming, diving, flying and calling: king eiders, Brünnich's murres, brants, guillemots, dovekies, fulmars and old-squaws. While the hunters walked around the lake looking for seals Axel and I sat on the high rocks and watched the birds.

The murres swam with their feet paddling briskly behind, churning up the water like old-fashioned stern-wheelers. They were not good fliers and had difficulty getting into the air. Before they could lift themselves they had to flap along the surface for about fifteen yards, slapping the water strenuously with their stubby wings. On high they looked like airborne penguins, flying in great wedge-shaped flocks, their short wings flapping energetically. On their cliff perches they looked even more like penguins, sitting bolt upright, fat and pompous, with white fronts and black dinner jackets.

Murres belong to the family *Alcidae*, which includes auks, puffins, dovekies and guillemots. The *Alcidae* use their wings to swim under water, whereas most water-feeders use their webbed feet. They have had, therefore, to adapt themselves to the dual purpose of flying and swimming. For under-

water use the wings cannot be too large and feathery, therefore they are not very efficient in the air. The Eskimos, who
have endowed all the animals with human personalities, say
that when the young murres leave the nest the parent birds
fly close beside them, holding the babies in the air with their
wings. It is true that they appear to do this, but their wings
are far too poor to be of any help. What they do, probably,
is to fly over, under and around the feeble-winged youngsters,
giving them encouragement and holding themselves ready to
break the fall if the new fliers fail.

The *Alcidae* compensate for their weak wings with extremely good eyesight and an unerring sense of direction.
And their feeble flying ability has kept them small and light
of body. The only exception was the great auk, which retired to remote, icy, rocky arctic coasts where no enemies
could molest it. There it gave up flying altogether, grew extremely large and fat and lived a happy, fishy life for many
centuries. And there man found it, a helpless supply of fresh
meat. The great auk was officially discovered and named in
1758 — eighty-six years later there were no more great auks.

The guillemots are tiny, dainty black birds with red feet,
called by fishermen "sea pigeons." They belong in the same
family as the murres, but have a delicate, artificial appearance,
like toy birds. The dovekies, or little auks, miniature rep-
licas of the murres, sat solidly in the water like little old men
in armchairs. Every now and then one vanished suddenly into
the depths. We did not see them fly. The king eiders are big,
noble, bold-patterned black and white ducks with brilliant
red and orange protuberances on their beaks. Brants are small,
dark geese. Old-squaw ducks, which we had already met at
our home camp, were here in hundreds, *anh-angh-ya*-ing en-

thusiastically, like an amateur chorus singing Gilbert and Sullivan — sadly out of tune and never together.

Fulmars are sea birds which make their living and their home on the ocean, only coming inshore in the spring to breed on high northern cliffs. There was a fulmar colony on Cape Hay, on the northern tip of Bylot Island, a hundred miles from the place where we sat, and the birds we watched were probably out on feeding expeditions from their far nests. Fulmars will travel several hundred miles in a day in search of food. A fulmar couple has but one chick a year, and even this one, nestbound for seven weeks, is often hard to raise, as the adults cannot find food when the sea is rough. Yet it is one of the most numerous birds in the world! Frequently one spots fulmars from the deck of an ocean liner, flying low and fast, nearly touching the surface of the water. They are dark gray and pale gray like the North Atlantic in winter, and they look like a creation of the sea.

The Eskimos have given souls to the fulmars, as to most other living creatures. A fulmar (*kakoodlak*, "bird of the storm") plays a role in the classic Eskimo legend of Takana-luk Angaluk, the Great Woman a Long Way Down, who created all the animals.

There was a young girl who did not want to marry. Her father was angry. "If you do not marry," he said, "you will have to marry my dog." One night a stranger came. He had long teeth, but he was very handsome. He lay down by the girl and took her to wife. The next day, when the people woke up, they found that the curse had come true. The girl had married the old man's dog. The people took the girl and the dog to an island, and they lived there. The dog swam over to camp every day to get deer and seal meat for his wife.

The girl bore a litter of many children. Some were dogs and some were humans. The old man heard of the children and felt sorry for his daughter. He decided to kill the dog. The next time the dog came the old man put rocks in the dog's pack, with meat on top, and the dog drowned. The girl had nothing to eat, so her father came in his kayak to get the girl and her children. The girl told her dog children to tear his kayak to pieces, so the old man quickly turned back. But the girl saw that her children were starving and she decided to save them. She put the dog children in the sole of her boot; two blades of grass were their sails. They sailed away to the south and became white men. (If you look at a ship's hull from above it looks like the sole of an Eskimo sealskin boot. But how did they know about white men when this ancient story came into being — had they seen Norsemen?) Then the old man came again and took her, with her human children, back to his house. She lived with him for a while, and one day a tall man came in a kayak. The girl hid. The tall man called, "*Ooeeneegoomashuikukkilik!*" ("She who will not be married.") She came out and went into his kayak. There she saw that he sat on a stool and wore goggles. The kayak stopped beside an ice floe. The man stepped on the ice and took off his goggles, and she saw that his eyes were red and he was very small. He was a *kakoodlak* (fulmar). She wept, but he said, "Don't cry. I will take you to my tent, made all of silverjar seals." When they got there she found that the tent was poor and mean, and made of fishskins. The old man, her father, began to feel sorry for her again. He got into his umiak (large skin boat) and went to her while the bird was hunting. The bird came home and found his wife gone. He flew after them, and called out that he wanted his wife back. But she said

scornfully that she would not go back to a little man who had
to wear goggles to cover his red eyes. So the bird flew faster,
and the wind came. The old man was frightened, but he
would not give the girl back. The bird flew still faster, the
waves got very high and the umiak started to capsize. The
old man threw his daughter overboard to save himself. She
hung on to the boat with her hands, and the old man cut off
her fingers up to the first joints. These turned into *netsek*
(ringed seal). She still held on, and he cut off the second
joints. These turned to *oogjoo* (bearded seal). The third
joints became *aiverk* (walrus). After that the girl sank. The
old man was very sad, and rolled up in his sleeping skins on
the beach. A great wave came and took him into the sea. He
sank to the bottom, where his daughter lived. Now she,
Takanaluk Angaluk, rules the sea animals and he sleeps next
to her and punishes wrongdoers. The dog husband lies across
the door, to keep people out. When there are no seals it means
that Takanaluk Angaluk, the Great Woman, is angry and has
locked them all up. Sharks live in her chamber pot.

Takanaluk Angaluk rules the affairs of men with a firm
and not too friendly hand. The Moon Man, Takerk Anutinga, whose story Pete had told us, is the good angel of the
Eskimos. He does what he can to aid people in distress, and
helps them to catch seals. But he cannot do anything against
Takanaluk Angaluk. The afterlife of the Eskimos is somewhat like that of the pagan Norse peoples. Those who die
heroically or violently, by drowning, murder, childbirth or
suicide (self-destruction used to be a natural corollary of Eskimo life and was committed when a man was old and could
no longer hunt), go to the moon, as do good people who
break no taboos. Takanaluk Angaluk receives at the bottom

of the sea the spirits of those who have not died a heroic death but have lost their lives through illness or starvation. There is no punishment for men, but women are treated roughly. The old man, her father, whips them and pulls their hair. The Eskimos firmly believed that these supernatural creatures existed, as well as the spirits that inhabited animals, plants, rocks and clouds, and that they could do good or ill to man. Yet there was never any form of worship. The spirits could be controlled only by magic, and they responded just as people would.

The fog lifted and the sun came out. Suddenly, surprisingly, mountains were all around us. Across the inlet were the high, white, shining mountains of Baffin Island, with pink and gold baby clouds floating around their peaks. Though at least twenty miles away they looked close enough to jump to. A thin gray line on the horizon to the east of us was the open ocean. The shore of Bylot Island, where we sat, was a forbidding stretch of high red cliffs dropping sheer into the sea. Jagged rocks protruded from them at crazy angles, and on their tops was ice, at their feet more ice. It was a beautiful land but desolate, dangerous, utterly indifferent to man. No wonder that the wanderers from Central Asia, coming to this vast, wild, lonesome country, had peopled it with spirits and given souls to their only companions, the animals.

I lay back on a rock shaped like an armchair and closed my eyes against the low, bright sun. I was nearly asleep — when about seventy-five pounds of furry, friendly Husky dog suddenly landed on me with a thud and started to lick my face. He seemed to be all tongue. We recognized him as one of the police team. These hand-raised dogs were noticeably bigger,

healthier, happier and more willing workers than the Eskimos'
hungry, spiritless slaves (Idlouk's were an exception — he
treated his dogs kindly though without familiarity). Pete had
told us, however, that when a hand-raised dog was given to an
Eskimo it went crazy within a few months and had to be shot.
Lacking the affection and gentleness it was used to, the dog
moped, became neurotic and later turned ferocious.

This enormous friendly dog had apparently followed our
footsteps all the way across the ice from Button Point, about
three miles away, and climbed the slippery, crumbling rocks
— just to find somebody whose face he could lick. He made
a great fuss over us, pushed us with his big wet paws, put his
nose in our eyes and growled playfully. Then he jumped back
and forth over the rocks, stopping to put his head low on his
extended forepaws and look at us expectantly. He could not
have said it more clearly. He wanted us to take a walk with
him. Imagine an Eskimo sled dog wanting to take a walk! We
obliged, and the huge silly animal leaped all around us, barking with delight. We met Pete, Idlouk and Kudlu on their
way back and they looked in silent disapproval at the ridicu-
lous display. Eskimos do not get sentimental over dogs and
obviously they thought that neither we nor the dog would
come to a good end if this sort of thing were encouraged.
They were right, too.

A seal was sighted in the lead where we had first hunted,
and we all leaped down the rocks and ran along the thin,
shelving ice edge. Poised and silent, we waited where we had
seen its dark head. The seal did not reappear. But we stayed
another hour, while fulmars flew low, straight and fast over
the water, kittiwakes dived and circled and the sun moved
across the inlet, reflected palely in the white ice.

I shall never forget the beauty of seal hunting at night — the quiet, tense watchfulness, the cold, clear air, the circling, hunting birds, the low sun which gave no heat but an otherworldly, pale-gold light, pure and unsensuous.

After seven hours of hunting we finally, sleepily, mounted the komatiks. In the cold dawn light our shadows were long, the ice crackled beneath us and the dead seals shook like jelly in the bottom of the boat. The two girls, Marta and Makpa, played a wild game of tag around the sleds all the way back.

In Makpa's tent we lit the primus stoves and fried seal liver, which we speared out of the pan with our knives and ate off pilot biscuits. I would much rather have seal liver for breakfast than Wheatena. The coffee was rich and strong and looked like Viennese coffee, with a lovely fluff of half-mixed powdered milk floating on top. The yellow morning sun shone through the light tent well, and none of us had a care in the world.

I X
The Akpa Cliff

IT was nighttime again and Pete was telling stories in Makpa's tent. There were many of us, and people were sleeping, working, thinking — some were listening. Ned slept, his long legs stretched over half the tent. An unidentified Eskimo lay near him, snoring gently, his head on Ned's knee. I sat in a back corner curled on a caribou skin, trying to mend my gloves with three inches of red wool given to me by Makpa. I was apparently more left-handed than I realized; all the finger tips of the left-hand glove had given way at once. Idlouk sat next to me writing in his diary, a formidably neat and thorough document. He had kept it for eleven years, a painstakingly exact record of what animals he had killed each hunting day, where and at what time, what tracks and other animals he had seen and what the weather was. This was part of the system that made him a successful hunter. He inscribed neat small characters of the syllabic alphabet, something like shorthand, which was invented by white men for American Indians some hundred and twenty years ago and adapted to the Eskimo language in the eighteen-eighties. The Eskimos never developed a written language and their soft, guttural sounds cannot be translated into our alphabet. The syllabic series, based on phonetics, was devised to enable them to read and write, and it caught on quickly. They have nothing to read except the Bible, the Prayer Book and the Hymnal, but they love writing. When they cannot visit one another they write long chatty letters, full of gossip. Idlouk was the only man in the Pond Inlet district who kept a diary.

"Jim Ford, an old-time Hudson's Bay Company trader," Pete was saying, "had a baby son. His wife was an Eskimo woman and the Eskimos respected him. An old man chose Jim's new baby to be his 'bones.' That is, when the old man died his spirit would not be doomed to wander the earth restlessly until a new baby was named for him, but it would pass directly into this child. When the baby was six months old the old man felt he was near to dying. He wanted to give the boy all his wisdom before he died, so that he would live on just as wise as ever in the new body. He had the child brought to him, and he talked to it for hours and hours, whispering all the ancient hunting lore of the Eskimos, things that Jim himself didn't know. When the child grew up, Jim swears, he acted just like the old man. He knew everything his 'bones' had told him; he even had the same look and manner."

The strangest thing about this story was that Pete believed it too.

What happened to the boy, we wanted to know, interested in the mixed fate of a half-Eskimo child brought up by a white man.

"He died," said Pete. "He was shot accidentally by his brother. Jim had two other children, too, who were killed. They were out on a trip together. The littlest Eskimo children aren't afraid to go out alone, and they all like to imitate their daddies. Some of them die that way, falling through the ice or getting lost. These children had dogs with them. They

came into a storm, had to lie up for a while, ran out of food —
and the dogs ate them.

"Jim had a lot of tragedy in his life. But he was the toughest
man I have ever seen. Once he had a post in northern Labrador (that's now part of Quebec Province). The Eskimos
there got a sort of religious fever and started going fanatical.
They decided that one of them was the new Messiah and they
held wild meetings every night, shouting hymns and dancing
around this fellow. Now, the Eskimos never had any crime
among them in the old days and it was the hardest thing in the
world to get an Eskimo mad or excited about anything. But
the Christian religion drove them a little crazy in the beginning, and they used to get themselves all worked up.

"Jim didn't care anything about this Messiah fellow and
was ignoring the whole thing — until the Eskimos tried to
rope him in on it. They told him he had to come to the meetings. He said, 'Not on your life.' So they got together in one
of their crazy meetings and decided he had to be sacrificed.
He saw them coming, about twenty-five of them, shouting
and waving knives. Jim got out of his house, closed the door
and stood with his back to it when they came on him. He
fought off all twenty-five with his bare fists, laid some of
them out and broke open the face of the 'Messiah.' He beat
them away after five hours, then he took the 'Messiah' into his
house and bandaged his bloody face. All the time he was fixing him up the fellow kept screaming, 'Keep away from me!
You're the devil!' That's a true story, but the Eskimos are
turning it into a legend. Down there along the coast of Labrador, if you ask an Eskimo to tell you an old story he will
most likely pull out his favorite, the story of Christ and the
Devil on Leaf River in Ungava."

139

"Now I will speak," said Panipookoochoo, using the formal Eskimo phrase for the beginning of a story. He had been listening attentively and laughing at the correct places, though he probably didn't understand more than three words. Panipookoochoo's language was expressive and fluid, the phrases rising and falling in a sighing chant. An Eskimo talks way back in his throat and loses his consonants somewhere in his bronchial tube. His *h*'s are mere breaths and his *k*'s could just as well be *t*'s, or something else, or nothing at all; they vanish down his throat and have just enough firmness not to be vowels. His syllables defeat every combination of letters in our alphabet. The soft, continuous, singing sound is enhanced by the fact that the language has no sentences. Words become longer and longer as syllables are added to modify their meaning (like *ooeeneegoomashuikukkilik* in the Takanaluk Angaluk story). Having no grammar to formalize it, the language is flexible and fluid. There are no abstract words and all verbs are verbs of action. The Eskimos, though extraordinarily quick and alert mentally, are not thinkers, in our sense — and their language is a reflection of their life and their racial character. It is a language of people whose lives are lived in their bodies and not in their minds.

It has no relation to any other language. Although the Eskimos are believed to have originated in Central Asia no trace of a similar people or language has ever been found there.

Panipookoochoo's phrases rose and fell with melting grace, and when he had finished Pete translated the story.

"Now I will speak. Once the *akpas* [murres] nested on a steep cliff near here. People were killed climbing this terrible cliff to get the *akpas* and their eggs. After many years the *akpas* had a meeting together. Too many people were killed climbing the cliffs, they said. The next time a man was killed they would move to an easier cliff. That summer a man climbed the terrible cliff and fell off and was killed. So the *akpas* moved to the Akpa Cliff, where they now live, and where men can get their eggs without danger. There, I have spoken.

"That's the way they all talk when they tell a story," Pete added. "They start their speech with a formal phrase, say it all the way through, then tack on a formal ending. No one ever interrupts a man who is telling a story — even if he's only talking about the seal he took last night."

The *akpa* story, he continued, is one of the few animal tales that the Eskimos continue to tell — because to them it is a fact, not a legend. The missionaries have discouraged them from telling most of their animal stories because, they say, animals cannot think and talk like humans, nor have they souls. Pete could sometimes get the ancient animal stories from them by telling them about the serpent in the garden of Eden, an animal which spoke and acted like a human — and it is in the Bible, which came from God.

The Eskimos used to believe that all the animals had souls. The soul was a little replica of the animal, which lived in a bubble in the groin. People could become animals and animals thought and acted like people. Some animals were interchangeable. The killer whale could come on land and turn into a wolf and the wolf could become a killer whale. It was easy for them because they acted the same. The walrus used to have antlers and the caribou had tusks. When men hunted walrus the animals sank the kayaks by piercing them with their antlers. And the deer gored the hunters with their long tusks. The people complained to Takanaluk Angaluk, and she changed the deer and the walrus. Now you can see white marks on the side of the deer's jaws where his tusks used to be, and the walrus has indentations in the top of his head to show where the horns were.

Not only did the animals have souls, but the world was full of spirits. The commonest were the *inoogaggoligakjuk*, land spirits. They were dwarfs, and they were not bad, though they sometimes took revenge if they were insulted. In fact they were just like people, only magic. Once, they say, there was a stone fox trap, and a man came to look at it. There was a fox in it. An *inoogaggoligakjuk* came along and said, "I have been following the fox tracks, hoping to get the meat, and my children want the ears to play with." (The fox is the dwarf's bear — he needs it for food and clothing.) The man did not wish to give the fox to the dwarf, so he turned away and went to his house. The dwarf also turned and headed for his house. When he got quite a distance from the man he turned and shouted, "Open your mouth!" The man opened his mouth. Then the dwarf called, "Bite down hard!" This the man did, and when he got home he found he could not open his mouth, and so he starved to death.

Another man met an *inoogaggoligakjuk* who also asked for fox meat. The man was kind and gave him the fox's flesh. As he went toward home the dwarf called after him, "Pour water on your snow house." The man did so. All the people laughed at him and said he was crazy. That night a wind came and blew all the snow houses down. But the man's house stayed up because it was anchored with ice from the water he had put over it.

The intermediaries between the people and the spirits were the *angakoks* (witch doctors), who could talk to spirits and drive illness and madness out of people. They did horrible tricks to convince people of their magic.

"An old woman," Pete said, "told me she saw this happen: an *angakok* took a hunting spear for whales, went with it out of the tent and came back with the head of the spear in his eye and the rest through his body, the thong sticking out of the left buttock. The men in the tent took the thong and pulled, but could not get the spear out of him. The *angakok* went outside again, alone, and came back holding the spear and scraping the blood off the thong. Another witch doctor cut the skin off his face down to the chin, so it dangled down his chest like a beard — then he stuck it back on his face. Another could take off his wife's breast with a knife and pass it around the tent, and then put it back on her again. Some of the *angakoks* were ventriloquists and some were hypnotists and some were sleight-of-hand artists. But they only did these things to cure sickness."

Well, at least it would surprise you out of the hiccups.

Idlouk had finished his diary and was making cats' cradles on his hands. He wasn't very good at it and the string kept getting into a knotty tangle. He laughed at himself. "I need Kidla," he said, and handed the string to Panipookoochoo. The cheerful-faced Eskimo took the thin string in his big, coarse, warted fingers, twisted it in and out with incredible speed, then suddenly drew his hands apart. Between them was a stylized, complicated animal, its mouth opening and closing, its feet moving back and forth.

"*Amarok*," he said (wolf). Then he made another, an *ishoognak*, jaeger.

Learning cats' cradles must kill a great deal of time. You

could probably tell the character of a man by his ability to do cats' cradles. Pani was a lazy man, Idlouk was not.

Pani made a long succession of beautiful animals and fish with the bit of string. Ben watched closely. "You find those patterns in the wild parts of India," he said, "and in Polynesia and all up the coast of Asia, and in Africa, and everywhere there are primitive people. They all make the same patterns, though they give them different names according to the animals, birds and fish that are most familiar to them."

The cats' cradles led to demonstrations by all of us of hand tricks, match tricks, coordination tricks. What were we waiting for? We had planned (what a laughable word that had become) to go out to the Akpa Cliff early in the evening to see the birds which nested there. Now it was six o'clock the next morning and we had been in one tent or the other for fourteen hours. Every time a new visitor came in another pot of tea was put on. We were starting on our eighth pot of tea when Pete asked Panipookoochoo a question. The Eskimo murmured an answer.

"He says they're waiting for us," Pete said casually.

We thought we were waiting for them. But it did not matter — one way or another we would have waited. We all got up at once and within five minutes were out on the sea ice on three komatiks, along with ten Eskimos. We crossed the little harbor to the open lead where we had hunted in the night, now sparkling blue in the morning sun. On our sled were four people and a heavy rowboat. Only eight dogs pulled it, scrawny little dogs but plucky and hard-working. Their driver whipped them unmercifully. The dogs ate snow as they ran, a quick lick now and then. They tried to pick up

144

bits of garbage, a seal flipper or a dead bird. If one succeeded in capturing a morsel it was whipped out of his mouth. Their natural functions had to be performed while running, and if one necessarily lagged behind he was pulled along helplessly, whimpering and howling — and then whipped for good measure when he got back in line. These little dogs were not going to live long.

But the driver was only slightly more heartless than most Eskimos toward his dogs. The average life of a dog in an Eskimo team was six or seven years; after that he was shot because he was no longer able to pull hard enough, worn out by too much work and not enough food. It was the worst sort of slave system. But the dogs were awfully nice about it. They had no revolutionary agitators — they didn't even bite.

On the far side of the harbor the dogs had to pull the sleds up the steep, rocky promontory. One of our unfortunate creatures got his trace caught under the sled runner as we went up the little cliff. He was dragged under the sled and we were sure we saw the heavy runner go over his neck. He howled in agony, but the driver did not stop. Gradually the dog, still crying, managed to work his trace loose and crawl to the front again. Once among the other dogs his howling stopped, his tail went up and he pulled sturdily as if nothing had happened.

One dog coughed terribly and unceasingly. Sometimes he could not breathe — yet he never stopped pulling. Much later, when we returned from the Akpa Cliff, he was found coughing blood and was killed by a rifle shot in the ear. Ben cut him open and found that his lungs had almost completely rotted away. Unthinkingly heroic, he had worked until the very end. The carcass was carried far out on the sea ice where the other dogs could not smell it. There gulls would pick it clean.

The lake in the further harbor had widened considerably since the night before. The spring ice was unreliable this near to the open ocean. Under the influence of wind, tide, fog and rain it moved irregularly in and out of the little harbors. It might be that on our way back we would find no ice at all — or pack ice might have moved in solidly from the ocean.

The only way around the harbor was a narrow snow shelf under the cliff, barely wide enough for a komatik. We all got off and clambered over the rocks, since our weight might have toppled the dangerous shelf into the water. On the far side the ice was solid and the komatiks raced in the hot morning sun. The red rocks towered above us, the snow gleamed, eiders and old-squaws flew back and forth honking and squawking and the men threw snowballs at each other. Rick had a dreadful collection of stone-hard snowballs in the bottom of the boat — this life appeared to bring out the brat in the most civilized of us.

The cliffs grew higher and sheerer. At the tallest of them Pete, ahead of us, fired a shot into the air. A cloud of pale glaucous gulls came out of the rock like smoke, and six ragged black ravens flapped heavily to the top of the cliff.

"That was the old Akpa Cliff," Pete called back to us. "The one that was too dangerous."

We rounded a curve and suddenly the air was full of noise and birds. Above us and around us was an unending, graceful swirl of kittiwakes, wheeling, soaring, landing, departing, calling constantly in high, sad voices. There must have been at least five thousand of them. Flocks of murres whirred away from the rocks, swift and straight. They streamed endlessly out of the cliffs and their numbers darkened the sky. How could there be any more? How could there have been that many? But still they came. Finally only a few pairs remained —probably they had nests and could not leave. Most of the kittiwakes were nesting, and the cliff face was dotted with pairs. They perched facing each other, beaks nearly touching, the male always a little above the female in a pretty attitude of conjugal tenderness.

A few grounded murres were trying to escape over the ice. But murres can only take off from water, and these were helpless as the men ran after them. When they were caught we discovered that they were all wounded. The rock of the cliff face was so rotten that often the birds, landing or taking off, dislodged stones, which fell on the ledges below, killing or wounding other birds. Dead kittiwakes lay all around the base of the cliff, and there was a scattering of jagged pieces of red rock on the snow.

We walked to the base of the cliff with Ben and discussed the possibility of climbing it. Ben is an expert mountaineer. He has climbed some of Alaska's dangerous, almost inaccessible, high peaks, including the first ascent of eighteen-thousand-foot Mt. St. Elias. He looked up at the five hundred feet of red, crumbling gneiss.

"I wouldn't go near it," he said firmly. "Not only would it come off in your hand when you took hold, but it's so slimy with bird droppings that you couldn't get a foothold. It's the worst rock I've ever seen."

It didn't seem that the *akpas'* present home was much of an improvement over their last.

But Panipookoochoo took off his boots and started up the

cliff in his stocking feet. Nonchalantly he hopped from ledge to ledge, hardly using his hands. With his peaked hood, his dun-colored anorak and his gray sealskin trousers he looked like a small deity of the rocks, perhaps an *inoogaggoligakjuk*. A rope dangled from the top and Pani touched it from time to time, but he didn't appear to place any reliance on it. It had been there for ten years, Pete told us, and was more dangerous than no rope. Pete was watching Pani eagerly, and finally he followed the Eskimo up the cliff, climbing more slowly but just as fearlessly. And three Eskimo children crept up the rock and played on the crumbling ledges, laughing as they jumped from one to another.

Pani and Pete climbed several hundred feet. Pete had his camera and crawled out on the most exposed ledges, photographing kittiwake nests. Pani was looking for murres. As native helper to the police he had been delegated to band some of the birds for a government wildlife survey. But he was obviously not interested in banding birds. He was looking for murre eggs, an Eskimo delicacy. He found two, put them in his beret and put the beret back on his head. Luckily for the murres Pani was about a week ahead of the egg season.

When they came down we had tea. As we lay back on the caribou hides Pete told us another story about the Akpa Cliff. "This one is supposed to be true," he said. "A man did not like his son-in-law and wanted his daughter to marry another man. He took the boy to the Akpa Cliff and let him down on a rope from the top, to collect eggs. The man intended to throw down his end of the rope, and the boy knew he was to be murdered. He called up to the man to wait for a minute. Then he found a narrow ledge and looped part of the rope around a rock above it. The man threw the rope over the cliff and went home, thinking the boy was dead. All summer the boy lived on the ledge, eating eggs. He caught *akpas*, skinned them and collected rain water in the skins. When autumn came and the water began to freeze he made ice steps with the water he had collected. He climbed on these steps to the top of the cliff and went home. Another man was living with his wife and the father was there too. Nobody said anything when the boy came, but the old man was frightened and would not allow the boy to have a harpoon, or any weapon. The boy made a thong out of sealskin. Then he got an icicle, to which he added water to make it longer. The old man asked him what the icicle was for. 'To hang my sealskin thong to dry,' answered the boy, 'since I have no harpoon on which to hang it.' Every day he added more water and made the icicle longer and sharper. But the old man was no longer afraid. One night, when he was in bed, he threw off his covers and his belly was exposed. The boy slit him open with the sharpened icicle."

The story had a faint ring of truth, distorted, as in a dream. But we were in the dream too. One half expected Pete and Pani to come across the boy sitting among his murreskins on a high ledge.

We left the Akpa Cliff after tea, to look for the floe edge. Its location was uncertain. The pack ice on the ocean was loose and shifted with winds and tides. Sometimes the ocean was open within two or three miles of the shore and the solid ice of the inlet; at other times the pack ice moved in and there was no open water within sixty miles of the land. Panipookoochoo had told us that the floe edge was close inshore now, so we went over the inlet, heading towards Baffin Island. As we neared the open ocean we came to a landscape of desolation, of ugly, tormented ice, twisted by tides and wind. Ice pans tilted crazily, and tortured, convoluted chunks of rotten ice floated in free water. Not long ago, we were told, a man was hunting on the floe edge in spring, and the shelf broke loose. He floated on an ice pan all the way to Greenland, four hundred and fifty miles due east.

We traveled along the edge of this fearful, frozen surf for about a mile. Gradually it calmed down and we came to a beachlike area where the ice shelved gently into the water. A narwhal ponderously arched its back out of the water, too far away for a shot. Then, closer to the ice, a huge whiskery head lifted itself out of the ocean and stared at us — a walrus! Four men seized their rifles and ran down the floe edge, uttering hoarse, barking cries. They all knelt together where they had seen the walrus, sighted and waited for the animal to rise again. They kept on barking.

"They're supposed to be sounding like lady walruses," said Pete.

"Suppose that was a lady walrus out there?"

"Well, maybe she'd come in for a gossip."

The walrus rose again about a quarter of a mile further down the beach. Again the hunters ran, again they knelt, four tense, motionless figures against the enormous ocean. It was a striking picture of primitive, predatory man. In camp these same Eskimos had looked wretched — sallow, too small, not very clean. But out on the sea ice they became themselves, pure, efficient, strong, almost noble.

The walrus came up once more, stared the waiting hunters in the eye for an instant, then went back to its clam bed (walruses, dangerous though they are when angered, live in-

nocently on a diet of clams, which they dig with their tusks).
The Eskimos laughed, half exasperated, half admiring.

We saw no more walruses, but there were many seals. Idlouk shot one immediately after the departure of the walrus,
and the sound of the big thirty-thirty rifle echoed and re-
echoed from mountain to mountain far down the wild coast of
Baffin Island. He stood his harpoon on the peak of a small
hummock, rested his telescope on it and sighted to see whether
the seal, about two hundred yards out, had sunk or floated.
With unconscious grace he posed himself against the gleaming
floe edge and the gray, quiet ocean. Behind him were the
mountains, endlessly repeating themselves, desolate, untouched. Idlouk looked as if he were alone on earth — but
not in the least disturbed by the fact.

After that seal the hunters had bad luck. Seal after seal
was sighted, only to disappear before the rifles could be
aimed. One stayed up long enough to be shot, then sank instantly, leaving a pool of blood on the water. The hunter ex-
claimed, then laughed. Was there nothing they could not
laugh at?

At nine in the evening, we headed back to Button Point.
In our weariness everything was surrealistic. The low sun
occasionally winking through striated clouds on the frozen
mountains of Baffin Island looked like sun coming through
half-closed Venetian blinds on a hot summer day. The
scenery was a mixture of whites — the mountains sulfury
white, the sea ice blue-white, the floe edge shining pure white,
the sky shifting layers of gray-white, darker and lighter. On
our sled Idlouk whistled slowly, deliberately, with great style,
"Tramp, tramp, tramp, the boys are marching."

By the time we had reached camp and finished supper it was

half past ten. We had been up for more than thirty hours. But I could not let go of the night. I stood alone outside the tent for a while, half dreaming. There was utter quietness, except for a longspur's sweet soaring warble and the murmur of Eskimo conversation, low and gentle, from the next tent. Each phrase ended in a long downward cadence, like a sigh. What a lovely, singing language it was, devoid of grammar and way back in the throat, very soft and loving. Pete was talking in there and his voice was in rhythm with theirs. He sounded like another Eskimo. I envied him, but wondered what his fate would be. This was not a white man's world.

X
The Toonijuk

I LEFT the golden night and the lullabylike conversation, crept into my sleeping bag and slept for thirteen hours. At noon the next day Axel and I stumbled sleepily into the boys' tent for breakfast.

There was nothing to eat. Dogs had got into the tent while we had been out at the ocean the night before, and they had finished off our food, even the cheese. The cheese was wrapped in airtight aluminum foil, so they could not have smelled it. Even without the aluminum foil they couldn't have smelled it. We had been using it to thicken the soup. The murres which we had planned to have for lunch were gone, and Rick's sealskin boots, every hair of them. A big hole was gnawed in Idlouk's caribou skin which the boys used for warmth under the air mattresses. Worst of all they had eaten the bird specimens we were to have taken back to Josselyn — a guillemot, a Brünnich's murre, a king eider and a European ringed plover, a rare wanderer which chooses for its breeding grounds the far colder but sunnier Canadian tundra in preference to its own stormy northern land. The dead birds had vanished entirely, bones, feathers, even the cotton stuffed into their beaks.

We all knew which dogs had been there — the big, friendly, police-team dogs, afraid of nothing, the only dogs who did not cringe and slink away when you held out your hand. The worst one was our playful friend from the rocks. He thought we all loved him, and he would push his way under the tent flap, nudge us with his heavy head, knock over the stove with his waving tail, slap at us lovingly with his big muddy paws. In the beginning we had thought he was cute, but lately he had become exasperating. We all threw things at him.

The most trying times were the necessary trips to the little hollow back of our camp. The dogs trotted silently behind, close as shadows. In the hollow a circle of attentive, eager dogs crept gradually closer, ears forward, eyes bright and staring, quiet as wolves. At first they had seemed pathetic — poor things, they must be desperately hungry, all skin and bones under that lovely fur. But now we carried pocketfuls of stones to keep the creatures away.

The morning after the robbery we had seal liver and pilot biscuits again in Makpa's tent (the dogs respected Eskimo tents). We were out of food and there would be no more hunting. The floe edge had gone elsewhere; the sea was dead white, unbroken ice as far as we could see. It was raining and fog was moving in from the ocean.

"We might as well go back to Pond Inlet," Pete said casually, making no move to go. We were satisfied. We had accomplished the scientific aim of our trip, as far as possible. We had identified fourteen bird species, some of them rare, most of them not to be found near our home camp. We had made a rough count of the number of birds on the Akpa Cliff and the rocks of the coast. Rough indeed! — one guess at the number of kittiwakes was three thousand, another one hundred thousand. The murre guess varied between five and ten thousand. We had seen at least a hundred fulmars, two to three hundred king eiders and a sprinkling of the others, including the ringed plover, parasitic jaeger, Canada goose and common eider, birds unusual in this area. We had tried to find out which birds were nesting, but we had apparently arrived a week or two ahead of the nesting season. An almost insuperable difficulty of watching nesting birds on this part of the island is that the nesting season always comes after the ice has broken up but before the water is open enough for boat travel. This is not accidental — many northern cliff-breeding birds put off nesting until their homes are virtually inaccessible to any animal, including man. This has nothing to do with season, but with ice conditions. It appears to be a primitive form of reasoning.

We had gained firsthand knowledge of three outstanding facts of arctic life — the total lack of time sense; the fundamental laziness (a native didn't need to do much hunting to keep his family fed and clothed — why should he work harder than necessary?); and the vast, unending sociability. These were attractive traits and no doubt good for the soul. But they were strange to conscientious, schedule-ridden Outsiders. The first was the most difficult to cope with. Used to living on a regular twenty-four-hour schedule, none of us could manage to stay asleep long enough to make up for the many hours we had to be awake. The tranquil, gay timelessness of perpetual daylight was beginning to tell. We had had our holiday by the sea and now we were tired and ready to go home.

This was lightly said but not easily accomplished. We five Bylot Islanders sat in our tent over our fourth pot of tea and considered the problem of how to get the others moving.

155

Should we strike our tents and all move into Makpa's tent, making such an uncomfortably big crowd that they would have to move? We knew what would happen then — they would just put on another pot of tea. We tried it anyway, leaving our tents standing for safety's sake.

Makpa's tent was already full of people. We were welcomed jovially. "*Tupik kalaitsuk*," said Idlouk. (A tent is never full until it bursts.) Another pot of tea was put on the stove. One more Eskimo came in, and another and another — and finally there really was no more room. Someone tried to get in and couldn't. We heard laughter outside, and in under the tent wall came Panipookoochoo's head. The head stayed there half an hour, and during that time it did not stop laughing.

Imperceptibly we prepared to leave and after seven hours we were ready to strike the tents. Suddenly I felt that Button Point was something precious, not to be lost. When the tents were down the plateau was sad and empty, already lost. As our komatiks skidded down the steep shelf to the sea ice I did not want to look back.

We were already several hundred yards out on the ice when Panipookoochoo came running down the slope, stumbling and sinking deep into the rotten snow. He shouted and waved his arms, and we stopped to wait for him. So out of breath that he was unable to speak, he pointed to the back of Idlouk's neck. We looked. An adhesive strip labeled "Ben" was stuck on the back of the hood. Pani doubled himself up with laughter, then made his way back to the shore, still laughing. He could not bear the thought that we would have discovered his last joke when he wasn't there to laugh at it.

Fog closed around us. We could not see more than five or

six feet ahead, and the other sleds had vanished, even their sounds swallowed in the heavy mist. Axel and I were on Idlouk's sled. The dogs trotted at a fast pace and Idlouk confidently called out directions to them — but we might have been in the middle of the ocean, going in circles or headed for Greenland. How did he know where he was going?

Idlouk pointed to his head and laughed. "I just know," he meant. Then he showed us cracks in the ice, indicating that they ran parallel to the shore. Land was close; he pointed to the piles of debrislike pressure ice which the tides had pushed onto the beach. As he did this a lonely boat, face down, loomed through the fog, and we saw the vague outlines of a tent.

The arctic landscape was full of signposts, invisible to us. Eskimos seldom got lost, even in the deadest, quietest fog. In winter, when they traveled in fog with no stars, wind or ice cracks to guide them, they studied the *sastrugi*, wind ridges on the dry, powdery snow. Remembering the direction of the last wind, they used its marks as guides. Kudlu had once taken Pete forty-five miles over the sea ice during a winter fog and had hit Pond Inlet within a quarter of a mile.

After several hours we stopped and went ashore. There were the remains of an ancient camp here, Pete told us, perhaps even dating back to the Toonijuk, the prehistoric people who, the natives say, were living in this land from the Bering Strait to Greenland when the Eskimos came.

The Toonijuk were not Eskimos and no one is sure of who they were or what was their final fate. They are said by the Eskimos to have been very large, and possessed of some queer and disgusting habits. They liked to eat rotten meat, and the women would tuck the meat into their clothing, to be made fetid by the warmth of their bodies. Not knowing how to cure skins, they would wet the hide of the caribou and wrap it around their bare bodies in order to dry it. Their beds were made of skins that had neither been cleaned nor stretched. When a man had a severe headache a hole would be drilled through his skull, from which blood and matter oozed. This operation cured the headache. Greenland Eskimos (according to Knud Rasmussen) describe the Toonijuk as people who wore no clothes, but had feathers on their bodies, or bearskins. Sometimes the lower part of the woman looked like a dog. They lived in underground houses with no sleeping platforms, and they did not know how to hang up their cooking pots. In order to make them thin, fleet runners, men would be put into bags made of the skin of the bearded seal and filled with worms. The worms sucked their blood and made them slender. At Eta, in Greenland, was found a generation ago the skin of a little auk, filled with worms. Eskimos said this was left behind by a family of the big strangers who had fled into the interior. The Toonijuk were said to have been good hunters: a hunter had only to beckon to his prey with his forefinger, and he was so strong that he could carry a bearded seal on his back and break rocks with his lance.

But the Toonijuk were not dangerous; on the contrary, they were timid and terribly afraid of dogs; they were also stupid and slow-going. The Pond Inlet Eskimos say that these big people never attacked Eskimos but fought among themselves until they killed each other off (but other Eskimo tribes claim to have stalked the stupid giants and killed them one by one, like game). They disappeared from the Canadian Arctic long before the memory of the oldest Eskimo, and only dim, distorted shreds of tales remain. When Idlouk was asked when the Toonijuk were here he could only answer, "Long ago, before my grandfather was born." That means, to an Eskimo, beyond memory.

What should the Eskimos know of the Toonijuk? From grandmother to grandchild have come out of the dark past a few derelict tales of despised, repugnant subhumans. The Toonijuk are shadowy figures in the half memory of another primitive race which has no writing and no history.

But the Toonijuk existed — or people who may have been the Toonijuk. Relics of pre-Eskimo peoples (known as Sarquaq, Dorset and Thule) have been found in the Eastern Arctic. On the Bering Sea coast are relics of a culture dating back to 5000 B.C., with tools linking it definitely with neolithic man in Asia.

The summer we were on Bylot Island an expedition unearthed a complete Dorset village at least three thousand years old on Melville Peninsula, not far from us, along with remains of the even older Sarquaq race. Until 1902 an extremely primitive tribe of Thule people lived on Southampton Island, and some of their customs were those of the Toonijuk. Greenland Eskimos say that a few of the big hunters still live, and have retired far inland, fearful and wary as wild animals.

Who were they? Many thousand years ago, probably, fierce warlike nomads from Inner Asia overcame the remnants of an older culture and drove the survivors northward from their homes. Over the course of several thousand years these harried refugees made their way in successive waves of emigration across the Bering Strait and settled in the lonely, untroubled American Arctic. The rigors of the new world probably caused many of the earliest Asian tribes to deteriorate. Others improved their lot and developed over many hundreds of years into the highly efficient, well-oriented modern Eskimo.

But some of the early, deteriorated tribes survived, and lived side by side with the better adapted Eskimos, until the lowlier peoples were exterminated or died off. It is possible that some of these more primitive races, Dorset and Thule, were the giants whom the Eskimos call the Toonijuk. The stories of the Toonijuk are tales of real people. They do not have the quality of legend, although in some parts of the arctic the ancient people have been elevated to the position of fairy-tale giants and even spirits. But they are seldom described as wicked or powerful or magic; simply strong, stupid and disgusting. They sound like prehumans — or like degenerated humans.

But this is all only conjecture. The Toonijuk, whoever they were, are lost beyond recall. The Eskimos not only do not know who the old ones were, but they do not know where they themselves came from. They have no legends of the crossing of the Bering Strait, or of the people of Central Asia who were probably their ancestors, or of the mild and fertile lands from which they may have been driven. They believe they originated in some northern Garden of Eden. (The Baffin Island Eskimos place this paradise on Igloolik, a barren, frozen island in Foxe Basin.) Many centuries ago they came to this land, their background wiped from their minds as if it had never existed. Here they developed a specialized culture perfectly adapted to their frigid environment — and here they live today, the last survivors of an ancient, gentle race.

(About a hundred years ago some Eskimos made their way

back to the country of their origin and settled along the coast of northern Siberia, side by side with the northern people there, who are no relation. These Russian Eskimos are as tough as their American cousins, and on Bylot Island we used to speculate what would happen in a war if the Communist Eskimos came face to face with the Eskimos of democracy. Probably, we decided, they would sit down on the sea ice on a caribou hide and have a pot of tea.)

We climbed over the boggy, rocky tundra until we came to a small protected valley. A rushing little river ran through it. Idlouk picked me up and carried me over the water as lightly as if I were one of his little children. Then he went back for Ned, who is six feet tall, hoisted him on his back and hopped easily across from stone to stone.

On the gentle far slope of the valley we could discern vaguely through the fog mounds of earth in circular form. The deserted village, probably many hundreds of years old, was dim and eerie in the low-lying mist. These were the homes, perhaps, of a race which no longer inhabited the earth. We had entered a primitive, unknown, ghostly world, a country of myth. Death and quietness were around us; the only living creature was a big white arctic hare (in summer they turn brown, tundra-colored, like foxes and weasels, but this one was late) which hopped nimbly away into the fog.

We swarmed over the silent valley, disturbing it, calling back and forth to each other through the gray mist. We found that the earth mounds consisted of huge stones, half buried, which indicated the circular walls of houses. Excavations had apparently been made in the iron-hard earth; the houses were partly underground. A narrow tunnel about three feet high led into each house. Inside were lichen-covered flat stones: a platform at the back and a bench at each side of the door. Some of the houses had rotting bones along their inner walls — wide, flat bones of the Greenland whale. The roof might have been a complicated arrangement of overlapping stones, as is still seen in the houses of some of the more primitive Eskimos. Or it might have been of hide, stretched over the whalebone inner walls and piled with snow in the winter to keep the house at a constant temperature. We did not see how they could have dug so deep into the frozen earth with their simple implements of stone and ivory, or how they had managed to transport the enormous stones of the walls, even with dogs and sleds.

The Toonijuk, the Eskimos say, built their underground houses of heavy rocks which no Eskimo could lift. They used the rocks for walls and whale ribs and shoulder blades for the roof. At the entrance of the house two whale jawbones were placed.

But we could see that the derelict village, whatever its origin, had been used by many Eskimos, and recently — probably up until the time the caribou ceased grazing on Bylot Island. In form the houses were similar to those used now in winter. The Baffin Island Eskimos do not live in snow igloos, though they build temporary ones when they travel. Idlouk told us that with another man he could put up a snow house in ten minutes; by himself it would take about twenty-five. But their permanent igloos are usually of stone. When they can afford to buy lumber they build inner walls of wood, which they line with paper torn from old magazines, for insulation. (Pete said that these papered walls were irritating.

You find yourself trying to read them, but you have to read upside down or sideways. And in the middle of a fascinating story you come to "continued on page 58." Page 58 cannot be found — most likely it has its face to the wall.) The Eskimos still use caribou hide for the roofs, or heavy canvas if they can get it, and snow is loaded on top to keep below-zero temperatures from penetrating. The entrance is a long, low tunnel. On the left as you come in — always on the left — is the woman's part of the house, with a big soapstone seal-oil cooking lamp shaped like a half-moon. In the back half of the house is the sleeping platform, of stone or wood, covered with caribou and bear skins. A tiny opening at the back is covered with greased, translucent seal-gut casing.

Our forsaken village bore clear signs of its most recent inhabitants. But the natives often built their camps on the sites of much more ancient settlements. And Idlouk confirmed what we had been told before we had come to the north — that there were Toonijuk villages on Bylot Island. Since there was no archaeologist among us we had no way of determining whether this was one of the prehistoric towns.

Though the mysterious ruins told us little we found something queer. Roaming through the fog-shrouded valley, we came to a high mound of stones. Some of them had fallen away, and peering into the dark hollow beneath we saw a few human bones. Ben leaned in to examine them and brought up a pelvis bone. He said it had apparently belonged to a large woman, much larger than an Eskimo.

Aside from the Toonijuk, if they ever existed, who else could have been here? Perhaps Norsemen. Those indefatigable explorers had settled in Greenland in the tenth century, and were reputed to have touched the coast of North America as far north as Labrador. It seemed an easy probability that some would have made landings further north (and much closer to Greenland). There they would have met Eskimos who were then moving in from the western side of the continent. There was even a possibility that the "big fighting people" who killed each other off in the Baffin Island Eskimo stories were Europeans. Tales about one race of men might have been superimposed on those about another, as can happen among a people who love to tell stories but have no way of recording them.

By now all the stories were semilegendary. But through the dreamlike, wandering tales, amid the magic and the coarse earthiness, there undoubtedly ran thin true skeins of history — rare discoveries for an anthropologist with the patience to unravel them.

We resumed the long journey. About four in the morning a cold east wind came driving in from the ocean, channeled between the mountains on each side of the narrow inlet, and wet chilly mist swirled around us, seeping into our clothing. The two girls, Makpa and Marta, had zipped themselves both into one sleeping bag and lay, an inert bundle, on one of the sleds. Pete hovered over the package like a mother hen, pushing it straight when it started to roll off, tightening the sealskin thongs that fastened it onto the sled. The bundle did not move. Curled into tiny balls, the girls apparently slept soundly for about ten hours. I was not so comfortable. I could neither curl up nor lie down and I was miserably cold.

My plight did not escape Idlouk. He was the most observ-

ant man I had ever known, and one of the most thoughtful.
Unobtrusively he was also watching the other members of
our group, and he knew almost to the second when it was
time to begin playing jokes. Idlouk was an intellectual, and a
man of fine tact. He did not have the brainless, all-embracing
gaiety of Panipookoochoo, but he knew which of us liked to
be silly and which did not, and even what kind of humor each
of us preferred. And when the wind grew bitter, the journey
seemed too long and spirits were low Idlouk knew it was
time to start all of us laughing, no matter how crude the jokes
must be. He cut a flipper from the inevitable dead seal tied
on the back of the sled, fastened it to the end of his whip
and dangled it behind. The dogs on the following komatik
rushed to get it. He jerked it sideways and they galloped
after it, nearly upsetting the sled. Back and forth the dogs
zigzagged, until Kudlu, driver of that sled, ran ahead and unfastened the main trace of our sled.

"*Waka glunga!*" shouted Idlouk, laughing as he jumped on
the trace to keep the dogs from running away. (*Waka glunga*
means "the most," and is used as an expression of shocked
astonishment.) While he was refastening the dogs to the sled
somebody stole his whip. Idlouk left the dogs and ran after
the offender, pulled him backwards off his sled and rolled
him in the snow. No matter what the jokes were the poor
dogs were always caught in the middle. They didn't think
any of it was funny.

But we were warm and wide-awake when we reached
Pond Inlet at ten-thirty in the morning after a fifteen-hour
journey. Jim Cooley, the junior constable, was sweeping his
front doorstep. Don Whitbread, the Anglican missionary, was
laying tiles on the roof of his new house. Even some Eskimos

were up. We had a faint guilty feeling of having been out on an all-night binge.

Most of our Eskimo sled companions disappeared immediately into tents, not to reappear for twenty-four hours. The eight undersized dogs who had pulled so valiantly on the trip to the Akpa Cliff and again on the way home were staked out by their master without being fed. Idlouk and Kudlu had fed their dogs out on the ice just before we came into Pond Inlet. But the master of that underprivileged little team had either been unable to get a seal or was too lazy. His dogs lay sadly on the muddy tundra, heads between their paws, eyes wide open. I felt like giving them my breakfast Cornflakes and coffee.

Kudlu came into the HBC house while we were eating and exhibited to Ben a severe case of burned eyes. He had forgotten to wear his ice goggles and his eyes were seared and red and half closed with pain. One could not stay in the glaring whiteness of this snowy world for more than half an hour before the eyes began to water, itch and ache, and snow goggles were a necessity. When the eyes were burned the liquid in them dried and you felt as if there were gravel under your lids; it was an exquisite torture. Ben rubbed ointment into one of the bad eyes and Kudlu jumped and screeched. Then he laughed, saying, "Now I have only one eye." Ben started to put ointment into the other eye. "Now I won't have any eyes!" shouted Kudlu, and doubled himself up laughing. We laughed too — what else could we do? There appeared to be no disaster which was not funny to him. As we finished our coffee Pete told us about a grueling trip he had taken with Kudlu around Bylot Island one May. They were out for sixteen days, most of the time in blizzards. They had almost

nothing to eat as the weather was too thick for hunting, and
for five days the only seal they found was an inedible
tiggak, an old male. (The aging male of the ringed seal has
a bad smell and is disgusting to humans.) To keep the dogs
going in the blinding snowstorms they often had to plow
ahead of the team on snowshoes. The skin peeled off their
faces and their lips were caked with blood and dried skin.
Kudlu had a crack on his nose an inch long which started
bleeding every time he wrinkled his nose in a grin. This
was very funny to him. When they laughed their lips split
open and blood ran down their chins, which made them
laugh harder. They agreed that it was the most hilarious trip
they had ever taken. Joking and laughing at difficulties was
the Eskimos' unconsciously philosophic attitude toward misfortune. It always worked.

It was impossible to get back to our home camp that day.
The sun had melted the snow on the sea ice around Pond
Inlet so that it was a blue-green lake. We had to wait until
the surface water evaporated or ran off into the leads. In the
meantime we tried to get back on a normal schedule of sleeping and eating. It was difficult. The second day we were at
Pond Inlet Ned and I had a fantastic conversation.

"Is this supper or breakfast?"

"Well, I have had two meals since yesterday afternoon,
when I got up. That makes it breakfast — I think."

"But you didn't get up yesterday afternoon. I was up
at eight in the night and you were still asleep."

"That must have been eight in the morning. I was definitely
up at two-thirty in the afternoon."

"That was the day before."

"No, it wasn't. The day before we were still at Button Point."

"Then I must have slept twenty-five hours. Is this eight at night or eight in the morning?"

"I think it's eight at night because I was at church at eleven and that wouldn't have been eleven at night — would it? And I haven't slept between church and now."

Finally the others broke it up. But we still weren't sure.

X I

The Lord Is My Shepherd

ON that disputed Sunday morning Axel and I, curious to see an Eskimo service, walked to church at eleven o'clock, just as the mission bell was ringing. The bell always set the dogs to howling and this morning, as usual, they sang their daily hymn. As we walked down the beach Eskimos were coming out of their tents, neatly dressed and looking sleepy. The only thing they were on time for, apparently, was church.

The Anglican mission was a new white frame house, green-trimmed and red-roofed like the others. About twenty Eskimos sat in quiet rows on wooden benches in a sunny, pleasant room. Don Whitbread, their minister, a stout young man with bright blue eyes and a cheerful countenance, spoke the morning service in the Eskimo language. His congregation gave the responses without looking at their books.

"We have erred and strayed in our ways like lost sheep," they murmured (we were reading the English version.) "We have followed too much the dictates and desires of our hearts. We have left undone that which we ought to have done, and we have done that which we ought not to have done. And there is no health in us. But thou, O Lord, have mercy on us, miserable offenders."

The "miserable offenders," Christians only since 1930, appeared to be enjoying themselves. The atmosphere was rest-

169

ful, the children were docile and the adults attentive. During the Lord's Prayer a baby cried; unself-consciously the mother took it out of her hood and put it to the breast. The baby was naked from the waist down, but its top half was swathed in layers of faded sweaters and on its head was an elegant, intricately patterned bonnet of caribou fur.

Between the prayers hymns were sung. These the congregation also knew by heart and they sang with gusto. The minister's voice was deep and full-throated and he accompanied the hymns with a large piano accordion slung over his shoulder. The big, jolly, red-cheeked young man, with his booming voice, his accordion and his merry eyes, looked more like a ballad singer than a man of God. The Eskimos obviously derived great pleasure from the sonorous words of the service, the beautiful old hymns and the cheerfulness of their minister. Most of them, we learned later, loved church and went to service every day when they were near a mission. Many read several chapters of the Bible each morning when they were away. Idlouk was not only faithful to his daily Bible reading but held Sunday church services in his tent when he was with us on Bylot Island.

We stayed after the service to talk to the missionary in his living quarters, which were clean, pleasant and neat. Living on a tiny salary, Don did all his own cooking, housework and carpentry and he had built the mission house himself, with some native help. The interior decoration was colorful if somewhat incongruous. The kitchen walls were dusty pink with yellow trim, the living room ivory with light-blue trim. In the living room were rugs of sealskin and polar bear, a tinted photograph of King George VI and his family and two striking photographs of arctic scenes. A tiny study off the living room was crowded with a large desk, files, tomes on musicology, an abacus, a radio and an ancient wind-up phonograph. A dusty pile of old records included arias from Italian operas and Johann Strauss waltzes.

During the winter, Don told us, he kept a school for children, for two hours on two days of the week, in which he taught English, arithmetic and a little geography. He also had a six weeks' course in basic English for adults and children, and he gave music instruction to the few he could find who had some musical talent. In his little school he tried to explain some elementary facts of history and world affairs, but here he didn't get very far. The white man's complicated troubles seemed laughable to the Eskimos. This peaceable race has never had a government, or any laws save those imposed by a hard and indifferent nature, or any leaders but the few, like Idlouk, who by their skill and wisdom set an example to the others. Crime is almost nonexistent. They have never wished to fight anyone, individually or collectively, and they think that we are foolish and nervous, forever going to war with one another.

Although Don was popular his school had few pupils, and they did not stay long. This was not his fault — schooling is a problem all over the arctic. The children love school and most of them would willingly stay at their books all winter. Their minds are agile and retentive and, since habits of obedience and courtesy are ingrained from babyhood, they are remarkably docile students. But if they were to go regularly to school it would mean that they would have to leave their home camps, travel many miles and stay with the missionary for weeks or months at a time. Eskimo camps in the sparsely populated north are spread over big distances.

In this whole administrative district, which is larger than California, there are only one thousand and eight people and four white settlements. If the children came to school from distant camps they would not have the opportunity of learning from their parents the basic skills without which the Eskimo cannot live in the north. It is far more important for an Eskimo child to learn to hunt than to learn the English alphabet. Don, like other white men we met in the north, believed that all Eskimo children should be given a little basic education whenever they could get to a school — that is, whenever their fathers came in to trade — and that a few more talented children should have regular schooling and go on to higher education. Eventually, then, there would be a small group of educated Eskimos who could take over much of the work which is now done by white men — trading, distribution of family allowances, care of the sick, teaching and missionary work. This work could be done much better by Eskimos, who know the needs and customs of their people, than by white men, however well intentioned.

In spite of Don's interest in schooling, however, his main province was religion. During the winter he traveled to outlying camps, where he taught Sunday school all day every day. The natives flocked to hear him and vied with one another for the honor of putting him up during his stay. This, we gathered, was only partly due to religious enthusiasm. There was not much to do during the long winter darkness and visitors were welcomed, particularly entertaining visitors like Don, with his accordion, his hymns, his Bible and his easygoing teaching. Don knew this — that was why he visited in the winter.

He told us about one of his trips the past winter, which illustrated the Eskimos' friendly respect for him. He was traveling with Kudlu as his guide and the full moon was high. They came to a section of tossed and tumbled sea ice — and at that moment the moon's light started to fade, although there was not a cloud in the sky. Within two hours they were in complete darkness, in a wilderness of broken, twisted ice and a cold of fifty degrees below zero.

"*Takerk sertok*" (the moon is black), said Kudlu, laughing, as they picked their way painfully through the pitch-black night. Neither was afraid and in fact they thought it funny that they had not remembered it was the night of the total eclipse of the moon. (The white men didn't need to teach the Eskimos anything about the sky. Eclipses, the slow wheeling of the planets and the positions of the stars are familiar and friendly phenomena to the smallest child. The natives have plenty of leisure to watch the winter skies and nothing up there frightens or surprises them. Christians they may be, but the stars are their friends, the souls of the dead, and when the aurora borealis brightens the sky with waves of silver the people of the air are playing football, and when a meteor falls someone up there has spit towards the earth.)

On their return from the trip Kudlu declined to take the money which Don had promised him in advance for acting as guide. "I had a good time," he said, "and I don't need the money." He was being tactful about the fact that he was a wealthy man and Don was a poor man. Kudlu's fox trapping had been unusually successful that year and he had plenty of credit at the HBC to feed his family. In addition he possessed eight thousand dollars left to him by his father, Hérodier, the French trader. The promised payment was eventually donated to the mission, with Kudlu's enthusiastic assent.

We were much impressed by the naturalness of the relationship between this sympathetic missionary and his charges. And he probably was typical of modern missionaries. Missionaries, we learned, had brought to the natives the only teaching and doctoring they had ever received before the Canadian Government began to take a belated interest. And many of these dedicated men respected, like Don, the gaiety, honesty and courage of their gentle flocks.

Others, we had been told, had brought nothing but doubts and problems to the souls they wished to convert to Christ. In many ways they had changed the character and customs of the people. We already knew of their suppression of folk legends. In smaller ways, too, the church had introduced a constraining morality. Women, it was insisted, should wear dresses. The native costume of the Baffin Island woman is unusually beautiful. She wears a snowy white parka, short on the sides and extending front and back halfway down the legs in a graceful embroidered curve. Below this are sealskin trousers with the shadowed, silvery fur outside. On her feet are boots of sealskin, the soles heavy, black and waterproof, the uppers scalded pure white and softened by her own teeth. Over the tops of the boots are the cuffs of her white flannel socks, gaily decorated with bright embroidery and ties of hand-woven wool. But she must now wear a shapeless, sleazy cotton dress which peers out untidily below the parka, hiding the silverjar trousers and the handsome boots and destroying the symmetry of the graceful costume. Women, it is sternly asserted, must not show their legs, even modestly encased in sealskin.

The church has also insisted that Eskimo babies should be baptized and receive Christian names. But how much more fitting that a native hunter should be Oodlateeta than Paul; that an ancient black-haired grandmother, full of legends, should be Oolayoo than Deborah. How incongruous that Idlouk, the Unborn Seal, should have been christened Joseph. And what a wonderfully rhythmical mouthful is Panipoo-koochoo, otherwise known as Joe.

Being meagerly paid, a few missionaries are said to have resorted to unethical means in their efforts to procure money from the natives. Women' clubs throughout Canada collect garments in charity drives and send them to missions in the north, to be distributed to needy Eskimo families. We heard that missionaries had been known to *sell* these shabby clothes to the Eskimos. On one post many hunters, in a poor hunting year, had exceeded their credit limit at the Hudson's Bay Company post. The trader could give them no more credit, so they went to the missionary. He offered them credit if they would leave their guns as security. This left them without any means of making up their debts, so the missionary sold all the guns — for the good of the mission, he said.

One missionary's wife said it was sinful that the Eskimos did not contribute more to the church. They are very poor, she was told, and they need everything they can earn to feed their families. Well, she retorted, they smoke, don't they? Why don't they stop smoking and give all that wicked to-bacco money to the missions? Actually Eskimos often give larger contributions to the missions than they can afford. And if they like the missionary they help him in countless small ways without expectation of pay.

Some missionaries do not like the Eskimos to dance, even though they now perform only the innocent English round dances which their ancestors learned from whalers. Once a police constable arranged a dance for the Eskimos on his post to celebrate the end of several weeks of grueling coal mining. As was their habit the natives all went to church first, after they had come down from the hills. There the missionary, in a fiery speech, told them they would all go to hell if they went to the dance. Nobody went.

The Eskimos, who, before they became Christians, had no fear of death, are now afraid of hell. Beyond death, they have been taught, lies a horrible fate. "If you are bad," said one missionary to a hunter, "you will go to hell when you die, and there you will be pushed up the barrel of your own rifle." To a woman he said, "In hell you will be shoved through the eye of your needle."

The Eskimos were apparently docile to all the missionaries' teachings, whether false or true. But they did not love every missionary, and they showed their dislike in small, subtle, but effective ways. There had been a missionary at Pond Inlet who would not drink out of a cup that had touched an Eskimo's lips; who regarded the natives as inferior, dirty and barbarous people whom it was his distasteful duty to lead into the way of Christ. On the way home from a trip with Kudlu — the same tactful Kudlu who would not let Don pay him — the dogs' main trace broke and the sled was left on the ice while the dogs galloped at full speed toward Pond Inlet. Kudlu picked up his gear and sprinted after them, while the missionary followed at a distance, shouting at him to go more slowly. Kudlu ran for an hour, covering about six miles. Then he stopped to make tea and wait for the missionary, puffing and furious, to catch up with him.

"Didn't you hear me call you?" shouted the angry white man.

Kudlu turned an innocent and smiling face as he handed him a cup of tea(Kudlu's own cup). "I didn't hear you," he said. "I was trying to catch the dogs." He knew he couldn't possibly have caught the dogs. He just wanted to give the missionary a little trouble. It was not even beyond him to have broken the trace on purpose.

In spite of a few bad missionaries and poor teaching, however, Kudlu was an enthusiastic Christian. He and most of the others had taken up the white man's religion with almost suspicious ease, and walked away from their legends, their spirits, their taboos and their magic without so much as a backward glance.

Don was disturbed about this. Interested in their folklore, he encouraged them to tell him stories and sing him songs, which he wrote down. Most of their dances, he said, had been hunting rituals, performed only by men and accompanied by a drum of caribou hide stretched over a whalebone hoop. But on Baffin Island they rarely danced any more, and the ancient meanings were almost forgotten.

Their music, too, was nearly lost, drowned in the flood of sea chanteys and folk songs which the whalers had brought them from Europe. But a few of the older Eskimos still knew the old songs. We wanted to hear one, so Don called in Idlouk Tana (the Fat), a lazy and dirty old man, to sing a song for us. Idlouk Tana's clothes, skin and teeth were all one color, a muddy, indeterminate brown. His ears were pointed and had no lobes, and he looked like a fat, elderly leprechaun. He sang, without spirit, a rhythmical, monotonous five-note melody in the pentatonic scale originally from Asia and used also by American Indians. Don translated the song for us. It was a paraphrase of one of the tales Pete had told us, about a man who married a snow goose and wished to accompany her when she went south at the end of summer. Like all the legends we had heard the song was a sequence of adventures, a ballad, half dreamlike, half earthy.

"I want to go a long way away, to the land of the birds, where there is no winter, and I will return to this land in the spring," chants the singer. He must pass through five difficult and dangerous trials before he can go and return. Because he has great desire to complete his journey and because he is very clever he will overcome them. He must go through a narrow rock passage, not wide enough for a man. By contorting himself, he works his way though it inch by inch. He must pass between two fire stones. (Before the white man came fire was made by hitting two stones together rapidly.) He makes a quick dash before the stones grind together. He must walk over a burning seal-oil lamp. He steps on the blobs of fat that have not quite melted, just as he would step from one pan to another on the rotting spring sea ice. He must negotiate a seething pot filled with boiling stew. The steam blinds him, but he finds pieces of meat as they come to the top and leaps from one to another before they sink again. In the last verse he sees the back of his wife as she leans over the seal-oil lamp. In his trance she appears as two hills with a valley between them, through which he must find his way.

"That verse," Don interrupted, "is, I imagine, symbolic." He paused, then added hopefully, "Most of these Eskimo songs and legends are symbolic." He asked Idlouk Tana to explain the meaning of the last verse. The old man did so at great length. Don turned to us, blushing. "It seems it is not symbolic," he said.

None of the Eskimos' tales, we had noticed, contained abstractions or symbolism, nor any trace of mysticism — although they were full of magic. The natives were as direct and natural in their folklore as they were in their daily lives, and death and sex were natural adjuncts to a primitive and dangerous existence. It was easy to see why some of the missionaries disliked and feared the legends and had forbidden the Eskimos to tell them. To our delicate, fastidious and puritanical culture the Stone Age attitude towards life seems crude and much too physical.

When we left the Anglican mission we went to call on the two Catholic priests, Father Danielo and Father La Verge, both Oblate fathers. Their home, on the slope of the hill above Pond Inlet, was a small white church with a Gothic steeple. One half was the chapel, with a striking altarpiece, a painting of the crucified Christ looming over the inhuman, icy mountains of Baffin Island. The other half was the fathers' living quarters, small, poor, but very neat. It contained a formidable library of theological volumes in Latin and Greek and a scattering of recent books about the Eskimos and the arctic.

"How is your cold?" Father Danielo asked me politely as he bade us be seated in the tiny corner of the house that served as living room and dining room. The four of us could barely squeeze into it.

"Much better, thank you," I answered, surprised. I had dosed myself with Pete's nose drops and cough syrup so I would not sneeze in church, and didn't think anyone could have noticed that I had a cold. (The germ had come north with us and rotated happily among us the whole six weeks, gaining momentum.)

"We heard you caught it on the way back from Button Point," the father said. They knew our names, and everything we had done on Button Point, and where we came from, and what our mission was in the north — almost everything but our home telephone number. You can't hide in the north. A mysteriously fast grapevine transmits news to every camp and post within miles, and every pertinent fact about a stranger is known even before he arrives.

With graceful French hospitality the fathers offered us sacramental wine and store cookies, delightfully unaccustomed luxuries. The Catholics have very few converts in the Pond Inlet district, we learned. The Anglicans got there first. In other sections of the Canadian Arctic the Catholics had beaten the Anglicans. The Eskimos are fairly evenly divided between the two, with a scattering of Lutherans and Moravians.

In spite of his perennially empty church Father Danielo, a bearded Breton, was cheerful and philosophical. He had been in Pond Inlet for twenty years, knew and liked the Eskimos and was much beloved by them. He realized that the mysticism of the Catholic religion was impenetrable to an Eskimo. How could their straightforward, nonabstract minds ever grasp the mystery of the Eucharist?

"Why do you stay here?" we asked him.

"As long as we have one soul," answered the priest, "it is worthwhile to stay and care for that one soul."

While Father Danielo was calm and resigned, Father La

Verge, younger, more fiery and full of Gallic spirit, was not quite ready to accept his fate.

"What can they think of the white man's religion," he cried, "when they see two missions in one settlement, each preaching an entirely different set of rules?" He was disturbed at the hold the puritanical Anglican missionaries had over the Eskimos and he believed that they spoiled the natives with their rules and taboos and their eternal hymn singing and Bible reading. However, he was ready to admit that the Eskimos derived a positive pleasure from the simple rites of the Anglican Church. The Catholics could offer them only a spiritual mystery which few Eskimos were capable of understanding.

But the Catholic missionaries in the arctic, we learned from others, were in general more tolerant and less preachy than the Protestant. Most of them were Oblate fathers. For a century this order has been sending missionaries to the Canadian Arctic from France and Belgium. These men come with a spirit of courage, dedication and eagerness to like and help the natives, and they stay in the north all their lives. Later we met an Oblate father who had spent his first five years in the arctic learning to live and hunt with the Eskimos. Then he established a school. But instead of teaching religion he taught the children the ways of their fathers.

"Don't you want souls?" he was asked.

Father Charlie shrugged his shoulders. "There are already too many bad Catholics in the world," he answered. "If an Eskimo really wants to come into the church and can convince me that he understands the sacraments — well, I'll consider it."

The two Pond Inlet fathers also were not in the least

downcast about the scarcity of souls in Pond Inlet. They led good, useful, hard-working lives, got along excellently with the Anglican missionary, were popular with the Eskimos — and they were in love with the north.

After saying good-by to the spirited and hospitable Frenchmen, we walked over the marshy tundra back of Pond Inlet. On a high brown hill we came across a fairly new cemetery whose corpses had not yet started to poke out of the ground. Eight or ten graves were marked with uneven rectangles of stones and wooden crosses knocked awry by the wind. They were all Eskimo graves except for one tiny oval of stones beneath which lay the bones of an eleven-day-old baby, son of a previous missionary. It was a bleak, sad place for an English baby to be buried, with bare, endless tundra around it and only the desolate mountains of Bylot Island to be seen across the long stretch of cold blue sea ice. A jaeger swooped low over the graves, hunting, and a red-throated loon, flying straight as an arrow, uttered an antediluvian *quawk* as it passed us.

"Bury me where the wild birds in heaven can hear my sad cry."

Walking back to Pond Inlet, we passed a tall, impressive crucifix planted firmly in the earth on the top of a hill. It dominated the little settlement and bravely addressed itself to the barren scene, pitting our little man-made religion against the tremendous, inhuman forces of the north. A courageous and hopeless gesture we agreed, thinking of the English baby.

But on second thought the gesture was frightening — because the little man-made religion and all the other little man-made things were slowly and inexorably taking over. We moved like a glacier, we and our civilization, inevitably bringing print dresses, Sunday school, a sense of guilt and canned beans into the land of the wolf, the seal and the Stone Age hunter. I don't truly know whether our civilization is better or worse than what was here before — but it is inescapable.

After dinner that Sunday night six of us went over to the Anglican mission. Don had invited us for tea and cupcakes and we arrived about eleven at night — not an extraordinary hour for a visit in the north. Axel and I thought it was to be a social call and we were surprised when the missionary handed each of us an antique, dog-eared folder. Inside were wrinkled papers of all sizes and ages: fuzzy carbon copies of the words of hymns. Don strapped on his accordion, stood up before us and said, "Choose your hymn."

We started timidly. But soon we opened our throats wide and sang with wholehearted enthusiasm. The singing had an intensity of feeling that I have never seen in an ordinary church service. After several hymns I asked if we could all go into the church room and sing. There was an old foot-pump organ there and I longed to get my hands on a keyboard. The organ had a wheezy sound, as if it were out of breath; its bellows squeaked desperately; chords trembled, shuddered and died beneath my fingers. I pumped enthusiastically through five verses of three hymns, then tottered away from the organ feeling as if I had climbed an Alp. Don told me that he never used it in his services because by the time he had finished pumping through one hymn he was too much out of breath to speak.

After the hymns Don gave us Bibles and we read John, Chapter 14, each of us reading one verse around the circle.

That is the chapter which contains, among other controversial verses, the oft-debated phrase, "In my Father's house are many mansions." At the end of the reading Don said formally, "Now we will discuss it." He didn't need to say it; long before the end we were all at a high pitch of enthusiastic dissent and longing for an argument. The discussion instantly got on the subject of the soul saving of the Eskimos, and with a combination of naïveté and cynicism it became extremely heated. Withal there was an extraordinary warmth and closeness of feeling among us. We argued for an hour, then suddenly we stopped. Don passed cups of ink-black tea and plates of gingery cupcakes made by himself and decorated with brilliant green and orange frosting.

Peace descended on us. It was odd and profoundly touching that we seven and the Man of God, almost strangers to one another, could unite in such inspired accord. It could only have happened in such a place as we were then —in the minister's new little house, built with his own hands on the wild tundra. During the entire evening we had been full of love, and we asserted our human friendship against the cold, strange, enormous north. Perhaps that is one of the true aims of religion.

As we left the minister's house a dog howled on the beach, and we were drawn back to the lonely world of the arctic. Another voice joined, and soon the wailing, musical voices were all around us. Why did they howl? Was it an instinct buried in the mists of wolf inheritance, and no longer of any meaning?

The Huskies, though tame and trained, were not individually attached to human masters. Lacking the close affection of a human, they might, like wolves, depend on one another for friendship and security. Maybe they howled in unison to affirm their solidarity — as we had sung hymns. The barbaric voices cried out to the lonesome sea, then they sank down, one by one, until the beach was silent as the frozen ocean.

XII
Lazy Days

DURING our few days at Pond Inlet I was the only white woman, and it devolved on me, whether I wished it or not, to add at least a suggestion of the feminine touch. I didn't look like the Hollywood conception of a lady in the wilderness — in fact a short distance away and from the back it was hard to tell which was I and which was Idlouk Tana. But without looking the part and certainly without thinking about it, I supplied something that the white men of the north had not had for a long time. I walked in a small aura of domesticity, and my light-handed, inefficient rule was accepted with surprisingly warm gratitude and unthinking chivalry.

I had discovered that eating well in the north was simply a matter of going into any kitchen — one's host's or one's neighbour's — and cooking. So I started the days by putting coffee on the stove and opening a can of bacon. Pete always woke up when the bacon was sizzling. The blaring radio could not wake him, but he was not used to the gentle sound of bacon on the fire. I further saw to it that we ate three times a day and that there was something on our plates besides bread and jam. I never knew how many would sit down to a meal — anywhere from three to ten people. I never knew at what time we would eat. None of this mattered to me or anyone else. The atmosphere of Pete's house was as relaxed as that of an Eskimo tent.

One day I picked a bouquet of buttercups and avens for the kitchen table, and the reactions of wonder and delight that followed were out of all proportion to the gesture. It would never occur to a white man in the north to pick flowers — nor to an Eskimo woman either.

Even such a small event as receiving a cup of coffee from the hands of a woman, to a man who was used to getting up and pouring it himself, produced a happy, surprised look on his face. I had a responsibility, and was warmed by it. But it did not weigh heavily upon me.

In fact the housekeeping rapidly began to deteriorate. Merkoshak, the HBC native helper, was off at Button Point hunting walruses. Makpa, the maid, apparently considered herself on semivacation, and kept most curious hours. Four people — Axel and I, Pete and Bren — were living in a house designed for two. (The others of our party stayed at the police house, also designed for two.) In addition the Hudson's Bay Company house, as in most northern settlements, was the center of social life, and there was a continuous stream of white men and Eskimos in and out, all day and all night. Tea and coffee ran as if from inexhaustible faucets, the kitchen table always carried an assortment of bread, crackers, jam and cheese, ash trays spilled over, mud was tracked all over the floors. The can that was used for indoor plumbing overflowed horribly one morning. The drinking water in the barrel went down to the last brackish inch. We ran out of coal and Bren had to scrounge over the post for bits of damp lumber to keep the stove going. The bread was all eaten and we had to take some from the police; then they ran out and

we were down to a few crusts, hard as wood. (We ate them.)
There was no more ice and the icebox, warmer than outdoors,
smelled dreadful.

Makpa, the maid, was a tiny seventeen-year-old with a flat,
sallow, Oriental face. She was always spotlessly clean and
beautifully dressed in her elegant Baffin Island costume, with
pure white sealskin boots on her dainty feet. She hardly ever
spoke, except to Pete, who treated her like a spoiled younger
sister. Her expressionless face lit up when he talked to her,
and she answered in a low, caressing voice, her happy smile
making her almost pretty.

For twenty-four hours after we got back from Button
Point Makpa didn't show up at all. Then she came, had a cup
of tea and a smoke, and vanished without touching the dirty
dishes piled in the sink. At eleven at night she came again,
washed the dishes and a huge pile of laundry, scrubbed the
floor, cleaned the rugs with damp tea leaves and finished, at
three in the morning, by baking eight loaves of bread. They
were burned on the outside and damp on the inside. One
thing about the north — you never got bored by dull routine.

Makpa was one of the few examples I had seen of Eskimos
ruined by coddling. They were easy to spoil, being both
adaptable and lazy, and generally the white men were commendably strict with them. Pete, for instance, would lend a
destitute Eskimo just barely enough credit to keep him from
starving, and tell him to go out and hunt. This attitude kept
the natives from getting shiftless. But Makpa, like a little Oriental kitten, had made herself special privileges. It was obvious
that this elegant, neat, lazy girl could never again live the life
her people lived. The delicate balance was tipped. She was
no longer a true Eskimo, but neither was she anywhere near

being a woman of our civilization. She was in a state of
limbo. At seventeen it was all right. The whole world was
hers. What would life be like for her at forty-five?

We asked Pete if Makpa ever thought about marrying.

"Of course she doesn't," Pete answered. "She's much better off this way. She's a woman, now that she's seventeen, and
she has her own tent. She makes money working for us, she
can dress well and do what she pleases. If she were married
she would have to live in a dark, cold house and cook over a
seal-oil lamp and have a bunch of sniffly children and sew,
sew, sew all day long."

"Suppose she married a white man?"

"That's *impossible*," said Pete with emphasis. "I don't know
any white man, except Jim Ford, who could live with an
Eskimo woman. They just don't have the same attitude
towards life. A man from our civilization would be dragged
down by an Eskimo wife here in the north. And if he took
her away she would die of misery and loneliness Outside."

Eskimo boys and girls, Pete told us, customarily married at
seventeen, after a long courtship. Marriages were arranged
almost at birth, and for a year before the marriage was con-
summated the girl lived in the house of her future in-laws. If
it was found that she was pure and good, and could chew a
boot and fry a bannock, she was accepted. Unless they happened to live near a mission there was no marriage ceremony.
The boy and girl simply set up their own tent, usually in the
camp of the boy's father. A month before childbirth the girl
was put away in a separate tent, where she remained, sometimes unattended, until the child was born.

But, Pete added, marriage was not quite so hard on the
women now as it used to be. They had conveniences — sew-

ing machines, primus stoves, a few ready-made clothes and occasionally canned foods. And once in a while there were even love matches, in which a boy and girl arranged a marriage without consulting their parents.

"Once," he said, "there was a boy here at Pond Inlet who came to me and asked for writing paper and pencil without telling me what for. He was very excited and nervous. When he had written a note he sent his sister to deliver it to the girl he was courting. After a while his sister came back with an answer. The boy broke into smiles and asked if I would give him a package of tobacco and some matches. He ran out of the house quickly, forgetting to take the girl's answering note with him. I read it. It said, 'If I could have a cigarette and a match I would say *yes*.' "

What an innocent and delicate courtship! Makpa didn't know what she was missing.

In spite of the complications of housekeeping, our days at Pond Inlet were easygoing and sociable. Axel and I wandered often over the tundra to watch birds or pick flowers. We always came back to find the HBC house full of visitors. The radio schedules, in the middle of the afternoon, invariably brought most of Pond Inlet in to pick up personal messages and listen to the gossip of the arctic, and they usually stayed on for several hours.

Pond Inlet communicated with radio operators at Arctic Bay and Clyde River. Messages were forwarded from one cold, isolated arctic station to another mostly by amateur radio operators. The whole Canadian Arctic (in fact most of the world) was linked by these radio enthusiasts, and no matter how remote, you were never alone. The radio conversations, chatty and informal, gave us a sense that the enormous north was a small town.

"Well, I guess you people want the baseball scores," said the disembodied voice at Arctic Bay, one hundred fifty miles away. "Just one second here till I get my pipe going. Boston won over Cleveland in sixteen innings yesterday. In the National League the Giants . . ."

I didn't listen. Baseball talk belonged to the New York City world of taxi drivers and television.

"Are Axel and Kathy and Ricky still there?" the voice said suddenly. (Canadians go in for diminutives.) "I have messages for them." The messages came from home, via New Jersey, Indiana, Halifax and Padlopung.

Pond Inlet had a one-way set. We could hear the voice at the other end, but messages had to be sent out in Morse code. Bren would tap out a question in the little office where the sending apparatus was located, then he would race back into the living room to hear the answer. Back and forth he ran — tap, tap, tap, then silence, until the distorted voice of Bob at Arctic Bay roared through the static.

When all messages had been sent and received Bob said, "Seventy-threes and eighty-eights," just before signing off. Everybody laughed. Seventy-threes are "best regards" and eighty-eights are "love and kisses." It was obvious to anyone in the arctic who happened to be listening to Arctic Bay that there were women at Pond Inlet. Bren tapped out a message in return. Probably he was sending back some eighty-eights. Love and kisses from Mary and me must have traveled freely all over the Eastern Arctic while we innocently watched birds on Eclipse Sound.

Evenings were long and peaceful, full of tea and conversation. People wandered in and out, sat down to read a book, joined the conversation, left in the middle of a sentence. The radio was always on, Pete read the poetry of Byron, Doug dozed on the couch. Occasionally, tired of tea, I opened a can of cool fruit juice. I would have preferred beer, and mentioned this once to Doug.

"We had beer here once," said Doug reminiscently. "A plane brought a case in. It was gone in a week."

"Don't you miss it?" Before going north I had had a mental picture of hard-bitten traders, trappers and prospectors drinking away their loneliness through the bitter winter night.

"I suppose so," said Doug, without conviction. "To tell the truth we don't think about it much. The Eskimos aren't allowed to have liquor and they don't want it anyway, so we kind of get out of the habit. Also you get a different type of man up here nowadays — you get men who really want to do something for the Eskimos, not just exploit them and then sit around and drink up the profits."

The men in the north might have a different attitude toward the Eskimos nowadays, but while we were at Pond Inlet we never noticed any of them doing any work, except Don, who was laying tiles on his roof, and Jim Cooley, the junior constable, who was taking a mail-order law course. Actually there wasn't much work to be done. The police were responsible for enforcing game laws — almost an impossibility because the Eskimo population was so widely scattered. They had to ferret out crime, of which there was almost none. Their chief activity was that of a welfare agency: to issue food vouchers to Eskimos for family allowances (every family in Canada receives this allowance, which varies according to the number of children), to keep birth and death records and look into cases of destitution and disease. But this work was carried on during the winter, when the police, on their long patrols, could be sure of finding everyone at home. Now, in the late spring season, the natives were scattered all over the coast, far from their home camps, hunting walrus and narwhal. Pete and Bren traded skins, kept credit accounts and honored the family-allowance food vouchers in the HBC store. The Hudson's Bay Company posts in the far north depend heavily on these government-sponsored orders to keep them in business. But that work left the traders with a great deal of free time, particularly in late spring, when the only skins coming in were a few silverjar seal, the store shelves were nearly bare and the Eskimos were catching their own food.

So the spring season was the lazy season for white men, and they were free to watch its subtle flowering, to hunt with the Eskimos and to talk and talk and talk with the strangers from the south.

After four days of this disorganized, friendly life Idlouk judged that the ice was safe for traveling, and we set out for home on a warm, sunny morning. As we left, all of Pond Inlet's dogs howled in an eerie, contrapuntal farewell, and we heard them still when the houses were as small as toys across the tumbled pressure ice.

We looked ahead with misgivings. Beyond the coastal pressure ice calm blue-green water glassily reflected Bylot Island's sharp black and white mountains. It looked as if we were traveling toward a bright lake with small cakes of white ice floating on it. In the next moment the sled would sink, leaving not a ripple on those menacing reflections.

Idlouk, confident and nonchalant, whistled the Doxology,

interrupting himself to grunt, *"Oonh-eh!"* at the dogs in his best Stone Age voice. We passed the rough shore ice and entered the lake. It was only surface water, several inches deep. But it had softened the ice, and the sled runners cut deep tracks in the rotten surface. Every now and then we passed a much-enlarged seal hole, a vicious dark whirlpool surrounded by thin brown ice.

The surface water softened the dogs' pads and then the crust on the rotten ice, shattered by their feet and sharp as broken glass, cut them cruelly. Soon there were scattered trails of blood behind us. Idlouk took his seal knife from the komatik box and cut small pieces from a scraped, softened sealskin. Quickly and deftly he fashioned little shoes for the dogs' bleeding feet. The dogs, tails down and heads hanging low, unhappily suffered their master to tie the shoes on their feet with sealskin thongs. They hated the little boots and ran with their legs spread wide as if they were trying to get away from the leather.

Near the midway point of the trip, about eight miles offshore, Idlouk suddenly pointed to the ice beside us. We looked down — and saw a fly. It looked like an ordinary housefly, hopelessly out of place. A little later he stopped the sled and walked about fifteen yards over the ice to a pile of old snow. He came back with a tiny piece of whitish fluff — fur from a baby seal.

Idlouk did not have good eyes. His glasses were five years old and he had to bury his nose in a book to read. But he knew how to use his poor eyes. Small signs, unnoticed by us, gave him clues. He had recognized the pile of snow as the igloo that a mother seal had hollowed out for her helpless baby underneath a snowdrift. And he took a chance, to impress us, that there would be some sign of the seal still there. In early spring, he told us with his now easy-to-understand combination of languages and gestures, the hunters catch seals, often mother and baby together, by jumping on these igloos and cutting off escape to the breathing hole. Sometimes a hunter jumps in the wrong place and lands in the hole himself. This is the occasion for much laughter.

Idlouk spotted many seals with his bad eyes, some as much as half a mile away. He stalked one, but the seal was wary and its head went up every five or six seconds when he got close. Idlouk threw down his shield, lay on the ice, waved his feet in the air and lifted his head every five or six seconds. I would have thought he was a seal. But the real seal was not impressed. It dived. After that Idlouk went after no more seals, though he watched each one carefully for a few minutes through his telescope. He explained with graphic motions that the seals were too wide-awake, and would dive before he could get within rifle distance.

Rick described the seals' diving mechanism as Idlouk posed gracefully on a snow hummock with his telescope and we rested on the komatik, our feet in a puddle of pale-blue ice water. Seals exhale before diving. Humans *inhale* before they dive, letting the air out gradually as they go down. But the seal goes very deep and very fast, and it has to have a mechanism to prevent its getting the bends when it comes up again. The moment it sinks, the seal's normal surface heartbeat of about one hundred fifty a minute drops to ten. During the course of the dive the oxygen content decreases from twenty per cent to about two per cent. This would be a dangerously low physical condition for a human, almost near death. But the seal handles it all right. It functions perfectly, swims fast, hunts its food, escapes its enemies — all this with its ears and nostrils closed. After about fifteen minutes, though, it must come up for air. As soon as its nose is in the air it takes a few deep breaths. The carbon dioxide is exhaled and normal metabolism restored within a few seconds.

How, with ears and nostrils closed, can the seal find its food and know its enemies? Not much is known about that, Rick told us. The seal's eyes have to be adapted both to underwater and surface vision, so they probably are not too good in either situation. But it has whiskers. They are attached to large sensitive nerves, and probably the seal feels vibrations with them. There is a record of an old gray seal which, when captured, had obviously been totally blind for a long time. But it was healthy and had a full stomach, so it is thought that its whiskers kept it alive. It's even possible, though it hasn't been proved, that without its whiskers a seal would not only starve but drown as well. With its ears and nostrils closed and its eyes unreliable, only its whiskers can tell it when it has reached the air. Had we ever seen a cat with its whiskers cut off? It bumps into things and acts lost and frustrated. And a rat will drown without its whiskers.

All the time Rick was talking Idlouk posed motionless, apparently waiting for us to notice him. Intent and serious, every self-conscious inch the proud hunter, he was watching a distant seal which seemed to be sleepy. Then, when he realized we were paying attention to him again, he turned, smiled and started pulling fur from the trimming on his parka and floating it to the ground. He indicated that he was testing the wind. It was an absolutely windless day. Idlouk, it seemed, was showing off. He had an odd grin on his face when he motioned to Rick to go after this unwary seal. Rick, happy and proud, set off with rifle and seal shield and stalked the seal with utmost stealth. When he got within shooting distance he lay down on the ice and aimed carefully. Then he raised his head and whistled. The sleepy seal dissolved into seven black ravens. Idlouk laughed for half an hour over his successful joke.

Once the dogs inexplicably started a mad race. After five minutes of wild galloping — the komatik careening perilously, Idlouk shouting and waving his whip in the air with great dramatic effect — the dogs dragged us up a steep bank of pressure ice and nearly dumped us into a large, nasty, brown seal hole. Bakshu, who had not been paying attention when the race started, spent the entire run underneath the sled, howling dreadfully, and finally succeeded in breaking his trace. Idlouk laughed heartily as we extricated the tangled dogs and readjusted the loads on the sled. If we had fallen into the hole it would have been even funnier. We suspected that Idlouk had not really tried to stop his dogs. He was in a joking humor. Beside the seal hole was a large red shrimp, part of a meal left behind in the seal's hasty departure. "Pretty big seal you got," said Rick. Idlouk giggled hoarsely and made the motion of harpooning it.

Near our home camp we came to an open-water lead about thirty feet wide. The dogs trotted close to its thin, shelving edge. A large piece of ice broke off under our weight, and Idlouk laughed as a sled runner hovered for an instant over dark water. A seal peered out of the lead. Idlouk stopped the dogs, grabbed his gun and his harpoon, which had a long sealskin thong attached to it, and ran along the dangerous edge. The seal looked again and he fired. He lifted his harpoon high in a powerful, harmonious motion, ready to throw it into the seal to pull it inshore. But the seal sank suddenly in a circle of bloody ripples. Idlouk cursed softly — or was he blessing it? Eskimos often murmur a blessing for the seal if it escapes. They feel very close to the little animals which are their livelihood.

Then he saw another dark head a hundred yards behind us and ran after it. For an hour or so he chased elusive seals, while we trotted tiredly after him, stumbling into holes, our cameras and binoculars bobbing heavily up and down as we ran. Idlouk was never disappointed. *"Ayta"* (too bad), he would say, grinning, as he watched the seal's ripples widen on the water. And he would run down the lead after another.

We had seen a lot of sea ice in the past eleven days — would we ever get home? It must have been seal hunting which developed the Eskimos' wonderful sense of fatality and timelessness, I thought impatiently. Besides, my feet were wet.

"Ayta," I said experimentally. I felt a little better.

A heavy fog crept over us, and Idlouk gave up his seals. We sailed along in a white world, the only reality the dark lead of open water beside us. Overhead appeared shadowy gray and white arctic terns, ghost birds, almost not there. It was the first time we had seen this far wanderer. The long-winged, graceful arctic tern spends its winters below the Antarctic Circle and nests on the tundra above the Arctic Circle. It flies an estimated twenty-five thousand miles a year in the longest migration known, and lives in perpetual daylight almost the year round. One can only guess at the reason for this exaggerated migration. Perhaps the bird has been pushed farther and farther in both directions over thousands of years due to competition for feeding and nesting grounds in the Temperate Zones. Or it may be a throwback to days when the climate was gentler in the polar regions, and the bird has never got around to changing its habits. Many seemingly absurd migrations are thought to be survivors of ancient custom or necessity — habits that no longer have any meaning.

Whatever the answer to the mysterious question I could understand the wild bird's preference for this fresh, empty land with its thin, clear air, its light nights and its feel of eternal springtime. If I were a bird I would spend my summers on the tundra too.

XIII
Time of the Poppy

SUNDAY, July Fourth, was hot, bright and mosquitoey. The temperature was forty-two degrees in the shade and much higher in the blazing sun, reflected back at us from snow and ice. We were now so well adapted to the cold that this weather felt like midsummer. We peeled off several layers of our many-tiered clothing, got out the 612 and resigned ourselves to an uncomfortable day.

We had come to the north prepared for a terrible invasion of mosquitoes. But, as an optimistic Eskimo poet wrote, "Cold and mosquitoes, these two pests, come never together — and such is life." To our relief we found that the country was too cold and dry to support many mosquitoes. The earth of northern Baffin and Bylot islands is called "dry tundra." (What, we often wondered, sinking to our knees in wet, mossy ooze, is "wet tundra"?) Very few mosquitoes found it to their taste, and they bothered us only on the few warm days. They were *Aëdes*; the word means "odious" and the mosquito is a carrier of yellow fever in the tropics. But these northern *Aëdes* were not very efficient. They were slow and clumsy, and many of them did not bite at all. That was because they were mostly males. They were swarming, preparatory to breeding, and they didn't feel like eating.

I sat outside the tent in the bright sun doing laundry. As I hung the tent lines with a colorful festoon of dripping, soap-smelling woolen clothing the wavering sound of children's voices singing hymns floated over the still Sunday air. I left the chores and went to Idlouk's tent. Opening the door a crack, I peered in, afraid to interrupt. Idlouk and Kidla, with immediate delighted hospitality, invited me to join the service. The white tent was hot under the high morning sun and the six children sat in a solemn row on the sleeping platform, dressed in clean, neat clothes. Kidla quietly nursed Susanna, and Idlouk, facing the family, read the morning service with serious devotion. At the end of the long service, replete with prayers, responses and hymns (all verses), Idlouk handed me a beautiful English Bible. Then he read a chapter from his own dog-eared Eskimo Bible, explaining the verses carefully to Kidla and the children as he went along. They were eagerly attentive; not a child was bored or fidgety during the whole hour and a half.

When it was over I tried to explain to them, through Leah, what the Fourth of July meant to Americans. It was uphill work. They did not understand what it meant that one country "owned" another, or the meaning of revolution. Men fighting one another over the taxes did not enter into the Eskimo scheme of life. The Bible was easier than politics — the strong, archaic stories in the Old Testament had a spiritual similarity to their own solemn, earthy tales of the creation.

No work was done on Sunday in the Eskimo tent. I stayed a little while longer to give Leah a music lesson on the tin whistle (we had advanced to "Frère Jacques"), then blew smoke rings for Nua and played finger games with Rootay. "This Little Pig Went to Market" and "Here Is the Church" were familiar to the two-year-old, and her mother repeated them in Eskimo for me. While I played with the children Panilu, Idlouk's seventeen-year-old son, bounced the naked baby Susanna on his stomach. Susanna's skin was white and her face sallow, like all the Eskimo babies we had seen. The Eskimo race is not dark-skinned, though the adults are brown-faced. Born pale, their cheeks turn bright red as soon as they are big enough to be out of their mothers' protective hoods. Later their faces and hands become dark brown from constant exposure to the burning sun and ice and the bitter winter winds.

The baby laughed as she bounced, and suddenly she began to whimper. Quickly her mother took her and sat her on an empty coffee tin. Eskimos begin toilet training at birth, and for occasional accidents inside the hood there is a wad of dry, absorbent moss more efficient than a diaper. This early training obviously does not warp the children's personalities — because no sense of strain or punishment is attached to it.

Idlouk's tent was clean, and as neat as a small tent could be with nine people living in it. On the sleeping platform were caribou hides and a confusion of faded quilts and clothing, many times mended and patched, and all clean. The shallow, blackened seal-oil cooking lamp was in its proper place, on the left as one entered. Along its straight edge a wick was laid, roughly spun of arctic cotton (a sedge grass gone to seed. We had seen a meadow back of Pond Inlet white with the tufts, like a cotton plantation). Over it hung a rack of black cooking pots. When Kidla cooked, her fuel was provided by a large piece of seal blubber which was suspended from this rack, slowly melting, drop by drop, into the lamp. But the low flame was not burning this day; bannocks and seal meat had been cooked the day before for Sunday eating. Bannocks, an

Eskimo staple, were heavy dry cakes made of flour, baking powder, seal oil and water and cooked slowly in a frying pan over the feeble flame of the lamp wick. Their only virtue was that they wouldn't freeze and kept practically forever. The seal meat looked equally unappetizing, dark gray and soft from at least twelve hours of cooking.

The ground was covered evenly with clean small pebbles which the children had collected on the beach. When Idlouk and Kidla smoked they used an empty peanut tin as an ash tray — nothing was thrown on the floor. The only smell in Idlouk's tent was the familiar rich smell of seal oil and animal skins. That was so much part of our lives now that we did not notice it. A small stuffed doll of wool plaid, made from one of the boys' old shirts, was pinned to the tent wall. The sun shone warmly through the white canvas, fat gay Rootay pounced on one big brother after another, Idlouk whittled at a piece of soapstone, Kidla sang quietly to her baby and Leah plaited wool for a belt. It felt like Sunday.

I looked at Idlouk's carving. He was hollowing a little dish, a replica of the big cooking lamp. The soapstone was porous and soft, and could be shaped with an ordinary pocketknife more easily than wood. Idlouk fitted a ridge of narwhal tusk, carved into dainty miniature teeth, into a slot along the straight sides of the dish. He looked up at me as I watched, and indicated that the ivory ridge was an imitation of the flame along the wick of the real cooking lamp. Then he smiled and handed it to me.

"For you," he said.

I was touched by his gracious gesture, and thanked him in Eskimo and English. Kidla, smiling, helped me with my pronunciation, while the children giggled softly.

After lunch Axel and I walked inland. As we topped the hill above our camp the northwest wind met us like a sudden burst of high summer, hot, strong and sweet with the smell of young plants. The dry wind came from the interior of the island; it baked the hilltops and made the valley bogs and puddles retreat. In the eleven days that we had been away the tundra had quite changed. Most of the snow was gone, and the new moss was thick, lumpy and bouncy — we felt as if we were walking on pillows. Everywhere was the sound of running water, of small streams finally freed from winter ice. It was difficult to judge up and down and level on the tundra because of the sameness of color and lack of landmarks, and often the quick little brooks seemed to run surrealistically uphill from moist, boggy depressions. Over all was the deep roar of the tremendous Aktineq River, rushing down from its inexhaustible glacier and taking the mountains with it into the sea.

The earth was still moist from recent snow, but it was so warm that one could walk barefoot on it. A profusion of low, many-colored flowers gleamed like stars through last year's yellow grass. This, the time of warm, wet earth and constant sunlight, was the period of the tundra's most enthusiastic flowering, and the blossoms of high spring were bigger, bolder and brighter than the modest blooms that had graced the cold earth two weeks before. Daisy fleabane (no relation to our daisy) grew in clumps, its delicate white petals sharply thin, its center shining yellow. Avens, wide-eyed, very pale yellow with a deeper yellow center, clung close to the ground and stared straight at the sun. The thick red mosslike foliage of arctic bell heather now bore blossoms, tiny white bells, like lily of the valley.

Most beautiful of all were the arctic poppies. Their fragile pale-yellow blossoms nodded gracefully on long slender stems, and bent to the ground with every breeze. This frail-looking offspring of the tundra can grow only in the arctic and on high mountains in the Temperate Zone — it does not like an effete climate. We found the dainty poppies blooming hardily on the tops of the windiest and coldest ridges, amid sand and pebbles, where nothing else would grow.

When I remember the arctic springtime I see first this tender flower, unfolding sun-colored, like hope, in a cold land.

Beetles crept through miniature jungles of arctic heather and willow, spiders scuttled over the rocks, mosquitoes and flies hovered in clouds over stagnant pools. Rick had set insect traps up and down the tundra hills, together with thermometers, to determine differences in species and populations at different levels and temperatures. He found that populations and species were fairly constant at all levels, and that the insects of the tundra were, like the birds, more generalized than those found in the Temperate Zone. Those with special needs and tastes had dropped out on the way north, and here were found insects similar to those of high mountain areas of America and Europe, which can live on practically anything.

The commonest spider was *Tarentula asivak*, a big, ugly, gray wolf spider (not poisonous to man). The commonest beetle was *Curtonotus brunnipenis. Tarentula asivak* fed contentedly and almost entirely on *Curtonotus brunnipenis*, wrapping it in a cocoon for safekeeping. There was an odd spider, the ant mimic, whose relatives dwell mostly in the tropics. It seemed misplaced in a land totally devoid of ants. But, we learned, it resembled an ant, not to catch prey, but to deceive birds which don't like the taste of ants but *do* like the taste of spiders. Many of its predators came from latitudes where there were ants. There were crane flies, long-legged and delicate-appearing, which also breed in water or moist soil in high mountains of the Temperate Zone. There were springtails, primitive, wingless insects whose larvae helped to aerate the earth and which, in adult form, leaped easily about the tundra by means of caudal appendages folded beneath their abdomens. There were a few butterflies, among them the sulphur butterfly and the black and orange *Boloria frigga*, which helped to cross-pollinate the plants. The butterflies did not have the range in size of our butterflies, but were uniformly medium-sized — about one and a half inches of wingspread.

Insects were difficult to transport and had a tendency to bite, so we did not intend to take any this day. But on the way home I saw two beautiful *Boloria frigga*. They were mating and paid no attention to me, so I picked them up and laid them carefully in a matchbox. They continued their honeymoon undisturbed until I got them back home to Rick and the ethyl acetate bath. At least they died happy.

The month of June is called by the Eskimos *Erniwik* ("the young are born") and all over the tundra infant life had begun during our absence. Tundra-colored birds' eggs in shallow open nests were so frequent that we had always to watch where we stepped. A white-rumped sandpiper crept away from us, barely keeping out of the way of our feet. She trembled, fluffed her feathers, dragged her wings and uttered distressful little bubbling cries. I sat down to watch her while Axel walked away, hoping that she would be unable to count and would think we both had gone. I sat quiet as a rock. In a few minutes she walked delicately toward me, showing no sign of fear. About seven feet away she stopped, then settled on the ground, fluffed her breast feathers and wriggled herself domestically into a comfortable position. We had not seen the nest although we had walked right over it. I inched slowly toward her, not rising. She regarded me without curiosity and gradually I moved my hand over the nest. But not until I actually touched her did she finally, reluctantly, leave her eggs and creep off, dragging her wings and crying. The nest was shallow and open, carelessly lined with a little dry grass. Four dun-colored, irregularly speckled eggs lay in it, invisible unless you knew they were there. I picked them up and held them in the palm of my hand. Daintily the bird walked toward me, looked the eggs over thoroughly, as if she were counting them, then retired a few feet away and waited patiently for me to give them back.

A little further on a female golden plover showed us she had her nest. Her display was a creeping run with all feathers spread out, accompanied by an incessant, thin, high crying. After a few feet she stopped and lay flat on the ground, spread her wings wide and beat them slowly, looking piteously up at us. "See, I'm helpless," she seemed to say. Suddenly she saw her beautiful mate on a nearby knoll. He was making the same display, trying to distract our attention from the nest. But he only succeeded in distracting hers. In a flash she gave up her pose and dived at him. When she had driven him off she came back to us and tried again to lure us away. In the meantime we had found her nest; two large eggs lay in it, almost as big as hens' eggs. Brown, spotted unevenly with darker brown, they were part of the tundra. As we left the nest she accompanied us, simply walking, as if she were on a leash. She stayed close to us for some fifty feet and then she saw her mate again, standing innocuously on a hill. With an angry cry she was in the air, darting at him. This ungrateful behavior was apparently a product of frustration. Unable to get rid of us, but feeling an irresistible urge to drive *something* away, she picked on the nearest live object.

The tundra birds inevitably showed us where their nests were by their creeping and wing-dragging displays. The weasel, an intelligent mammal with a taste for eggs, uses the same reasoning we did to find nests. Seeing a bird displaying, it follows, then waits unmoving until the bird returns to its nest. Most eaters of birds' eggs, however, are not so clever. The only small-birds' nests we found destroyed during our six weeks' observation of sixty-five nests were two snow buntings' and one American pipit's — a weasel had got all three. In spite of the shortage of lemmings the small birds were not much disturbed by other predators. Either they could not find the flat nests which looked like tundra or else the birds actually succeeded in luring them away with hurt-pretense.

The psychology behind this display of ground-nesting birds is a puzzle. Some say it is an undirected instinct born of fear which makes the bird tremble, crouch and cry, showing every sign of intense shock. Others think it may be a sign of elementary reasoning ability. Josselyn told us that now the most widely accepted theory is that it is neither blind fear nor pure reason but a sharply directed instinct. The bird shows these signs of shock and distress *only* when she thinks her nest is threatened, never if she herself is threatened — in that case she simply flies away. As soon as the intruder is a safe distance off or the bird is satisfied that he is not dangerous the tactics cease.

This is one more instance of the astonishing specialization of birds, which are much more highly developed than any animal in the class of mammals. Not only have they keenly directed instincts, which have reached a high degree of variety and precision, but their physical structure, too, is delicately adapted to their role. Birds which do much flying, for instance, have hollow bones so they are light in the air. And their wings act as a bellows, forcing muscular contractions of the thorax, so they actually breathe more easily while flying than while perching. We humans, in comparison, are sloppy, imperfect creatures. Nothing of us works quite right. Our instincts, though strong, are few, misty and vague, and our physical structure leaves a great deal to be desired. The human brain, developed to a remarkable extent, has apparently grown at the expense of other functions, which have been retarded and in some cases have deteriorated. This dulling of instinct, however, has resulted in an extraordinary freedom of action and thought, exclusively human. We cannot envy the birds the set and narrow paths of their uncompromisingly efficient lives.

Way back on the tundra, on the high plateau that rose slowly toward the Aktineq Glacier, the land was bone dry and tenantless. We walked, entirely alone, over the unblooming ground, and suddenly two long-tailed jaegers screamed out of the sky, attacking us. Again and again they dived, almost touching our heads and uttering squeaky little cries, quite unsuited to their powerful and frightening figures.

Clearly they told us that they had a nest nearby, and we found it easily — not a nest at all, but the barest depression in the ground, containing one fat, mottled, brown egg. We tried the same trick which had worked with the sandpiper. Axel walked away while I sat quiet, trying not to notice the mosquitoes which immediately settled on my face and hands. But these birds were evidently more intelligent than the song-birds and shore birds we had observed earlier. They knew well that I was not a rock and they assumed that my intentions were dishonorable. They were not going to rely on any feeble wing-dragging ruse but intended to drive me away by force.

I did not move and after a long time they retired to a small hill about a hundred yards away. There they sat hopelessly, close to each other, waiting for me to go. Every now and then one of them flew around me again, calling in its high-pitched, wailing voice. Finally, apparently, the female worried about her egg. She favored me with one more shrieking dive, then landed close to the nest. Very slowly she approached it, not taking her eyes off me. She settled gently, her two black tail feathers arched with slender grace, her dusky wings and white breast seeming to melt into one another. But still she watched me, and at the click of the camera she was in the air again. We left them alone. I had never thought I would feel sorry for a jaeger, which is a bird that clearly can take care of itself.

As we descended over the low hills and sharp little ravines we noted the interesting effects of mud motion, known as solifluction — the movement of moisture-laden earth over a hard surface. The permafrost, hard as cement, acted as a smooth slide for the surface soil, and the hills of Bylot Island were slipping toward the sea and falling over themselves in folds, the mud hanging over deep ditches like cake frosting. Along the damp lower edges of the mud frosting arctic heather grew thick and rich, its tiny bell-like flowers looking like sugar. The steady downward flow of earth was partially held back by the shallow roots of grass and willow, but they could only slow, not stop, the inexorable slide. On the flanks of the hills were flat, upended rocks, like tombstones, and we seemed to be walking through a vast, open graveyard. The slow downward stream of heavy earth had probably, with the help of frost action, pushed these huge rocks upright over the centuries.

Most of Bylot Island's tundra hills were crowned with big rocks, where the mud had oozed off completely, leaving the bones of the earth exposed. These hilltop rocks were the richest areas of life on the tundra. There snowy owls and jaegers had perched, attracting the orange lichen *Caloplaca*, which played its part in crumbling the rocks into soil again. There, under the rocks, foxes had their burrows. The food leavings and droppings at the entrances to their lairs attracted rich vegetation, which in turn attracted lemmings, which were then eaten by the foxes. When the lemmings began to come back after the lean years they made their first burrows on these fertile hilltops, and the slower-reviving foxes came after them, to start the chain again. Geese had made their nests in the lush grass, mosquitoes swarmed and bred there, beetles were attracted and in turn brought spiders, who ate the beetles.

The rock crowns, created by permafrost, mud motion and the rhythmic thawing and freezing of the surface soil, were microcosms of arctic life. Victim and predator lived there in uneasy balance; organic and inorganic forces played their own slow game of destruction and creation.

In the boggy lowlands near the shore we looked for a clean pool in which to bathe. But most of the inland waters were clouded with algae, swarming with mosquitoes and edged with thick red mud. The color was caused by bacteria which drew iron from the water and oxidized it into rust. (The Eskimos say it is blood, and they have an extraordinarily vengeful and earthy legend to account for it.) We finally came across a puddle which looked deeper and cleaner. On its shore were stones, in its middle was a dark-gray miniature iceberg. There we took baths — real ones — with the pale sun shining on our backs and the cold water sparkling darkly. The mountains gleamed, enormous, beyond the white highway of the Aktineq Glacier and the white sea ice was covered with a network of thin dark-blue cracks, like a giant cobweb. The land was pure and awesome in its loneliness — yet the small life we had watched, so visibly swarming on its surface, made it seem friendly.

Josselyn, Bill and Mary had, during our eleven-day absence at Button Point and Pond Inlet, found about thirty birds' nests within a quarter of a mile radius of the camp, and were following their fortunes every day. The ravines and hillocks had received poetic names: Phalarope Pond, Golden Plover River, Lark Gully, Snow Bunting Creek. These names were signposts, not affectations, and they had grown naturally. It was impossible, we found, to give accurate directions. The tundra all looked the same, and one rock, hill or ravine could just as easily be another one half a mile away. "I saw two black-bellied plovers courting near the pond where we first saw the red phalaropes" or "If you go up the gully where we found the first lark's nest you will come to a creek with a snow bunting nest in its left bank" were our only ways of indicating landmarks — so the names grew.

Every day the round of the nests was made by two or more of us, and Mary kept a running record of the number of eggs in each nest, the date of the laying of each egg, as near as we could determine it, the date of the pipping and the length of time until the nestlings left home. So far as we knew, the nesting of arctic-breeding birds had never before been followed from start to finish in one spot. We would probably see the entire breeding cycle of many of them, from their first arrival on the bleak, snowy coast in June to the flocking on the warm, flowery tundra for the southward migration at the end of July.

The birds, for the most part, had little fear of us. Their instinctive display tactics were perfunctory and very quickly the females would hop delicately back on their nests and pose for pictures. They disliked leaving the nests — the eggs would chill soon in the cold northern air — and sometimes we had to push them away to count the eggs and look for cracks.

In the late afternoon of that July Fourth Axel and I accompanied Josselyn on the nest round. Mary had found a horned lark's nest the day before and had told us that there were young, probably hatched about ten days previously. "Try and find them," said Mary.

Our first difficulty was in finding the correct little white stake that marked the nest. It lay on a slope, named by Ben "Stake Heaven," popular with all the scientists because of its abundant life and its nearness to home. Everything, including nests, was marked with little white stakes, and we trod carefully through a maze of them, trying not to step on anything vital. Rick had planted his insect traps here and marked their locations with stakes. His thermometers, some buried in the ground, were also fastened to stakes. Bill's mud-motion stakes marched up the hill, wavering slightly where the slowly moving ooze had given them a push. The outlines of his snow patches, long since melted, were marked by a nightmare network of stakes. Even I had added to the confusion, by planting a stake next to a clump of pure white poppies for Bill to collect if he was interested in anemic poppies (he wasn't — said they were as ordinary as pale blondes among humans).

Finally we found the stake with the proper hieroglyphics on it. We looked directly at the ground about a foot below the stake, where the nest was supposed to be. There was no nest. But a little circle of ground was heaving gently. Looking closely, we distinguished the breathing mass from the unbreathing tundra. The baby larks, a random mottling of brown, pale yellow and grayish white, fitted neatly into their nest in a circle of soft feathers. Somewhere there were beaks the color of dark horn, invisible unless you put your nose in the nest. Josselyn touched the wad of breathing fluff. Suddenly it all came apart and five tiny creatures scattered in every direction, running competently. Josselyn picked up one and put it in a pocket for his collection. We quickly gathered the others and stuffed them back into the shallow nest, but they kept coming out between our fingers. Finally Josselyn had them quiet by approximating a mother lark's breast with his hand. The mother bird, which had been unusually shy, turned up at the last moment when everything was rearranged and flew in low circles around us, cheeping wildly, much disturbed.

One Baird's sandpiper nest, the first that had been discovered, had already graduated. Although the youngest was less than twenty-four hours old all four were out of the nest and making their way, wobbly fluff balls, over the tundra toward the beach. Sandpipers, in common with many shore birds, are precocial — they walk out of their shells with all their feathers on, almost ready to support themselves. They looked like bits of tundra come alive. Their red-brown backs were patterned with delicate threads of black and pale gray-green splotches so much like *Stereocaulon* that they seemed actually to have lichen growing on them. Their small black-rimmed faces were as pale as the whitened pebbles of the beach, and on their heads were soft reddish caps like pieces of old moss. Only their black beaks marked them as birds — miniature sandpiper beaks, long and strong and pointed for digging in marshes and wet beaches. A pair of nervous and worried parents tried to guide their random progress, but the babies gave them a bad time. The adults fussed constantly, uttering small chirping cries, like crickets, while the little ones went off in all directions and teetered and fell and sat down to rest.

A pair of Lapland longspurs had from the day of their arrival fed domestically in our backyard garbage hole. They had made a nest in an abandoned lemming hole under a bank about fifty feet from the cook tent. It was deep and carefully constructed, woven of coarse grasses and lined with white feathers. Today it held three young ones just born and a fourth in the process of hatching. These birds were not precocial. They were pieces of raw meat with a little fluff stuck to them here and there and shards of eggshell glued on their backs. They looked as if they should not have been born yet. (But within nine days they had all their feathers and were out of the nest.)

We found no more young. Most of the arctic birds were very late breeders — for the simple reason that it was too cold for eggs and nestlings any earlier. As a compensation their young matured quickly. By the end of August there would be hardly a bird left on the tundra.

Every day some strange new product of the tundra was found. This evening it was a *Dreikante*, a sand-carved stone. Ned had found the small, smooth, perfectly triangular rock half buried in the earth on top of a high ridge. The tundra had held it viselike for many years, while the strong, constant east wind had carved with geometric precision, using sand as its tool.

After supper Ned analyzed our drinking water under his little microscope. We could now add to our richly varied menu a kind of filamentous green alga (a low form of plant life), some large shrimplike creatures and numerous little worms, called nematodes. I shuddered at the worms. But Bill reassured me. They were the commonest and most numerous worms. If you could take away the entire contents of the earth except nematodes there would still remain the shimmering outlines of everything, in nematodes. (He did not add that some nematodes cause trichinosis.)

Josselyn skinned his baby lark. Inside out, with its skeleton exposed, the tiny creature looked like a half handful of nothing at all, and its soft skull was flattened under Josselyn's fingers. Delicately he scraped the brain out, removed the infinitesimal eyes, filled the skull with cotton and turned the skin right side out, while we held our breaths. We were sure that the little head would go to pieces and that all the tender, downy fluff would come off. But it turned out a real baby bird, dark beak as large as its head, new soft feathers fluffed out. It could almost be put back in the nest, except that Mama would wonder how it had got its feet tied together.

Then he turned his attention to a murre egg we had wheedled out of Panipookoochoo and brought back from Button Point. It was about four inches long, a giant egg for such a small bird, pointed at one end, wide at the other, and of a lovely pale green unevenly spattered with black spots. It looked like a Russian Easter egg.

"We should open it, and find a scene with snow and huts and angels."

"Well, you can't tell what we may find in here," said Josselyn carefully as he drilled a small hole in the side. He blew out the contents with a glass tube. A seemingly endless stream of yellow egg came out, but no huts or Russian peasants — not even a murre. Then he sucked a little fresh water into his tube and blew it into the egg to rinse it out, like a good housewife. He tucked the clean, empty egg in layers of moss and lichen and laid it in his big trunk, which already held trays of carefully packed birds resting on beds of cotton and mosquito netting.

About nine in the evening some of us gathered in the cook tent for tea and hot chocolate. These evening sessions usually developed into full meals, and they got longer and longer as we became more and more timeless, like the Eskimos. This evening the talk turned to Bill's digging and the underground patterns of frozen earth he had found in the course of it. The earth was thawing rapidly under the spring sun and the warm wind, and every day the holes were filled with water and he had to dig deeper. Would he ever reach permafrost we asked.

"I don't know," he answered. "No one knows how deep permafrost may be in any particular area. It may be hundreds of feet underground or it may be only six or seven feet. When you hit it you know it. The permanently frozen soil has an entirely different construction from the soil that freezes and thaws every year. What I am hitting now is only annual frost."

"*Annual Frost*," murmured Josselyn, who had been out of the conversation for a long time. "Sounds like a faculty party." And the serious discussion fell apart as if it had been blown away by the northwest spring wind.

Around midnight we began drifting off to bed. Axel and I heard voices and laughter in Rick's tent and walked over to see what was happening. In his tiny dwelling, three by six feet and only high enough to kneel in, Rick was entertaining Panilu, Kidla and Rootay. A primus stove was humming noisily and they were all drinking tea. Panilu and Rick were exchanging a rapid conversation above the small roar of the stove, though neither knew what the other was talking about. It was like a scene from *Alice in Wonderland*.

We walked down the beach and admired the sunset. Every evening one unconsciously expected the sun to go down and the sky to turn flaming red. But the sun never quite made it, and the suspenseful moment was prolonged all night long. There was no dust to color the sky and the low sun shone through air as thin and clear as outer space. Tonight the mountains across Eclipse Sound, forty or fifty miles away on Baffin Island, were exceptionally high and sharp-etched; one could almost step over to them. Tiny clouds floated high in the sky, the wispy cirrus clouds which were made of ice crystals. Our iceberg was sharply white against the pale-pink ice. Although it retained its outlines it was growing noticeably smaller. I wished that it would one day go over with a tremendous crash, or drift majestically down the sound out to sea. But like everything else in the north it was patient and undramatic, and bided its time.

X I V
The Gander Moults

W**e** could find no more snow geese. There were no signs of new nests and even the high-flying feeding expeditions had ceased. They were nesting inland, Idlouk told us, but even he couldn't find any. By the second week of July many of the young geese have hatched and the adults are beginning to moult. Young and old gather in family flocks, all earthbound. The young ones cannot yet fly and the adults, like other geese and ducks, moult all their primary flight feathers at once, so they cannot fly either. (Most birds take many weeks, or even months, to change their feathers and can fly during the entire period, though they look unkempt and don't feel very well.) The goose families retire to remote, unpopulated places, usually near rivers, so they can escape an occasional wandering fox by swimming. In its lonely inland retreat the bird has almost no enemy and can be safely earthbound for the short period of its moult.

Itsawik ("the gander moults") is the Eskimo name for the month of July and this, traditionally, was the time the natives had fresh goose to eat (but no longer, as the Canadian game laws allow Eskimos a daily bag of fifteen geese from September 1 to October 15 — when most of the geese have already left their arctic breeding grounds). Our guide told us that about twenty miles down the coast, in a place of deep and wild ravines above the banks of a big river, Eskimos had sometimes found snow geese nesting in quantity. Large, white and vulnerable as wing-clipped farmyard fowl, the greater snow goose seemed a pathetically easy prey.

Josselyn, Axel and I therefore set out lightheartedly over the ice on a wild-goose expedition, with Idlouk and his komatik. The sea ice changed daily and every time we went on a komatik the scenery was entirely different. The day we set out for Ooyarashukjooeet, Place of the Big Boulders (spoken by Idlouk this word was just a grunt and a sigh), Eclipse Sound was a wasteland. The winds and tides and soft spring fogs had created a scene from Limbo. Black cracks twisted over green ice; crazy-shaped purple lakes yawned before us, their thin brown banks dangerously undercut; slow whirlpools turned evilly in greatly enlarged seal holes; ice wreckage rose in tormented shapes from the endless flatness. In the east, where the narrow rockbound inlet met the ocean, stood two gigantic, gleaming ice towers, tall, slender and slightly lifted off the surface of the ice — entrance gates to a country of death. We drove along the edge of a wide lead, watching for seals. Slabs of ice floated in the dark water, some turned on their sides with their jagged edges in the air. They looked like pieces of a jigsaw puzzle and one had a faint impulse to fit them into the sides of the crack where they belonged.

Over the purple water arctic terns hunted, swiftly graceful. In the fog, coming home from Pond Inlet, the terns had been misty bird spirits. Today, in the clear sunlight, they were bright and sharply defined, with red feet, crimson bills, black caps, clear-gray backs and snow-white breasts. Josselyn had his gun out, but he sensed that Idlouk wanted to shoot one. A strong current of understanding ran between these two men, who seldom tried to speak to each other. Idlouk jumped off the komatik, stopped the dogs and aimed at the terns as they wheeled and dived. With the first shot one fell dead into the open water. Immediately a second tern darted down and circled close around the murdered bird, calling its hoarse sad cry. Its mate, I thought sentimentally. But in a moment five or six more were there, wheeling and screaming. Maybe it was a polygamous tern, I thought, less sentimentally. Josselyn said that terns always act that way when one of them is killed. One does not know why. Perhaps they are trying to help. We had seen crows try to aid a wounded companion. But crows are both more social and more brainy than terns. Maybe the terns were simply looking for a free meal.

Idlouk shot another tern; this one was only wounded, and fluttered frantically in the water until Idlouk fished it out with his long whip. He picked up the quivering bird, pinched the area around its heart with his thumb and forefinger and killed it by stopping the flow of blood. Josselyn was astonished.

"That's the ornithologist's way of killing wounded birds," he said. "It prevents bleeding and keeps the skin from being spoiled or the bones broken." He asked Idlouk where he had learned it. The hunter told us that he had seen his father do it. The purpose was much the same as the ornithologist's — the meat should not be bruised or torn and the skin must be whole and free of blood, so it can be used to line clothing.

Idlouk took one seal in the lead, a big male. When he cut it open to detach the gall bladder an almost unbearably putrid odor gushed into the clean, cold air. "*Tiggak*" (stinker), said Idlouk, wrinkling his nose and grinning. This peculiarly

The spring ice was unreliable near the open ocean, and moved irregularly in and out of the little harbors, under the influence of wind, tide, fog and rain.

seal was shot at the floe edge, and the sound of the big thirty-thirty rifle 1oed from mountain to mountain far down the wild coast of Baffin Island.

The dogs, harnessed in a rough fan shape, trotted easily across the desert of ice, their long sealskin traces hardly taut.

The dogs' pads were cruelly cut by splintered ice, and Idlouk deftly fashio little shoes of sealskin as we traveled. He sliced thin strips of leather to lace th up the ankles, and cut holes for the claws. The dogs hated them.

unpleasant smell is typical of elderly male ringed seals. Before *Phoca hispida* got its respectable name it was dubbed *Phoca foetida* by early classifiers. Dogs can eat the noisome meat of the *tiggak*, but humans cannot get it past their noses.

Idlouk tied the fetid creature on the back of the sled, put his gun away, cried, *"Hut-hut-hut!"* (hurry up) to his dogs, and we sped over the crackling ice. Sitting on a warm caribou skin and facing backwards to keep my face from the cutting wind, I stared directly at the bloodstained, evil-smelling, fat seal, the long slit loosely laced together with slimy gut. I felt no faintest sense of disgust. Was this the same city-bred girl who shuddered when she stepped on a caterpillar and could not squash a fly with her bare hands?

We had lunch on the naked blue ice, in a bitter wind. Far down the sound, on the distant Baffin Island shore line, there was an illusory city — snow patches on bare low hills, with a mirage of ice towers above them, looked like Manhattan from the New Jersey shore on a misty summer day. Heat waves shimmered over the frozen sea.

We spotted a snowy owl on a hillside about a mile away. This was the first time any of us had seen this greatest and most spectacular of tundra bird predators on Bylot Island. We turned inshore, hoping to find a nest, but by the time we had landed the owl had gone. We walked inland over a high and desolate ridge eroded into countless gullies and canyons, looking for it. The hilltops had too many stones on them, all owl-shaped. We didn't miss one with our hopeful binoculars.

After four hours we found it — in the same place we had first seen it. A huge bird standing two feet high, its white feathers flecked with soft brown, it was perfectly a creature of the tundra. It stared at us blankly, flat-faced, as we approached. When we were a hundred yards away the bird lifted itself into the air with one quiet stroke of its wings and flew softly and silently, like a piece of fog, to the opposite hillside. It looked much more suitable there, on the wide brown tundra, than it did atop a telephone pole in Long Island.

We hunted a long time for its nest. On all the neighboring hills the bird had perches, marked by pellets and small, soft feathers, but there was no nest. We picked up some pellets, the old ones light gray and crumbling, the new ones brown and soft. These were for Rick's formidable pellet collection. He planned to return home with about a thousand owl pellets, to analyze what the snowy owl lived on — and consequently what lived on Bylot Island. I should have liked to see his wife's face when she opened that trunk, full of dead mice.

Back on the sled again we moved slowly, close to the coast, looking for the landing place. Along the beach, parallel with us, moved a dirty, starved-looking pack of dogs.

"Iglookishak dogs," said Idlouk disgustedly. The dogs, whose owners were too slipshod to stake them down, had wandered at least twenty miles from their home. They had been out on a spree, but now they were ready for supper. Anxiously they sniffed the air in our direction — delicious, fat, smelly seal.

Our dogs, seeing the strays, suddenly turned and galloped furiously inshore. We bounced over the lumpy frozen surf and piled in a heap on a rocky beach. Idlouk for once was angry. He whipped his dogs, shouted at them and forced them to pull the sled a few yards along the dry beach as punishment, before heading out to sea again. We traveled another half mile.

Then "*Woy-woy*," said Idlouk to his dogs in a hoarse, long-drawn-out tone with a caressing upward inflection at the end, like a blues singer. Decorously the chastened dogs turned inshore and trotted, neat and dignified, onto a narrow sandy beach. We had landed at Ooyarashukjooeet.

Above a little shelf of land we found a grassy meadow dotted with tiny flowers, white, yellow, purple, pink. Beyond it was a long tidal mud flat. A deep river ran through the mud and on its shores were many terns and ducks.

Eskimos had camped here before; we found a few tent rings and some decaying pieces of lumber, probably from an old boat. No doubt the camp was a leftover from the days when caribou still grazed on Bylot Island. But winter trap lines were laid here too, the hunters coming from as much as a hundred miles away on their komatiks. Idlouk named the Eskimo camp that had the trapping "concession" on Ooyarashukjooeet. Although there were no expressed rules, they were careful not to encroach on one another's trapping territories. An Eskimo would never touch the trap lines of another man, even in the dead dark of winter, far from home where no one could possibly find out. Honor and respect for personal rights were part of their lives.

While we ate supper the dogs wandered restlessly. Idlouk had succeeded in driving the strays a good distance away, but our dogs were still uneasy. Bakshu was as usual in trouble. He had a bark, a small *woof* which was not very convincing. Approaching a tired old campaigner with an engaging air of playfulness, he uttered his foolish little bark, batted the old dog in the face with one big paw, like a giant kitten, and was favored with bared yellow teeth and a low snarl. Bakshu backed away. But he did not give up. He tried it again and this time got a vicious snap. In an instant the puppy was on his back, whimpering, all four paws in the air. If there was anything that could be done wrong, Bakshu did it. He was always in bad with somebody.

Anyone who has ever gone camping knows that it consists almost entirely of hard work and discomfort. A benevolent dispensation of memory makes one recall only its joys, however fleeting and few. From the time we had landed until three hours later, when we tucked ourselves tightly into our three small tents, with polar-bear skins to keep us warm, we had not ceased the small but arduous chores of outdoor living. Then the dogs took over. Although Idlouk had hobbled them, one foreleg through the harness, so they could not wander far, they paced noisily over the campgrounds for several hours, growling, sniffing and snarling at one another over empty beef-stew tins and chocolate wrappers. Finally they gave up and we all went to sleep. Around five in the morning the mosquitoes started. The sun was shining brilliantly on our tiny tent, turning it into an oven. Somehow we slept again and awoke at eight-thirty, dripping wet, covered with mosquito bites and feeling dirty.

But after a few minutes in the bright, cool morning air all uncomfortable feelings faded. Breakfast was lovely in the sun, with the meadow flowers pale under its glare and the sea ice gleaming blue-white. All over the sea were large mushroom-shaped figures hanging a few feet above the surface and reflected upside down in the ice. An intensely real mirage of snow cliffs hung high above a wide, shining ice field on the Baffin Island shore across the sound. Like a seal in its *agloo*, Idlouk said, the land was coming up to breathe. *Puikatook* ("coming up for air") is the Eskimo name for mirage.

Josselyn had shot a ruddy turnstone, a heavy-set black, orange and white shore bird which had never been reported on or near Bylot Island. While he skinned it Axel and I walked over the broad river delta to watch the birds feeding on the mud. Here frost had created another of its faultless configurations. The pale-brown flat had a softly geometric pattern of frost forms — low, rounded hummocks of smooth mud with cores of solid ice. The rhythm of freeze and thaw had created these billowing structures. As the surface mud froze it expanded and pressed against the permafrost beneath. Unable to stand the strain the permafrost broke through, bubbling upward like a spring, at regular intervals of space. The mud bubbles looked as soft as sofa cushions, but the ice under the mud was old as creation, black and iron hard. On top of one hummock was a rotten-looking mushroom of gray ice about ten feet across. It barely touched the slippery mud and looked as if it were balanced on a pin. I tried kicking it over and nearly broke my toe. It seemed to be attached for all eternity to the ice core inside the hill.

Later all four of us started over the soft, rubbery tundra to hunt for geese. Since the birds were known to stay near water during their moult we followed the twisting course of the big river by whose delta we had camped. We asked Idlouk what the river's name was. "Gook," he said. The River Gook ran through a canyon so deep that we often lost sight of it. From high pinnacles we looked far down on fortresslike formations of eroded sandstone and cliff banks carved into caves and towers by the relentless water. They looked like the walled towns of the Pyrenees. Streams of mud slowly oozed their way down the canyon sides, carrying the hills into the Gook. (We found out later that *gook* means "river.")

As we climbed higher toward the inland mountains the land became desertlike. Sea shells and bones of the Greenland whale, whitened and ancient, were strewn on the bare hills, far above sea level. There had been beaches there — we could see the parallel ridge marks of prehistoric water lines. The land had been submerged by the slow-moving glacier and had bounced up (during many centuries) after the heavy ice had passed by. We asked Idlouk where the bones had come from.

"The Bible," he said promptly. "Genesis seven." (The Flood.) The Eskimos have a flood legend which predates their acquaintance with the Bible. Perhaps it came with them from Inner Asia, the land of all our ancestors.

Scattered over the arid land were small uneven rings of stones. We guessed that these were caused by frost action, but asked Idlouk. He frowned at them, the frown that meant this was going to be difficult for him to explain in his combination language. Then his face cleared. Little people, he said with his hands. Littler than children. People who ate only rabbits. Down at Canada Point, the western corner of Bylot Island, there was a whole camp of little tent rings with rabbit bones in them. But there were no little people any more. Did he really believe this? Perhaps he said it only to entertain us. Sometimes Idlouk was inscrutable.

But Captain Luke Foxe, looking for a northwest passage in 1635, reported that he came across an island in the Canadian Arctic — never since found by anyone else — covered with the graves of little people. The skeletons, surrounded by bows and arrows and ivory lances, were none of them over four feet high. . . . Maybe Idlouk was right.

Still, with all his wide and accurate knowledge of the ways

of the arctic and the creatures which lived in it, our hunter could pass in an instant from fact to fantasy. Truth meant little to him, and it would never occur to him (or to any other Eskimo) to say, "I don't know." Whether his statement was based on careful observation or a tale told by a grandmother or a story in the Bible, it was given with equal definiteness. Magic and legend had been part of his childhood, in the days when every cloud, insect, flower and animal had a spirit.

We would never understand Idlouk. He was of a people cut off from us by a barrier of many thousand years of progressive civilization, the counterpart of our Asian ancestors who drifted east and west out of an unknown, faintly remembered Garden of Eden before there was any God or any nationality. Crouched low on the ground over the pebble rings, his brown face surrounded by a rim of brown dog fur under the tundra-colored peaked hood, Idlouk looked like man as he must have looked when Prometheus first created him out of mud and water.

The tundra was as mysterious as he. Deep ravines were a tumble of rocks, a shelf of dirty ice and a slow trickle of watery gray mud. On flat bogs new grass was a mist of green. Black mud and the gleam of water showing through sparse young grass blades made the marshes look like rice paddies — with patches of dark, torn ice in them. On high, eroded plateaus, dry as the Arizona desert and swept by a powerful wind, poppies bloomed brave and beautiful among the whitened pebbles as if they did not know that nothing could grow there. Once we descended a steep hill and suddenly saw a lush green slope covered with buttercups. A brook murmured at the bottom of the pretty gully and it could have been New England in June. I drank from the sparkling water and got a mouthful of glacial silt. And on the other side of the flowery ravine was a gray, rotting snowbank.

How could one compare this land with any other? Always, in the midst of comparison, we were brought back to its essential primeval northernness. The fresh strong wind, the cold white sunlight, the tossed clouds, the soaring songbirds and the wonderful wild emptiness of the tundra gave us an intoxicating sense of freedom — not personal freedom, but nature's freedom from the domination of humans. No man, it seemed, had ever stepped here before.

Then we sat down to rest by a big rock — there, five feet away, was an ancient tobacco tin!

We had walked for six hours when we saw our first goose, far down the canyon on the shore of the river. It sat quietly, not looking, while Idlouk trotted down the steep hillside after it. When he got near, the goose nonchalantly slid into the river and swam to the other side. Idlouk went after it, plunging up to his thighs in the rushing muddy water. We stayed on our side while the hunter chased the goose up and down the ravines for half an hour. Idlouk was running, but the goose stayed out of his way, waddling competently before him over the most difficult terrain it could find. Finally Idlouk caught up with it. He could have picked it up with his hands, but he drove it into the river again and it swam over to our side. Good Idlouk! Tactful and understanding, he knew that Josselyn wanted to take this goose. The bird climbed over the stony shore before Josselyn, and finally crouched under a gray-brown snowbank, exhausted and unable to run any farther. There Josselyn shot it.

It was a moulting goose, the creature we had thought would be pathetically accessible. But we had to come all the way to the arctic, make a seven-hour dog sled trip and trot inland over the wild tundra for six hours in order to find only one!

Like most of the arctic creatures we had seen, the greater snow goose could clearly take care of itself.

We examined the bird. Some of the new black wing primaries were already poking through their opaque hornlike quills, and the tight neat tips looked like paintbrushes. The wings were eleven inches shorter than they would be when all the new feathers had grown, and flight was obviously impossible. The bird was extremely thin and had a haggard, bedraggled appearance. Its face and neck were rusty, but when all the new feathers had come in these parts would be temporarily snow white.

Idlouk was proud of the goose, but apologetic that he had not found us more. He had observed that geese were plentiful in one place for two years, then scarce for the next two. This, we knew, was *not* due to population changes. There are about fifty-four thousand greater snow geese in the world — all of them in North America, most of them wintering on or near Chesapeake Bay — and the number remains stable. For some unknown reason they apparently rotate their nesting sites. A biologist should follow Idlouk around the tundra and the sea ice for a year, and dig into the ecological causes behind his unfailingly accurate observations. . . . One might even find a reason for the little tent rings with rabbit bones in them.

Maybe, the hunter added, there were many geese a few miles further west. How much further west, we asked.

"One sleep away," said Idlouk with a ghost of a smile. We laughed. What was "one sleep away" to an Eskimo — fifteen hours, thirty hours, forty-eight hours? We told him that we thought we had better go home. Our wild-goose chase had ended in the capture of a wild goose and we were quite happy.

Walking back over the highlands, we were tired. But little, frail Idlouk strode sturdily ahead of us, almost in a dogtrot. He stopped only to wait for us to catch up or to show us something. He never missed anything, on the ground, in the air or five miles away, while his tiny feet tirelessly, patiently devoured the miles.

He gave us a new insight into the Eskimos' easy disregard of time. At Button Point they had been lazy and gay, as if on holiday, and it did not appear that they worked very hard for a living. But hunting is the native's entire reason for being — it is not only his livelihood but his passion. And hunting the few and wary creatures of the arctic — goose, seal, fox, bear — requires strenuous effort. The hunter must be ceaselessly alert, observant and patient. He must stand for hours over a seal hole in temperatures of fifty or sixty degrees below zero, or trot miles over the boggy tundra, or stalk on the sea ice with infinite care, or wade through deep snow in the winter darkness to tend his trap lines. He hunts in high wind, bitter cold, hot sun. Time means nothing to him and it matters not when he sleeps or eats.

Between the long stretches of boring, patient, tense, difficult hunting he must relax completely in order to gain new energy for the struggle for existence. He has learned to sleep anywhere, at any time. He can eat five pounds of seal meat at one sitting. He can talk with his friends and consume endless pots of tea while the sun wheels twice around the rim of the mountains. He is full of irresponsible gaiety, he plays jokes on his family, makes cats' cradles or sits doing nothing and saying nothing — without ever feeling that he is wasting time. Hours are nonexistent; the day is many months long and so is the night, and when necessary he will hunt again.

These remarkable little people, sometimes irresponsible and lazy, sometimes as wise, wary and quick as wild animals, have achieved an easy balance with their hostile surroundings which no white man, unless he is born to it, can even begin to emulate.

We had planned (why didn't we give up that word?) to go back to our home camp that night. But in the middle of after-supper tea rain started pelting down heavily. Within a few minutes it seemed that we were getting the entire eleven annual inches of rainfall. We retired hurriedly with our tea-cups into our separate, too-cozy tents. When the rain let up, Idlouk said, we would start home.

Before we lay down to rest after the long day we looked over at Josselyn's tent. It was heaving and shaking and looked awfully wet. Josselyn had seemed overtired after our nine-hour trot on the tundra, and we were worried.

"Are you all right?" we called.

"I'm fine — in here with my snow goose and my polar bear." This was the voice of our own civilization, sophisticated, ironic — yet absorbed by the primeval, legend-ridden land in which it surprisingly found itself. We no longer worried about Josselyn.

We dozed, and after an hour it stopped raining. Axel went to see if Idlouk was ready to go. He found our hunter buried in his sleeping bag, sound asleep.

Breakfast next morning was a cold, wet, windy, dirty meal. But even in a dank fog the tundra and the sea ice were full of enchantments. The thick sky glowed pale yellow and the wet meadow flowers had deepened their colors as if a painter had touched them in the night.

The fog lifted and we saw eight seals lying out on the ice. We struck camp in a hurry and set out over the ice on the komatik, Idlouk ready with his gun and shield. For several hours we hunted. That is, Idlouk hunted, while we tried hopelessly to keep the dogs from following him. There was no rapport between us and the dogs. The sea ice was full of seals that day, but with our helpless acquiescence the dogs succeeded in driving all of them to shelter.

Before he went after the first seal the hunter stopped the dogs, waved his whip over their heads and spoke sternly to them. Then he stalked carefully, upwind. I played Mrs. Simon Legree, slinging that snaky whip around and feeling powerful. The dogs paid no attention to me. They sat alert, not taking their eyes off their master. Every now and then one of them started forward and the others were on their feet in an instant. We ran from dog to dog, cajoling, threatening, waving the whip, pushing them down bodily, even kicking them a little. We knew all the right words, but they had lost their magic. So we turned the sled at right angles to the main trace and worked the knotty mass of traces under its runners, hoping they would act as a brake.

Then Idlouk's gun went off. The dogs started at a gallop, knocking down Axel, who was in the midst of them, and upsetting the braked sled. We jumped for it and hung on breathlessly as the sled bumped sideways over the ice and the dogs' feet sent blinding snow spray into our eyes. Axel had the whip in his hand, but it was so heavy with moisture that he couldn't even get its tip off the ground.

Idlouk was not particularly happy when his dogs leaped on him. He spoke very strongly to them, gave us a hypocritical smile and went off after another seal. When he was almost ready to shoot the crazy gallop began again.

"What do we do?" asked Axel as the dogs nearly dumped us in the seal hole. "Put a stake through the ice?"

"Put a stake through the lead dog," I said.

On we went over the sea ice, leaderless and helpless, while seal after seal dived into its hole before us. We felt like the Flying Dutchman, careening pointlessly and forever over the endless blue sea.

Finally there were no more seals. With relief we stopped for lunch. I taught Idlouk how to play hopscotch and he began to feel better. With just a trace of revengeful satisfaction he made me jump over the high-piled sled with both feet together, and leap through the whip as he swung it in a loop.

Near home we had our first taste of traveling over the sea ice when it was breaking up. The Aktineq River had undermined the ice cover for a mile or more along the shore, and the sea looked like a gigantic cobweb. We threaded a maze between deep black cracks. One runner slid into a crack and we tugged frenziedly to keep the heavy sled from spilling sideways. Coming to an undercut lead, we bridged it with the sled, and the dogs walked across, tails down, embarrassed. Onshore a dog howled and our friends came out of their tents to look at us and wonder what we were doing.

We came to a big lead thirty feet wide, running parallel

with the land and apparently impassable. Helplessly we watched the camp recede into the distance as we traveled along its shelving edge. Our friends went back into their tents — we were somebody else, they had decided, going somewhere else.

Ahead of us the big lead divided into smaller streams winding tortuously in and out of an ugly, high-piled mass of ice debris. The dogs regarded this crossing place with disfavor and looked unhappily back at their master. He flicked the snow with his whip and they leaped across open water and scrambled up steep hillocks, protesting all the way, while we pushed and pulled, trying to keep the sled from falling into the horrid little brown rivers.

The last hill was nearly vertical. The dogs reached the top and leaped all together in a tangled mass across six feet of open water. We pushed the sled up the hill after them; it teetered on the top for a moment, then hurtled down the other side. We jumped for it — and missed. The dogs ran happily toward home, while all four of us were scattered sprawling on the ice. Idlouk had no sooner hit the ground than he was on his feet running after the dogs. But we were left on the wrong side of the lead, clinging to the icy side of the steep little hill. I saw a little ice island in the middle of the lead and stepped gently upon it. I turned to speak to Axel and he shouted, "Watch out, your ferryboat is sinking!" I looked down. My little island was no longer an island and I was up to my knees in the water. I jumped quickly, landing on my face in slush, while the ice pan popped up impertinently behind me. The others were more wary.

I don't make a very good Eskimo, I thought ruefully, as I

ran to catch up with the sled, stumbling on the rough ice, my boots full of cold water. The whole scene was excruciatingly funny to Idlouk. He laughed all the rest of the wav home. So did we.

X V
Village on the Aktineq

WE arrived home almost at the same time as Ben and Ned. The two mountaineers had been on a week's expedition into the untouched mountains of Bylot's interior. We had watched them go, each carrying a towering pack of about seventy-five pounds, with the accouterments of mountaineering — snowshoes, crampons, ice axes, ropes, willow stakes — hanging all over it like an advertisement for a sports store. In the packs were weather-reading instruments and altimeters, binoculars and cameras, stoves, tents, sleeping bags, ponchos and food for two weeks. Their first objective was Mt. Thule, a little over six thousand feet, heretofore thought to be the highest mountain on the island. Thule was twenty miles inland across a wilderness of crevassed glaciers and crumbling cliffs. We surveyed the gigantic debris with a doubtful eye and wondered what their route would be.

"You take the first left turn," said Ben offhandedly, "then the second glacier on the right." Maps and compasses were of no use in those unknown northern mountains and the climbers would have to rely on the sun, occasional glimpses of the sea and landmark peaks to find their way. Off they went, lighthearted, ambitious and in very poor condition from the decadent days at Pond Inlet. We didn't expect them to get much further than the talus of the Sermilik Glacier, their starting point.

They had got up the Sermilik, climbed two mountains, descended the Aktineq and now, home again, were red-faced, strong and healthy. But they had had enough of Bylot Island's mountains. They had traversed rotten glaciers seamed with hidden crevasses, carefully worked their way up steep slopes of sliding, soft, broken rock, waded through waist-deep snow on the high flanks of the mountains. The weather had been unfailingly fine; the peak of Thule had been windless and burning hot in the clear sun. In fact they had suffered more from heat and sunburn than frost and wind. During the days, usually, they had slept — twelve unbroken hours — and during the nights, when the sun was low and the snow safer, they had done their arduous, boring climbing. The mountains and glaciers required no mountaineering skill, only stamina. Any extensive exploration of the interior of the island would have to be done in early spring when the snow was still hard and one could travel with dogs.

The only fact they had discovered of any interest to geographers was that Thule was not the highest peak. They had climbed another nameless one about three hundred feet higher. They had also confirmed the fact that the interior of Bylot Island did not, as shown on the maps, consist of a large icecap, but an unbroken wilderness of jagged rock peaks stretched over the entire island.

For the first time since we had come to Bylot our whole party was together for more than one day. The kitchen tent was always crowded, and the constant coming and going among the tents, the games and laughter of the Eskimo children, the howling of the dogs, the visiting and the gossip made us feel like a real village. The day after the two parties got back we had two further additions to our population. The same wretched, grinning old man from Iglookishak who had given Axel the wooden goggles came to bring us beautiful miniature snowy owls he had carved out of walrus ivory. And an Eskimo traveling from Pond Inlet to his home north of Eclipse Sound made a detour to gossip with Idlouk and hand us a sheaf of radio letters full of news from the strange, half-forgotten world way down there. We loved receiving radio messages by komatik — it was a charming contrast. Axel and I got a one-word greeting from friends in Copenhagen, a telegram from my cousin in New York saying, "Re 10,000 shares U. S. Steel forget if you said buy or sell important" (that one worried every amateur operator from New York to Pond Inlet), and a letter from Pete informing us that he had heard from Bob at Arctic Bay that Brit at Halifax had had a letter from my mother in New Jersey saying that the children were fine, had poison ivy and had gone horseback riding.

A few days later Idlouk pointed out a komatik, a toy sled at least a mile out on the ice. He concentrated on it, squinting and frowning. Then his face cleared.

"Aglaktee," he said (that is Pete's Eskimo name, and it means "the one who writes"), "with three people, two of them women." Natives never call themselves Eskimos, as it is a derogatory term. They are *innuit*, "the people," *inuk*, "a man," and *angna* "a woman."

Even with binoculars we couldn't check Idlouk's accuracy. It is clear why all the natives have been made rangers by the

Canadian Government. Their observational ability is extraordinary, sharpened to a fine point in this wide, bare country where so little moves, and so far away. The government issues rifles and a hundred rounds of ammunition a year to every hunter, with orders to spot and report any planes or unknown persons. It would be impossible for a stranger, native or white, to hide himself for more than a few days. Isolated as the Eskimo camps are, and sparse as is the population, these alert hunters miss nothing over the hundreds of miles of their hunting territories. They recognize the traveling native from afar by the size and shape of his team, his actions on the sled. And if they don't know the strange white man they will soon. News travels fast; the north is a land of gossip and the arctic grapevine is a remarkably efficient operation.

Pete came like visiting royalty, surrounded by his retinue, Makpa, Marta and the HBC native helper, Merkoshak. As a gift he brought fresh fish — arctic char, a small salmon which is caught in gill nets at the river mouths as it comes down from mountain lakes to the sea after the river ice breaks up in early July. This fish spends little time in the sea, returning upstream again in September before the rivers freeze. It spawns in the cold, high lakes in October and winters quiet and deep in the water beneath the heavy ice. We had no char on our island, because Bylot's lakes were only small shallow puddles which, if they did not dry up entirely in summer, would freeze solid in the wintertime.

Pete skinned and filleted the fish expertly, and we fried and ate them with canned butter, lemon extract and mustard. They were delicate and tender, and so fresh that they had no fishy taste.

Pete's visit, which had no purpose save that of sociability, was a twenty-four-hour fete. At breakfast the next day sixteen people crowded happily into the cook tent and three of us worked constantly at the stoves, turning out a continuous stream of pancakes, bacon and seal liver. Then, instead of scattering over the tundra on our daily collecting and observing expeditions, we all stayed in camp for conversation and games. Pond Inlet had taken over.

Makpa and Marta started jump-roping. Rick joined them, entangled his feet in the rope and fell on his face. "*Kooka!*" they shouted joyously, laughing at him. They called Leah into the game. But she was fearfully embarrassed when she missed her step, and quickly sidled away. What was the matter with Leah? When she was teaching Mary to plait a wool belt; when she practiced scales on the fife; when she led us to a bird's nest she had discovered — then she was sweet, gay, responsive and pretty. But some desperate inner fear, probably a residue of her frightening year Outside, turned her into a tongue-tied little waif when she found herself in a group. Today she looked poor and shabby and timid between the two beautifully dressed, self-assured Pond Inlet girls in their embroidered white parkas and silverjar boots. Leah wore the white women's clothing she preferred — long black wool stockings, down-at-heels saddle shoes, a sleazy, shapeless print dress and a cerise wool jacket that didn't fit.

How easy it was to ruin an Eskimo. As soon as the outside world came too close they changed. Makpa, it seemed, had been spoiled by coddling, Leah by coldness.

While the girls played with the rope Idlouk exhibited his slingshot, a sealskin leather thong widened slightly in the middle. He put a stone in the wider part, held the two ends in his hand, swung it twice in a wide circle and let go. Several seconds later there was a small splash in the lagoon far down the beach. He did it again and hit an old-squaw. The duck was really surprised — Idlouk pretended to be.

Kidla approached us with a pair of sealskin kamiks (boots) she had made for Bill. While her husband was bending over Bill's foot, seriously absorbed in explaining the merits of the heavy black waterproof soles, Kidla ungently clipped a snap clothespin on his ear. Idlouk jumped and gave a mild Eskimo shriek — then doubled himself laughing, as did his wife. That was the beginning of another of those running Eskimo jokes: "Pin the Clothespin." You had to do it when the victim wasn't looking, otherwise it didn't count. It was also necessary to be there when it was discovered so that you could laugh too. The clothespin game went on continuously all the remaining days of our stay on Bylot. Sometimes Idlouk left the cook tent with seven or eight clothespins fastened on various parts of his clothing, followed closely by a group of giggling scientists waiting for him to realize there was something wrong. It got so that if we wanted clothespins to hang out our laundry we had to go over to the Eskimo tent and pick them off Idlouk's parka. The hunter was as indefatigable an addict of this game as we.

It took Pete about three hours to say good-by. Finally he went, but he got only as far as Idlouk's tent. We followed him there, and another hour passed, serene, lazy and pointless. By imperceptible degrees Pete got his entourage on the komatik — and suddenly they were off at a gallop without a backward look. But they didn't get very far. At suppertime they were still a quarter of a mile offshore hunting seal along the big lead. We heard occasional shots until late at night.

We had wasted a whole day, but felt no remorse. Oh, the lovely, untroubled timelessness, sometimes irritating, sometimes boring, but always peaceful!

For supper we had soup made of the heads, tails, skins and bones of Pete's fish, cooked with potatoes, carrots, onions and dried herbs. Ben poured a long stream of Worcestershire sauce into it, which didn't hurt it any.

"The *soupe du jour*," he said, shaking pepper freely into the odorous pot, "is what you didn't eat *hier*."

Ben, a cook with a free imagination, had by choice taken over most of the camp cooking. Into the soups went larks, snow buntings, chile sauce, bacon rind, goose bones, vegetable water. Into the uninteresting dehydrated vegetables and tasteless canned meats went brown sugar, vinegar, mustard, chile, curry powder and herbs. Usually it was delicious, once in a while it was awful — always it was a surprise.

Late that evening I washed my hair outdoors in a brisk east wind and a temperature of thirty-eight degrees. The sea ice glowed in the pale sunlight and the cold night was full of peace. No dogs howled; even the Eskimo children were quiet in their tent. Half our party had gone off with Idlouk on the komatik for another wild-goose chase to Ooyarashukjooeet. Our village had suddenly dwindled to nothing, and the lonely tundra was all mine.

The next day Axel and I went with Josselyn on a bird-collecting trip. Josselyn had his shotgun and we were to be his beaters. As we walked we watched the thin, almost invisible life of the cold tundra, our Temperate Zone eyes by now accustomed. Looking across these dun-colored, treeless, seemingly empty moors, we were never disappointed. The tundra colors were delicate and low-toned, varying shades of brown and gray and rust and yellow, with occasional sharp black and white. The birds and insects showed the same narrow limit of color variation, the same subtle shading. It was a subdued beauty, that you had to look for.

We had looked for it and found it. By now we had made the tundra our home, and the pebbly hills and the grass-filled gullies and the mossy marshes and the rusty puddles were as familiar to us as the streets of our home towns — and just as populous and friendly and beloved.

When we reached the top of the first hill a breath of hot air hit us, a disturbing dry wind that smelled like high-summer drought. It was a Temperate Zone smell that did not belong in the arctic, a reminder of midsummer at home, a warning that we must leave soon. But a tiny wisp of cloud floated across the blazing sun and we were suddenly cold again. The unpredictable variation in temperature gave us a good feeling. The land was free to the sky and wind and sun and clouds, and there was nothing here to enchain either heat or cold.

When we reached the heights above the camp we fanned out to flush birds. I spotted a female snow bunting and called to Josselyn. He got his gun up with what looked like slow deliberation — and had shot her while the echoes of my voice still sounded in the clear air. The bird had a large incubation patch: the entire belly was clear of feathers and the skin was thickened, with lines on it where the feathers had been shed. The purpose of this was to give the eggs and young direct heat from the mother's body. All breeding arctic birds had bare bellies; on the cold windy tundra their babies needed good radiators.

Josselyn ran his finger up the bird's white feathers, rippling them backwards. The base of every feather, invisible from outside, was deep black, soft and downy. This also is a peculiarity of arctic songbirds with white feathers, and is probably a means of retaining heat. White birds that feed and swim in the water — geese, gulls and terns — do not have this black undershirt. Instead their feathers have a glossy, water-repellent texture to keep them warm and dry in the icy water.

Josselyn touched all the moist or bloody spots on the dead bird with corn meal to dry them, stuffed cotton into the beak and throat so that no moisture would come out of the mouth, placed the bird in a transparent plastic cone and dropped it into one of his dozens of enormous pockets. Josselyn was a walking ornithological laboratory. He always carried with him all his instruments for cleaning, curing and making up skins, as well as cartridges, camera film, telephoto lens, filters and lunch. More remarkable, he always knew where everything was.

We saw the male snow bunting near where its mate had been shot. Josselyn would not take this bird. Though it could not incubate eggs the male would feed the young — and by this time there undoubtedly were young. Axel, whose powers of observation were almost equal to Idlouk's, found them. The nest was under a rock, well hidden and safe from all intruders except Axel. Through a long, narrow, rock doorway flush with the ground we could see three downy nestlings. My hand was the only one small enough to go through the tiny tunnel. I reached in and pulled out a little bird with a gray fuzz on top of its head like an old man's hair, and black wing feathers just beginning to sprout from their transparent hornlike cases. I held the shivering baby in my hand while they photographed it. On the ground it pattered uncertainly in circles for a few seconds, then went unerringly back into its tunnel.

On the high, windless, barren plateau above the river we found the jaeger nest again. It had been despoiled. The egg was gone and so were the jaegers, leaving feathers strewn around as a memento of the fight that must have taken place. We surmised that a dog had been there — probably one of the hoboes from Iglookishak. It was sad that the beautiful, bold birds had lost their nest. There are fewer and fewer wild predators, and their place is taken by man and his satellites.

We did the nest round on our way home. Axel had found the first old-squaw nest the day before. It was the kind of nest that you had to trip over in order to find. The mother, completely invisible on the tundra, would not leave her nest to display and lure away an intruder. She crouched silently, not twitching a feather, and since her nest was a down-filled depression exactly her own size her mottled brown back was nearly level with the earth. We pushed her off the nest and found seven large white eggs in a bed of soft dark-gray down plucked by the mother from beneath her breast feathers and practically impermeable to cold. (When the duck leaves the nest of her own free will she covers the eggs with the down so that they are not only warm but invisible.)

There was no sign of a male old-squaw. We knew where he was. He was down on our drinking-water lagoon, contaminating it, cavorting with his friends, talking loudly and eating continuously. Handsome and conspicuous, he would be of no use on a flat tundra nest. He could not even feed his wife — ducks have to feed themselves. The female duck, therefore, has to do all the child-care work alone. She usually makes her nest near a puddle so that she can snatch quick meals without going too far, and as soon as the young are hatched she leads them to the water.

Looking at the seven fat eggs, we wondered again about the mysterious relation of reproduction to food supply. Clutch size is dependent to a large extent on how much the adult can find easily to eat and how much it can find after the young are born, to feed them. Owls, for instance, lay more eggs in abundant lemming years, when the food is there for the taking; sometimes none at all in times of scarcity. But ducks do not feed their young, and their food supply is fairly constant and easily available. How do they know how many eggs to lay? The clutch size of duck broods is nearly always the same, and large, although nowhere near the number the bird is physiologically capable of laying.

Its size may be dependent on the survival rate of the nestlings. Generally birds whose nestlings are systematically devoured, as the ducks' were by foxes, lay more eggs than those which have few enemies. The fulmar lays but one egg a year, well out of harm's way on high arctic cliffs. The arctic tern lays only two eggs, right out on open beaches — but the tern has no enemy except an occasional lemming-hungry jaeger. The duck, with a skillful and hungry enemy stalking it over the tundra, must make provision for the fox's wants as well as the survival of her race.

One of the golden plover nests had begun to hatch and the young were in four stages. One egg was still smooth and pristine. Another had begun to pip, and through the tiny hole we could hear the bird squeaking. A third bird was half in and half out, and looked messy. The last was a full bird, a most beautiful, perfect young creature. Its body was soft gold and black. It had slender, delicate, extremely long feet and tiny, half-formed golden wings. Its large head had a strong black adult beak in place of the gaping, amorphous bills of most nestlings. (These precocial shore birds, like sandpipers, are not fed by their parents but find their own food almost from birth.) Its immense dark eyes were surrounded by pale feathers that would later turn glowing white, like those of its parents. By the next day, probably, the tiny, elegant creature would be down on the beach a quarter of a mile away, competently collecting its own food. And in a month it would be fully fledged and ready to fly south with its young companions. Unaccompanied by adults, it would fly through midwestern Canada and the United States, over land it had never seen before, to hit a random spot in South America. To this same spot it would return year after year, unerringly. The parent birds would take a short cut, flying down the eastern coast of North America to Nova Scotia, then taking off over open ocean on a twenty-four-hundred-mile flight to South America. Golden plovers, not being swimmers, can alight only momentarily on the waves to rest, and they accompish their heroic flight in forty-eight hours!

In a small enclosed hollow near the river we came on a scattered pile of fresh snowy owl wing feathers. There was no sign of a body, only the long white brown-flecked feathers, some of them with serrated edges. This owl, in common with most others, has a convenient arrangement of primary wing feathers. The outer edges, which are exposed to air when it flies, have serrated edges — so that the air will not whistle through them, and the owl can fly soundlessly. The purpose of the silent flight is, not that the victim should be caught unaware, but that the owl may hear the faint rustlings and scratchings of its favorite food, the lemming. Since these owls hunt all through the arctic winter night it is necessary for them to hear as well as see their prey.

We could not guess what animal had surprised this powerful bird. Bylot Island had a secret life, of which we saw occasional aftersigns. Its hunters were there, constantly in action but extraordinarily wary.

We were tired, as we finally turned homeward, from the hours of straining our eyes for invisible little birds, scanning every inch of low-toned tundra, watching for a slight variation in the landscape that might mean a nest or a crouching bird. As we came down the last hill I lifted my eyes almost for the first time that day. To the east were the great mountains — Castle Gables a wild black tumble of rocks with sheer cliffs falling into the sea, Thule a giant black and white cone behind it. Thule, as I will always remember it, had a feather of cloud on its peak, and a drift of mist softened the ferocious lines of Castle Gables. The Aktineq Glacier, its ice now torn and gray, led almost irresistibly into the beautiful mountain wilderness. Before us lay a long gray pebbled flatland, ending in the yellow-gray angry river. Then came the wrinkled expanse of Eclipse Sound. A ragged-edged lake had opened where the big Aktineq streamed into the sea, and a wide dark seam led out of it, disappearing into the distance toward Pond Inlet.

It was still spring on Bylot Island. Summer would not start officially until the sea ice had broken up. But we were seeing the end of the growing season. Bill had already collected all the plants which could occur on Bylot Island. And now the tundra around us showed signs of the drought that would make the land a desert by late August. The saxifrage, flower of early spring, lay in limp dead clumps, its blossoms withered and pale red, its leaves dry and brown. The thick rich fringes of arctic bell heather, drooping heavily over mud folds on the hills, had lost their spun-sugar look. The poppies, most beautiful of all, died beautifully too, their petals turning deep green and curling inward from the tips. The moss was brown, wiry and very thick — uncomfortable walking.

As we came off the hot dry hills a cold damp breeze came to meet us, the prevailing southeast wind of the coast, that brought the chill of the sea ice with it. Our camp always had a seaside feeling, a cool wetness in the air. The chilly evenings (the cold came on about six o'clock) felt as if they should be dewy. But there was no dew. The days were too cold to evaporate enough moisture to condense on the ground at night.

The weather, to us Temperate Zoners, was strange. The average humidity, Ben found in his daily readings, was eighty per cent. In New York we would have suffered horribly. But here the moisture-laden air was so cold that we did not feel the high humidity. On the rare days when the temperature climbed above forty degrees the humidity fell abruptly. The average absolute temperature during our six weeks' stay was an almost constant thirty-six degrees Fahrenheit in the daytime and thirty-four at night. But the effective temperature fluctuated wildly, depending on sun, wind, reflection, humidity. It got as hot as ninety-one degrees one day; another day it was down to twenty-eight and five-tenths. Daytime was usually much warmer than night even if the sun was hidden by clouds. Rainfall was slight, though we had a great deal of fog and drizzle. And the wind, with a few awful exceptions, was mild.

In the hour before supper Josselyn rapidly made up three birdskins, a pipit, a sanderling and the rare European ringed plover. The pipit, a dainty dun-colored bird, weighed only twenty-three grams (there are twenty-eight and a quarter grams in an ounce). The sanderling, rarely taken in its breeding plumage, is a little shore bird familiar to our beaches in winter. It had never been recorded before in the Bylot Island locality.

While Ben and I watched Josselyn's speeding, unerring fingers with the unswerving fascination of onlookers at a ping-pong game, Axel wandered around the neighborhood with his binoculars, not expecting to find anything, but hopeful.

Suddenly he called, "Josselyn, here is a gull with a dark head!"

Our three heads turned at once. There was a Sabine's gull, resting quietly on a peat ridge about fifty yards away. It was a slim bird, refined and fashionable, with a long white forked tail, slender wings with coal-black tips, a smoky gray head. This rare and beautiful gull came possibly from the Bay of Biscay, and was not known on Bylot Island or the adjacent mainland, though it nested in other parts of the arctic. No one knows its main wintering place, and it breeds so far north that it has seldom been taken in breeding plumage. It seemed to have come to rest in our camp just for Josselyn. He was cutting the infinitesimal wing tendons of the pipit, but with quiet deliberation he set down the denuded bird, picked up his gun and waded out into the green marsh.

I made supper that night. I was practicing Ben's everything-but-the-kitchen-sink method, and we had the remains of the fish soup, enriched by Swiss cheese, cabbage juice, leftover bacon and corned beef, dehydrated pea soup, onion flakes, potatoes and chile sauce. It was a formidable soup. We had fried potato cakes made of dehydrated mashed potatoes, dehydrated eggs and dehydrated milk. We had fried birds — the Sabine's gull, about three and a half inches long, a baby lark, a pipit, a snow bunting and a golden plover, all so small that we could understand why hungry foxes didn't bother with them. We had fried seal liver and candied carrots. For dessert we had chocolate pudding. There wasn't much that even the ingenious Ben could do about desserts except mix them together, and even then they tasted exactly the same. I had made the pudding in the morning and set it out on a snowbank to cool. When I went to fetch it I found that my icebox had become a warm brown puddle, so we had chocolate sauce instead of chocolate pudding. Somehow I managed to use fourteen pots. We were living extravagantly. On our table was a tundra bouquet of avens, poppies, arctic bell heather and moss pink, planted in wet green moss in one of the pastel plastic dinner dishes.

At eight o'clock was the radio schedule, to which we had been hopelessly faithful all through the weeks, as had Pete and Bren on the hill behind Pond Inlet. Axel and I climbed Radio Hill, sat on its windy peak and started our pathetic sending of monotonous phrases off into nothingness.

"Bylot Island to Pond Inlet. Bylot Island to Pond Inlet. Bylot Island to Pond Inlet. Over." No answer — only the sound of the sea, as in a conch shell. Then the same phrase again, over and over, for fifteen minutes. All we did was waste batteries. It was frustrating but not frightening, as we were never without visitors for more than two days. If anything happened to any of us it would be known in New York

City and Boston within a week and all the Eastern Arctic would come to our rescue.

When we came down Ben was ecstatic — as ecstatic as that calm person ever became. "Look at my vegetable garden," he said. "It's coming up!" He had planted radishes, onions and sweet peas ten days before, and little shoots were poking courageously through the dry, crackling, unfriendly soil. From time to time we had watered the garden, but no matter how much water we poured the earth was, within five minutes, as dusty and crumbly as before.

Now, what a homely touch, to see the brave young vegetables in the midst of the vast cold tundra. We predicted that before we left we would eat our own onions, grown on the northern tundra barrens for the first time in the history of mankind.

"When can I thin them?" I asked eagerly.

"Don't ever!" said Ben, horrified. "They keep each other warm."

The little vegetables never came to anything. The sun burned them and the frost bit them. Within a week they were turning yellow and by the time we left they had all died. But not before Ben had eaten an onion — a threadlike brown root.

That night the sun was deeper gold and the sky pinker and hazier than usual. It had suddenly turned cold and there was a smell of fall in the air. We crawled quickly into our sleeping bags, piled them high with all the clothing we had taken off and settled down comfortably to read. The little tent window was covered with transparent plastic film fastened with clothespins (rescued from Idlouk's parka). Through it the sun shone with a diffused golden light. At our heads were sizable pillows constructed of coats and sweaters. On the night table (grocery box) were cigarettes, crackers, dried prunes, a little clock and the carved-ivory owl that we had got from the Iglookishak artist. The picture of our children smiled down from the tent pole. I read Chekhov stories — in all the weeks I had not got through half the volume — and was entirely happy.

The next day was Bastille Day. It felt like November — a raw, gusty wind, dark-gray clouds, a dank fog sitting on the horizon. We had had summer for two days and now, it seemed, it was autumn. I untangled myself from my warm sleeping bag at half past nine (we were keeping Eskimo hours these days and Axel was still asleep), exchanged one set of clothes for another, brushed my hair and ran to the cook tent — all in exactly three and a half minutes. The water in the ten-gallon can had a thin film of ice. Josselyn was already in the cook tent, hunched shivering over the inevitable powdered eggs and dried milk. Mixing eggs was a long, boring task which Josselyn had taken on himself. He was the best egg mixer we had; when he was not there the eggs invariably had lumps in them. They were horrible enough as it was, without lumps — flavorless, with the consistency of pudding. I lit the kerosene heater, which immediately filled the tent with its warm, smoky smell. As I started the bacon and cereal we had a desultory, casual conversation.

"One forgets about the little luxuries of home," said Josselyn with the air of one about to deliver a pompous platitude. "We have running water in our house."

"My, you *are* lucky. But we have glass windows."

"Well," said Josselyn, "that's New York City."

During breakfast it started to rain, and a big wet wind battered the tent. One side leaned dangerously over the stoves and I kept bumping it with my head. Every time I touched it I started a stream of water down the inside. The tent was of thin lightweight material, closely woven so as to be water and wind resistant. But it was built for secluded spots in the woods and valleys of the Temperate Zones and it could not stand the buffeting of the arctic east wind dashing freely across miles of uninterrupted sea ice. A big rip appeared in one corner where the guy rope was tight. Helpless, we called Kidla. She came with her needle and caribou thread and sewed it together with her strong, gloveless little hands, laughing while the freezing wind threw clouds of rain in her face. We loosened all the guy ropes and added more, riveting them to the ground with piles of big stones. At the end the tent had fourteen guy ropes and looked like a huge green sick spider, listing, sagging and shuddering.

We left it as soon as possible, not caring if we never saw it again. The four of us walked down to the pebbly flat river delta to look at terns' nests. The wind blew rain in our faces and low clouds scudded over the broken gray sea ice. On the cold wet beach dainty harebell grew, shining through the mist, the color of an early morning sky. The mountains loomed before us like black shadows, forbidding and mysterious, and gray arctic terns wheeled and darted through the rain, screaming hoarsely. Axel had found the first two nests a few days before. Now the terns pointed out three more to us. They could hardly be called nests. One or two sand-colored eggs lay right out in the open beside a rock or a clump of saxifrage, with no covering of any kind, not even a depression in the sand.

A flock of Baird's sandpipers, young and adults together,

fed busily on the beach oblivious of the gusty wet wind. They were flocking, getting ready to fly south after only five weeks on the tundra. But the terns had only started to nest.

"If those birds are ever going to get back to the Antarctic," I said, "they had better get cracking."

"In more ways than one," added Ben.

The dilatory terns had hard luck. Within ten days we had found twenty terns' nests on the beach; on the eleventh day only eight were left. Twelve had been destroyed by one dog, escaped from its stake, in one night. Bylot Island was no longer a free land for the far-wandering arctic tern. Woe to the wild creature, fearing no enemy, who comes against man and his friends.

I spent the rest of the fierce wet day in the cook tent, trying to type with half-frozen fingers, which I had to warm over the kerosene heater every few minutes. Nua, Pauloosee and Rootay came in the afternoon and stood in a diminutive row beside me, silent and smiling. I showed them how to use the typewriter and each one wrote his name while I held the little fingers. They were pleased, and low giggles bubbled out of them. I gave them chocolate and they retired to a corner, chewing and reading their names out loud to one another. Idlouk's children, it appeared, had learned the English alphabet — probably Leah had taught them. After ten minutes they murmured, "*Kuayanamik*," and departed, zipping the tent flap up and down lustily a few times. Five minutes later Moseesee came in. He wanted to type his name too. I gave up working and accompanied the little boy back to his mother's tent.

It was perfectly dry and much warmer than ours. The

heavy canvas had withstood the rain, in spite of numerous holes, and the moisture-laden earth was hidden beneath the dry floor of pebbles. The spirit of the Eskimo tent was, as usual, sunny. Kidla was cutting a sealskin into kamiks for me while Rootay, bare-bottomed, raced back and forth over the sleeping platform, jumped on her mother's shoulders and stamped on the skin Kidla was working. Kidla smiled patiently and went right on working. We never saw Kidla or Idlouk that they were not busy, except on Sunday. They made nearly everything they used — whips, traces and harnesses for dogs, seal-oil lamps, sealskin and caribou clothing, fish nets, even the wooden implement to make the fish nets. They were always busy at something, yet always amiable and relaxed. When I mentioned to Josselyn one day that I hadn't had time to do any carving on a piece of soapstone Idlouk had given me he said, quietly ironic, "No, I guess you haven't. You have to have nine children to have time for things like that."

Now Kidla measured my foot with her hand and cut the sealskin by eye with her razor-sharp ulu — the Eskimo woman's knife, shaped like a food chopper, which she uses for everything. We had seen Idlouk shoot the seal and skin it, then had watched Kidla expertly scraping the fat off the skin, a delicate operation, as one must not scratch or cut the hide. (Leah couldn't do it right yet, and her mother laughed tolerantly at her mistakes, even though they spoiled a good skin.) Every few minutes Kidla had sharpened the ulu blade on a whetstone, running it quickly and deftly toward the hand that held the stone — why had she never sliced a piece off her hand? When the skin was smooth and clear of flesh she had pegged it out in the sun, fur down, to dry. After drying, it was stiff and hard, and she dulled the blade of her ulu and worked it over the crackling skin to take the first stiffness out. Then she twisted it between her strong hands, inch by inch, until it was as malleable as suede.

Today, when she had cut out the soles of my boots, she chewed them along the seam lines to make them soft enough for the needle to go through. Her thread was sinew from the backbone of a caribou, and her stitches were commendably neat and tiny. She used a steel needle. The HBC had emancipated Eskimo women from the beautiful, clumsy ivory needles.

The soles were of a heavier sealskin, *oogjoo* (bearded seal), and some of the flesh had been left on to keep them water-resistant. The legs of the boots were of silverjar with the fur outside — the dressy boots of the Eskimo women. Kidla cut thin strips from the nearly white belly skin and set them diagonally down the front of the legs, to make an attractive pattern of slim light lines among the silver-gray rings. I had no flannel socks for embroidered cuffs, so she tore up an old shirt of Nua's and made plaid wool cuffs for me.

I love the cuffs. When I look at them now I can see the trio of plaid-shirted little boys marching, arms over one another's shoulders, across the spring tundra.

The soft, sighing sound of Eskimo conversation filled the tent. All the time she was working Kidla talked — to me, to Rootay, to Leah. Her speech was slow and lilting, her voice low, and she gave the impression of utmost graciousness. Her face was serene, but her eyes sparkled, and when she smiled she had a wonderful beauty. Leah translated for us in her shy, whispering voice. We all sipped tea and Rootay chewed contentedly on a pilot biscuit, strawberry jam oozing through her fingers. Before I left Kidla gave me three pairs of silverjar mitts she had made for me and my small children. Those for the children fitted perfectly on Kidla's delicate brown hands. She was greatly amused that children the ages of Moseesee and Pauloosee should have such gigantic hands.

As I rose to go they rose too. We practically curtsied. Gracious, polite and old-fashioned as mid-Victorian ladies, Idlouk's wife and daughter were also most perfectly feminine — just the way women ought to be.

Behind the tent a pregnant bitch, Kingmiachuk, was chained. She was so near her time that Idlouk had left her behind when he went off to Ooyarashukjooeet. I went to see if she had had her puppies yet. She had dug herself a deep hole, but she would not go in it, and she was deeply unhappy. Stretching her chain to the limit, she jumped up and down and howled continuously, and this she had been doing night and day since she had been left behind. We always thought it meant puppies. But all she wanted was to be with her brothers and sisters and uncles, pulling a sled.

There were still no puppies in the hollow, but there was a new note in Kingmiachuk's howl. Instead of being sad and complaining she was wildly excited. She knew what it took the rest of us an hour to discover — Idlouk's komatik was coming back.

The party spent nearly two hours crossing the rotten ice near the shore. All the sea ice was terrible, they said. The trip home had taken eight hours (without hunting). Several of them had fallen in and the komatik had nearly sunk on some of the floating ice pans. Rick had kicked a recalcitrant dog

and broken his toe. He did not know how to kick like an
Eskimo — the dog had not even turned around.

"Have to amputate," said Ben ominously, examining the
swollen toe. "Up to here," he added, pointing to Rick's neck.

That night Kingmiachuk gave birth to eight puppies. It was
a freezing, wet night with a strong wind. The dog cleaned
each puppy continuously and thoroughly, and in spite of the
mud and the rain her brood was spotless. She was touching in
her efforts to keep the tiny wet creatures warm, nudging
them under her and arching her body to give them better
shelter. Idlouk came out when the first one was born. He
patted the mother on the head and murmured something com-
plimentary, then he put a fence of boxes and tin basins around
her hole to keep the wind off — it was unthinkable that an
Eskimo should take his dog and her puppies inside his tent, no
matter what the weather. Five of the puppies were males. Idlouk killed the three females and the children delightedly
seized the carcasses. They played ball with the little wet
bodies for two days.

Idlouk had to get over to Pond Inlet before the ice broke
up. His family was running out of staples and he needed fresh
supplies from the HBC store. (Idlouk could keep his family
in food from the sea and the tundra, but not in the luxury to
which the HBC and the fur trade had accustomed them.) He
had to get his outboard motor; in two or three weeks the ice
would be gone and he would need the boat for hunting and
traveling. In addition he wanted to take some fish. The whole
family craved fresh fish, and the dogs thrived on it. But the
violent wind and the gusty rain and the flying fog kept him

here, and he was clearly worried. Although full of laughter as usual, his eyes kept straying to the mottled, rotting sea ice. "This afternoon . . . tonight . . . tomorrow," he said, as the weather worsened.

Rick and I wanted to go with him. We didn't care how rotten the ice was — we had Idlouk. We would put our lives in his hands with absolute faith. He would not only save us, he would make us laugh as well.

X V I
Whose Land?

WE waited for two days while the wind blew, the rain fell and the sea ice melted and cracked before our eyes. On the third day the sun gleamed yellowly and the high clouds were light and thin. Idlouk loaded his boat on the komatik, hitched the dogs and we set out — Rick and I, Idlouk and his son Panilu.

The ice was breaking up in long straight lines under the prevailing east wind and the pull of the tide. To get to Pond Inlet we had to travel crosswise over these lines, so we rode uphill and downhill on a gigantic washboard, jolting, slipping and splashing. We were more off the sled than on it, which was good, because there was, as usual, a cold wet wind off the ocean. We had finally found the secret of keeping warm on a komatik: do something. It didn't matter what — push the sled, eat, drive the dogs, take pictures. The slightest activity kept the chill off and the spirits high. Panilu sang and Idlouk whistled as we bumped along — no hymn, but a lilting Norwegian sea chantey.

The heavily laden komatik buried its runners in one jagged, gluey ice hummock after another. The dogs stopped each time and turned their heads toward their master. "We'd like to pull," they seemed to say, "but we just can't. What shall we do?" And we all jumped off and jerked the sled back and forth until its runners were free of the sticky ice. As they saw us working the good dogs pulled again. Suddenly the sled broke free and went over the top. We all leaped on quickly, every which way, as it careened down the other side and crashed into the next hill.

Bakshu was not in on any of this. He did not even bother to look back. Each time the runners got caught he sat down instantly. He waited until the other dogs had done the hard work, then got up and trotted along behind them, his line slack. With this system he finally managed to catch his trace under a runner and break it. The young dog shook himself all over and dashed happily ahead. He leaped back and forth in front of his hard-working uncles and cousins, wriggling his whole body in puppylike delight, daring them to come and play with him. His bark was almost a laugh. "Look at me," he seemed to say, "out here having fun. And look at all you lugs in chains." The patient dogs pretended not to see him. But he rushed into the midst of them, got himself entangled in the traces, fell on his back and started howling. Idlouk mended the broken trace with a few deft slits of his seal knife and a clever knot, and put the puppy back in the herd. Bakshu was crestfallen. His master laughed at him and gave him a quick, secret pat on the head. Idlouk did not like us to see his affection for his dogs. Probably he thought it was not manly.

As we approached the Baffin Island shore, where the pull of the tide was greater, the ice grew more rotten. The last quarter mile took five hours and it was mostly over open water strewn with undercut, mushroom-shaped ice pans. The dogs swam from one pan to the next, the komatik was often under water and the boat tied on top of it barely floated. Often a dog would be caught under the ice and nearly drown before

Idlouk could pull him out. The dogs complained with their little perfunctory howls, but they struggled unceasingly. It was not in their mentality to give up.

Only Bakshu — poor miserable Bakshu — did not even pretend to pull any more. He walked behind the others, limping and shivering and feeling sorry for himself. He was dragged into the water, did not try to swim, was pulled out on the other side and lay down hopelessly on the tangle of traces. There he stayed, on his side, his back or whatever position he landed in — sometimes he was going backwards. He no longer even tried to howl. Finally Idlouk unfastened him. The puppy hung on a tiny ice pan, not quite standing but unable to sit because his sodden tail was so far between his legs. He tried to take a step, failed and sank onto his haunches, wet tail and all.

There we left him, trembling and utterly forlorn, a picture of absolute hopelessness. His forelegs were spread far out to each side, his beautiful fur was plastered darkly to his thin, trembling body, his nose nearly touched the ice — everything about him hung downwards. Hours later, when we had reached the shore, Bakshu was still on the same ice pan. He would float out to sea on the next tide and land in Greenland, a frozen statue of despair — the dog who did not want to be an Eskimo Husky.

Near Pond Inlet thin ice floated loose in open water, and there was no way to cross it, either by sled or by boat. We moved slowly down the coast, and a mile east of the settlement we found an ice pan insecurely anchored a few yards from the rocky shore. We had been journeying for twelve hours, and there we rested, unable for the moment to do anything more. The Norwegian sea chantey had long been silent;

the komatik was a mass of splintered sticks covered with a cobweb of rotten ropes and strings; the drooped heads and woebegone faces of our wet little party looked like Bakshu.

We had not been there half a minute before little brown laughing Eskimos came out of the brown rocks. They came from all sides, leaping towards us, as if we had rubbed a lamp. They crawled out to our ice pan, using an abandoned komatik as a bridge, took off their mitts and shook hands formally all around, then went to work, chattering softly. In a few minutes they had us off the ice pan and on dry land. Several of them loaded our boxes and packs on their strong, efficient shoulders. Others dragged the broken komatik onto land, tied the boat to a stone, unfastened the dogs' traces. Still others cut up the seal and fed the exhausted dogs. Even Idlouk and Panilu resigned themselves to the care of these happy people. The tense hours melted away as we walked over the firm, friendly tundra to Pond Inlet, greeted everywhere by grinning, hand-shaking Eskimos. It looked as if the whole Tunnunermiut tribe had come to see us safely ashore.

It was two o'clock in the morning. Over the settlement the moon was rising. It was the first time we had seen the moon. What a strange vision! The sun hovered barely above the mountainous Bylot Island horizon, the sky was full of yellow clouds and the sea ice was pale gold and the open water was shining blue. The moon hung over the hill, a pale, washed-out gibbous moon, frayed at the edges, looking like a fugitive from another world.

When we came to the first houses we saw Pete and Doug walking casually together down the neat graveled path as if it were midmorning. They greeted us off-handedly. We might have parted only yesterday. At the HBC house were beef

266

stew and soft newly-baked bread. Pete had seen us coming
five hours earlier and popped the loaves into the oven so they
would be ready for us. Supper ended with the familiar fluffy
coffee. We felt as if we had come home.

I lay on the sofa in the HBC living room pretending to read
the poems of Robert Browning. It was one o'clock in the
morning of the next day. Three Eskimos sat in the kitchen
and there was a soft murmur of conversation, flowing like a
slow river. One of them started to play a mouth organ. He
played "Red River Valley" and I sang it as he played. The
three Eskimos found this pleasing and laughed gently. The
musician went on to Christmas carols. I did not feel like singing Christmas carols. Outside the slow ice glided past almost
imperceptibly in the mist and the low clouds drifted as slowly.
In the kitchen the mouth organ lapsed into silence in the
middle of a phrase. The three men left the house as silently as
the slow-flowing ice; I did not know they had gone.

I felt quiet and sleepy and sentimentally peaceful. The long,
long day was a blessing — the gray ice moving on the quiet
sea, the pale sun moving along the foggy edge of the mountains, the Eskimos drifting into and out of the house, with
their harmonicas and their singing, loving language, the white
men always kind, always casual, taking me for granted as if
I had been here forever. There was a lot of time here, for
poetry, for music, for slow-flowing hours with a little talk or
no talk. The day was as long as you wanted to make it.

Pete and Doug came in and immediately turned the radio
on. "This is your Milkman's Matinee," said a bright, familiar
voice. I started. Was WNEW really still functioning somewhere? "Now Patti Page with 'Cross Over the Bridge.'"

"Are they still playing that old thing? They were playing that when I left." Pete and Doug laughed at me.

"You only left five weeks ago," said Pete.

But there should have been some new songs invented in the lifetime since I had left New York.

I got up and fetched coffee. When I came back the radio was tuned very low. It was hot in the house and we sat silent and sleepy, listening to New York City.

"It feels strange to go Outside," said Pete suddenly. "I went out once, five years ago. The funniest thing was trees. They looked peculiar, sticking up there with no guy wires to hold them."

"And it's noisy," added Doug. "I couldn't get used to the noise and all the automobiles. The first time I got into an automobile I thought it was going seventy miles an hour. I hung on and closed my eyes. I guess the guy was doing about thirty."

"You walk along the street," said Pete, "and nobody even sees you. Not like here. If you have a toothache here everybody knows it even at Arctic Bay and Clyde River."

"I had a little limp once," said Doug, "and everybody asked me what was the matter, and it got on the radio sched and next day Bob at Arctic Bay said, 'How's your leg?' Out there you could be dead on the street and nobody would even stop."

"I went to a movie once, when I was Outside," said Pete. "It was called *My Friend Irma*. When I saw that all I wanted was to come back north again."

Pete talked off-handedly. His manner was detached and faintly amused at the strangeness of Outside. But there was an inner nervousness which he could not hide. Pete was going Outside in three weeks — possibly for good.

The young trader had come to the arctic when he was six-teen and just out of school. He had answered a Hudson's Bay Company advertisement on a dare, and after a physical exami-nation, an intelligence test and an interview he had been sent to the arctic with eight others — out of one hundred twenty-five applicants. Since that time, seven years ago, he had been Outside only once.

The adventurous boy had quickly made himself at home on the wide tundra barrens and the frozen sea. He learned to live as the Eskimos did and soon could stalk a seal and drive a dog team with the best of them. The natives were his friends and he tried to help them — while realizing that they must re-main proud and independent hunters. He had become an ex-cellent trader, not because he was sharp or businesslike, but be-cause the natives loved him and trusted him — and because he would not give credit unless the hunter hunted. Without seem-ing to be active or bustling, he had got Eskimos trading skins who had never brought in so much as an old *tiggak* before.

He learned some rudimentary doctoring and for difficult cases he arranged a radio schedule with the nearest doctor, at Pangnirtung six hundred miles away. Advised step by step over the radio, he had operated successfully on a woman with a breast abscess and a baby with a mastoid infection.

He encouraged sculpture and gave good prices for beauti-ful work. But he would not stand for the shoddy knickknacks, falsely labeled "primitive," that were turned out almost on a production line by natives anxious to make a quick dollar in some parts of the arctic.

For all his youth and his easy, relaxed manner, Pete had authority.

He had made a good life in the north. It was his only real

home and the Eskimos were his only real friends. During the vital years from sixteen to twenty-three they had been the most potent influence in his life. He was gay, as they were, and proud and warmhearted and generous — and he had a kind of purity from the long youthful years in this land of mankind's springtime.

But Pete was an intelligent, well-read man, a twentieth-century man. He did not want to spend his life on an HBC post trading skins but desired to go to college, to study anthropology, to write professionally. He felt there was an inseparable gulf between the two civilizations and he did not believe they could ever mix successfully. (This is a typical Canadian attitude — in Greenland Eskimo and Dane have mixed successfully for several centuries and a new race has grown, superior to both.) Somehow, Pete felt, he had to come back to his own kind.

The young trader, so naïve, so sure, so unwise in the ways of the world, had a terrible struggle ahead of him. How would that kind, eager face look six months from now, and how soon would he come back to the north?

(Pete went Outside shortly after we left. He studied anthropology desultorily at a university, and railed against professors who taught dry facts but had never seen an Eskimo or an Indian. He argued with ignorant government representatives about how to treat the Eskimos. He skipped classes and ran around night and day in an old car. For eight months he was disturbed, unhappy and restless. Now he is back in the north again, trading skins — and doing more for his gentle friends than all the government officials and professors from whom he had thought to learn.)

Doug was another young man whose life had been so profoundly influenced by years of living among Eskimos that he probably could no longer leave the north. Slow-moving, offhand and relaxed, this calm-faced person did not seem at all like a policeman. He liked the natives and was easy, joking and kind with them — though as a policeman he occasionally had to be strict. He liked the long February and March patrols by komatik over the ice-hard snow, with the sky a pale, cold glimmer above. His longest patrol was eleven hundred miles — about two months by dog sled.

"It does get kind of chilly," he said, "and sometimes it's boring. But there's a little light in the sky and traveling is quick. And the natives are always glad to see you."

At the end of his three-year stint in the arctic Doug had immediately signed up for three more years. His wish was to go even further north, to Ellsmere Island, where there were no natives. At one time people had lived there, but for an unknown reason they had deserted the island and now, untouched for many years, it was rich with game of all kinds. Doug wanted to settle some families there. He had interested Idlouk, and the hunter was now anxious to move to this land which teemed with caribou and musk ox.

"But what would *you* do there?"

"They have an RCMP station there," said Doug. "Every few years they send someone up for a year. The Greenland Eskimos used to nip over the ice in the winter — it's only a hundred miles — and help themselves to musk ox. This is a sort of spot check, to let them know they'd better stay where they belong.

"Anyway," he added as an afterthought, "there are too many people around Pond Inlet. I want to be in a lonelier place."

These two young men were probably typical of the Canadians now working in the arctic. A large percentage of them are unmarried, most of them are young, all of them go north with a predisposition to like, help and try to understand the Eskimos. They find here purity, kindness, and peace, and they do not want it to be spoiled.

But there is danger for them — the danger of sinking their personalities in an alien culture, the danger of loneliness far more potent than mere aloneness. It is a life of too-great peace, of fatally attractive isolation.

Still, men like this are good for the north. One can criticize that Canada has sent traders and policemen, who have brought with them a trail of disease, unhealthy food and customs unnatural to the Eskimos — and that the government has not sent doctors and teachers to repair the damage. One can say that the little that is being done to help the natives is disorganized and that various groups — missionaries, police, traders — are out of harmony with one another. One can say, with truth, that Canadians in general are indifferent to the fate of their Stone Age wards (as we Americans are indifferent to the remnants of our Indian population).

But in spite of mistakes and lack of interest nearly everyone who goes to the north has good will. They are there because they like the country and because they like the Eskimos the way they are. There is a real, though fumbling, attempt by the men of the north and the Canadian Government behind them to keep the natives in their ancestral way of life as far as possible and still give them some of the benefits of our civilization.

It is not easy. Although to us the Eskimos were a miracle, to the Canadian Government they are a problem. Canada needs her Eskimos. No one else can hold the north for her.

These highly specialized, finely adapted little people are her trappers, her miners, her guides, her rangers. They can live easily in a land where no white man can exist without help from Outside. Without them there would be no mining and no furs, and huge areas of the north would be closed and deserted.

But from the very fact of Canada's need for the Eskimos springs the danger of their destruction. There are only a little over eight thousand Eskimos in the fifteen hundred thousand square miles of the Northwest Territories and the Yukon, and they are members of one of the few remaining Stone Age races which have not succumbed entirely to the dreadful blandishments of our civilization. The Eskimo lives in a delicate balance with nature and the slightest alien touch can destroy this balance. Now all over the north Eskimos are becoming dangerously dependent on white civilization. They learned long ago that the fox and the weasel, despised creatures, represented wealth to the white man. Before the fur business hit the Eskimo he had lived easily on caribou, seal, bear and fish — these supplied every need. Now he must tend his trap lines for five months of the year. Therefore his hunting time is cut down considerably and he must buy supplies from the trader. When the bottom drops out of the fur market the Eskimo is destitute. He has no money to buy guns or ammunition and he has forgotten the use of the harpoon and the bow and arrow. He and his family are used to the luxuries the trader has brought them, and no longer know how to live without them. He needs a motor for his boat, canvas for his tent, wood and iron for his sled, clothing for his children, flour and sugar and tea and tobacco and chocolate. Family food vouchers, recently extended to the Eskimo population, have made the natives even more dependent on white men's food, and further discouraged hunting. In addition the Eskimo population, which was stable for a hundred years of record taking (and probably a thousand before that) is now sharply on the rise. And game, under the decimating influence of the repeating rifle, is decreasing.

A new danger to Eskimos are the mining camps and air force bases, which employ natives as menials. Living on wages, they quickly lose the ability and the incentive to hunt; with that their pride is destroyed and they become miserable, dirty and careless. As more areas are opened to mining and air force bases more Eskimos will inevitably be ruined.

To preserve these few remaining Stone Age people, so important not only for their two-thousand-year-old culture but for their usefulness, takes extraordinary knowledge and wisdom. Slowly — perhaps too slowly — the government is taking steps to keep this valuable population intact. No traffic is now allowed in the Northwest Territories except for the legitimate business of trading (strictly controlled) or for scientific research, weather stations, air force bases and mining — and for religious conversion. No hunting or trapping is allowed to white men except the very few residents. All visitors from Outside must bring their food with them and cannot buy from the Eskimos, as game is already dangerously scarce. Young men are being trained in Eskimo ways so that they can go north as government representatives and try to solve the problems of mixing Stone Age civilization with twentieth-century civilization.

At the same time the government discourages Eskimos from leaving the arctic. Not many of them want to leave. Away from their cold, free country they quickly become shiftless, diseased, helpless and desperately lonely. Idlouk, he told us, once lay awake all night worrying about the nightmare vision of people living on top of one another in close layers (apartment houses, we gathered).

Perhaps these measures will save the race. There are not yet enough white men in the north to alloy this remarkably pure civilization.

"What have we given the Eskimos," I asked Pete, "except bad teeth and tuberculosis and false morals?"

"We've given them rifles and outboard motors and canvas tents and primus stoves and writing," Pete answered.

"But they were perfectly happy without them," I said.

"We've brought them new blood," said Pete. "The part-white Eskimos are much more healthy, lively and ambitious than the pure ones." This was a strange statement to come from a young man who didn't believe in mixed marriages.

He continued. "The Eskimos haven't changed their ways in over a thousand years. They are an arrested race. Any race that does not progress is bound to go downhill. They're all inbred and too small and not very healthy and pretty shiftless. And they were that way long before there were any white men here."

"Are we any better?" I asked. "We're all too nervous and busy, and we fly off in all directions. But they're happy and at peace and full of laughter. I think they picked a fine moment to arrest their development."

"They're not that good," said Doug. "There was a little colony on Milne Inlet, near here. When I went there on a patrol I found the people were destitute. The hunting was no good around their camp, though they had men who were good hunters and trappers. The funny thing was, they lived between two camps, both of which were successful. The even funnier thing was that they would not move to a better place. That's where they'd always lived, they said. They are hide-bound, almost all of them. They do just what their grand-fathers did. We white men are only conveniences to them. The natives think we are nice, but they don't take our advice. Hardly any of them, for instance, will bother to preserve food even though I've shown them how. It would be easy to smoke it or freeze it. They won't even build sheds or dig pits to keep fresh meat in — just leave it lying around where the dogs can get it. No wonder they starve in bad years."

"And it's awfully hard to teach them even the most rudi-mentary personal hygiene," added Pete. "Have you noticed their teeth? As for medicine — I remember that once a little boy was brought to me with a nasty abscess on his cheek. I treated him for three days, then sent him back to his family. About a week later I visited that camp and asked to see the boy. When I went into the tent, which was kind of dark, I saw something horrible. The boy was lying on a skin in the back, and *fur* was growing out of the cheek. When I went to him I saw that it was the skin of a rotten lemming. 'The *anga-kok* [witch doctor] told me to,' said the mother. All the oint-ment and antiseptic I had given the boy lay unopened at the bottom of a food box."

These stories only proved that they were deeply dependent on their own traditions, as is any people that has had almost no contact with the rest of the world. Yet they might also indicate absence of ambition. The Eskimos had no govern-ment and were docile towards one another, living by a set of rules so old that they were no longer expressed but simply taken for granted. Although this was a happy state it also showed a certain lack of spirit.

I asked Doug about crime.

"Hardly any," he replied. "In the first place they're mostly honest and in the second place they don't get mad easily. Sometimes a hungry Eskimo will steal something. Once in a while you get a murder, but it isn't really a murder — not an angry murder, that is. Every year a member of the RCMP who is a justice of the peace comes on the boat. He hears cases and imposes sentences. Usually the sentence is less than a year. But they don't like to send an Eskimo to a prison Outside — it's expensive and useless and just about death to the native. So the criminal is sentenced to work for the police on the post during his prison term. That means that he fetches water once in a while and keeps coal in the house when he remembers to. He gets free board and lodging and all the tobacco he wants, provided we have any.

"About five years ago, before I came, there was a murder not far from here. An old woman was dying and she was in terrible pain. She asked her grandson to kill her, in accordance with ancient Eskimo custom. He said he couldn't because of the white man's laws. But she finally persuaded him, so he tied a noose around her neck and held her until she died. He wasn't secretive about it — it didn't seem anything wrong to him. A trader over that way heard the story and called in the police. The boy was tried by a solemn court of nine policemen and sentenced to five years — not because of the murder but because he knew the white man's laws and didn't obey them. He worked out his time helping around the post."

But though they seemed mild, he continued, they could

take subtle revenge if they disliked a man. There was a constable who was scornful and tough with the natives. On a patrol he and his two native guides were held up by a storm and ran out of food. "Go out and hunt," said the constable. They said, "We have food," and handed him some rotten seal meat. The natives could eat it, but no white man could get it past his nose. So he ordered them again to hunt, and again they said they didn't need to. When they brought him back he was half dead from starvation. But not quite dead. They respected the white man's laws when they dealt with a white man.

If these sophisticated and subtle people belong to a dying race they don't show it. In his own land, unhampered, the Eskimo still is king. Though he has been changed he is not yet a gauche, blurred copy of a white man. He can still live easily and happily in his hostile country, and we cannot. The Eskimo is entirely conscious of this. Proud and sure and sweet-natured, he delights in helping those he likes, guiding them, carrying their loads, cheering them up, tucking them in at night, trying to teach them to live the way he does. With equal sureness he takes revenge on those he does not like.

In perfect balance with nature, unafraid of death or misfortune, gay, quick-witted and courageous — it seems that the Eskimos are man at his best.

But there is something wrong with them — they are soft. Friendly and adaptable, they have no foresight, no real faith in their own way of life. Living only in the present, they do not see the dangers the white man brings. They see only his gifts, and adapt them to their own civilization. Gradually they are becoming acclimatized to the white man's world and out of touch with their own. Our civilization is inevitable — and inevitably dangerous to them.

One day, all of a sudden, there will be nothing left of the Eskimo. He is like a mummy which has been preserved for thousands of years. Unwrapped and exposed to air, he will crumble to dust.

The fire was out and there was no more coffee. I shivered. Looking out the window I saw Bakshu through the light fog, picking his way fearfully and painfully from one drifting ice pan to the next. Twenty-four hours ago we had left him, evidently on his way to Greenland. But the puppy retained a residue of hope and a dim spark of courage.

"Come on, good Bakshu," I encouraged him silently, thinking about Eskimos.

Cold and sleepy, I made a pretense of offering to sleep on the sofa. It was ignored. The bed situation was fluid — something like musical chairs. Being a lady, however, I always got one. The others took turns staying up. They would have stayed up anyway.

Before going to bed I went out to the unheated kitchen porch to get some water. A little boy was sleeping there on an old torn sofa, coughing and shivering as he slept. I called Pete.

"Shouldn't we send him home?"

"He hasn't got any home," said Pete. "His father is dead and his mother was sent Outside to the hospital. Nobody knows where she is or what is the matter with her. Sammy just sleeps wherever he happens to be." Pete got a quilted cover and tenderly laid it over the little boy.

"He's a fresh kid," he said. His manner was casual — Pete's manner was never anything but casual. But I knew that, in an off-hand way, he took care of Sammy as he took care of the few other destitute natives too young or too ill to hunt. He fed them from his private larder, gave them credit at the store, which he charged to his own account, and never asked to be paid back. He was not soft with a lazy man, but he was (as are the Eskimos themselves) unendingly generous with a helpless one.

If the white men in the north were all like Pete there would be no problem.

X V I I
The Nights Are Long and Bright

AGAIN all sense of time had evaporated. I slept until half past two in the afternoon. By the time "breakfast" was finished the radio schedule was on. I typed the messages and volunteered to deliver them on my way to visit Don Whitbread. Going to the mission house, a five-minute walk, was not, I found out, simply a matter of walking there. It was an hour and a half before I reached it. I stopped at the HBC storehouse, where the two government geologists had set up housekeeping in the loft, intending simply to deliver their message. But coffee was on and one of them wanted to show me a crinoidean fossil — a three-hundred-million-year-old sea lily (distant relative of starfish and sea urchins). The crinoidean was a few dim wavy lines on a stone. For what the information was worth, it dated the surface vein of coal where it had been found. No uranium, no oil, no gold had they discovered — but the fossil of a sea lily. That was as it should be.

Pete came in to see the crinoidean, and later I went with him to an Eskimo tent to be measured for a silverjar jacket. Then I delivered a message to the fathers. They treated me to a hot brown bun fresh out of the oven, with honey, and talked in their lively Gallic fashion about literature and politics. For all their supposed unworldliness the fathers were much more in tune with Outside than anyone else at Pond Inlet.

The next stop was a shed where Idlouk was trying to fix his outboard motor, a task which had occupied his every waking hour since we had arrived. Eskimos are amazingly mechanically minded and nimble-fingered. A native who has never before seen a motor can, I believe, take a plane engine apart and put it back together again and then fly the plane. He can study the inside of a watch in concentrated silence for twenty minutes without touching it, and he will know all there is to know about a watch (we had seen Panilu do this). Idlouk's trouble with his little motor was not lack of mechanical deftness but a breaking down of parts. Kept in an unheated warehouse over the long cold winter, it would not respond even to the most agile fingers. Idlouk was worried, irritated and voluble. Important parts of his motor were broken; he could not replace them and had to fix them somehow himself. He wanted to go fishing. He *had* to go fishing. Above all he had to get back to Bylot Island before the sound was completely impassable. There were about two weeks every summer when all travel on the sea was impossible, either by boat or by komatik. With every fog, every rain, every tide those two weeks came closer.

At the end of his tirade Idlouk shrugged his shoulders and made a face of comic despair. "We have to stay at Pond Inlet," he said and laughed. *"Iyonamut!"* (It can't be helped" — a favorite Eskimo expression.) I was not worried. Somehow, even if he had to manufacture wings from his outboard motor and his ruined komatik, Idlouk would get us back to Bylot Island before our plane came to take us away.

Finally I reached the mission house. I drank black tea with Don and two Eskimos, fishing out tea leaves and lumps of undigested powdered milk with a bent tin spoon. Then I went out to the cold church room and played Bach chorales on the broken organ. For an hour I was in another world, far from the north, far from anything earthly, a world of pure musical abstraction, as I followed the intricacies of Bach's subtle counterpoint. The chorales are to ordinary hymns what calculus is to the multiplication table — yet more. For Bach poured his soul into the dusty laws of counterpoint and transformed them into glowing miracles of religious emotion.

The empty, icy world of the north is the place to play Bach chorales. The less there is around you the more receptive you are. Bach could have written his chorales expressly for me that afternoon at Pond Inlet.

Suddenly time caught up with me. Eskimos were filing in silently for the eight o'clock service. Pete and Bren and probably half a dozen others were waiting for supper back at the HBC house. We were to go fishing that night. I ran back along the muddy beach, for once in a hurry.

Remembering Ben's tutelage ("How much chile do you put in?" "Enough — and you cook it until it is done"), I manufactured in twenty minutes a strange mushroom soup with some alien leftovers floating in it, an overpungent chicken curry, mashed potatoes and heavily candied carrots. My head was still full of music.

About half past ten Rick and I started out in the heavy rowboat with Panilu. (Idlouk was still patiently working on his motor.) The tide had taken most of the ice away from the immediate neighborhood of Pond Inlet, so boat travel was just a matter of dodging ice pans and backing out of dead ends. Pete followed us in his long, slim white kayak. He wore his elegant silverjar jacket and a jaunty red beret. Behind him were black mountains and a fiery sky with heavy clouds, blinding gold on their edges, threatening the brilliant low sun. His kayak was surrounded by large white floating ice pans, and the whole improbably romantic scene was reflected in dark glassy water. It looked like a tinted photograph — "Land of the Midnight Sun."

Pete gave me his kayak. One dip of the double paddle and I shot past the cumbersome rowboat, headed straight for an ice pan. A second dip and I was suddenly headed back the other way. A kayak is an embarrassingly responsive craft. The smallest extra thrust of the paddle will send it spinning in circles. Very long in front and back, sharp-pointed, narrow, light as a bird, it hardly seems to touch the water. It feels alive. One has to cultivate delicacy in dealing with it.

I did so, and soon the kayak and I were part of the enchanted sunset, our wake slow red ripples on the spotless surface of the sea. Far away dogs howled; there was an occasional shot and dim, distant Eskimo shouts. *Oogjoo* had been sighted just offshore of Pond Inlet. The coming of the huge bearded seal to the inlet meant that summer was here. They came close inshore to shallow water when the ice broke up, to take refuge from the vicious, wanton killer whale. There they were exposed to slightly less vicious man.

But the hunting excitement was somewhere else. Here was all blissful peace. As we neared the mouth of the Salmon River, where we would fish, the sky and land were enveloped in a light golden mist which soon turned to rain. Everything noisy was far away and softened in the foggy half twilight.

The land rose in gentle hills above a bubbling shallow little river; beyond its mouth was a sweet narrow arc of sandy beach. On the hills were mounds in which were the ruins of old Eskimo dwellings, silent and overgrown with grass and moss. The whale bones that had been walls were scattered, the doorways had fallen in. Sandpipers flew low over the ruins, crying. Nearby were two graves. One of them had a head-stone with the inscription JANES 1927. The rest was effaced. Janes had been a trader who went berserk and threatened to kill any Eskimos who did not bring him skins. To protect themselves they killed him first. An RCMP constable asked one of the post Eskimos to take him by komatik to the place where the crazy man had been buried. The native took the policeman on a long trip, way inland, straight to the grave.

"How did you know where it was?" asked the policeman.

"I buried him," answered the Eskimo. The policeman felt a little queer riding back over the lonely white tundra with a corpse and one of its murderers.

Now Janes and his killers and the policeman were only faint memories. Over everything was a feeling of death and peace, as if man had been here a long time ago and had gone, and the land had taken over again.

At the river mouth Panilu and Pete were trying to lay out a long gill net festooned with cork floaters. Ice pans kept getting in the way. Panilu jumped onto the biggest one and paddled away furiously with an oar. But others glided in from all sides. So they moved the net closer inshore and anchored it in very shallow water with a heavy stone at each end. As soon as it was in place it began to heave with fish and one floater after another bobbed up and down. Pete, Panilu and Rick, standing in the solid, heavy-bottomed rowboat, started pulling fish out.

No one at Pond Inlet fishes with a rod — these people catch fish for food, not for fun. But I was contemptuous of the gill net and watched from the kayak with a supercilious air, thinking of my beautiful glass rod. That was until I tried taking fish out of the net.

"Come on," called Pete as I paddled lazily in and out of ice pans in the misty rain. "See if you can take one from the kayak." I did. I caught hold of one angry and desperate fish by the gills. It must have weighed at least ten pounds and it flopped over a dozen times while I held it, each time entangling itself more inextricably. I tried to untangle it with the other hand without tearing the net, balancing carefully in my light craft meanwhile, to keep from tipping over into the icy water. Finally I got the fish undone and held it in the air triumphantly.

But then I didn't know what to do with it. There was no place to put it (the inside of a kayak is almost an airtight fit), no way to kill it, and I couldn't paddle with one hand. I simply had to sit there holding a furious, thrashing salmon, all solid muscle, in one aching hand. With the other hand I pushed my wavering boat off ice pans as it drifted around the little harbor. After the others had laughed for a little while Pete came and took the fish away from me.

"Now you can get in the big boat and do it comfortably," he said. But I didn't want to. I loved the light, graceful canvas kayak. And it was bad enough to take fish in a net — one should at least make it a little difficult. I wove back and forth over the net taking my fish the sporting way while the others, sensible and efficient, pulled them out from their solid craft. I didn't get many fish, but I had a wonderful time.

After a while, wet to the skin, I went ashore and started cleaning the fish. I had never cleaned a big fish before and Rick showed me how. I buried my hands in the dark slit through the fish's belly. They came out filled with guts and covered with blood and I looked at them with faint surprise. Then, suddenly objective, I saw myself sitting on a muddy beach in a rainstorm in the middle of the night cleaning out the inside of a fish — how did it happen that I was as happy as I'd ever been in my life?

Tea water was always bubbling on the primus stove and food was spread out under a big rock out of the rain. But we paid no attention. The tea grew cold in our cups and the pilot biscuits melted on the wet rocks where we left them as soon as we saw the corks bobbing up and down again. We could not keep away from the net and we fished with a kind of passion, sometimes from the boat, sometimes from the kayak. A growing pile of silver-blue fish, dripping with blood, lay on the beach where we threw them, not looking, impatient to get back to the net again.

How beautiful the fish were, and how they fought, and how strong they were! In one way net fishing surpasses rod fishing: the fish is right there in your hand, and you look him in the eye and know just what you are fighting with. The only trouble is that you always win.

Once Rick pulled up a sculpin. It was a small gray horned monster, big-headed, blunt-nosed and covered with ugly bristles from its tail to its eyes. It figured, Pete said, in one of the Eskimo legends, in which an innocent and remarkably undiscerning girl married one.

While we paddled around the net he told us the story. "There were four women who had a Greenland whale's head and the bones of an eagle and a rock and the bones of a sculpin. These they pretended were their husbands. The woman who had the rock began to turn to stone. She sang:

'O boat, way over there,
Come here, I will make you my husband,
For my legs are turning to stone.'

The one who had the sculpin's bones for a husband turned
into a sculpin and hid under a rock close to the shore. When
the tide went out the next day she was cooking over an open
fire. The woman who had the eagle bones for a husband
found that the bones had come to life and were whole again.
She said to it, 'Go over on the horizon and bring me those
sun-tinted clouds, as I like them.' So he went the following
morning, leaving the woman braiding deer sinew. This was
for her mother, who lived below the cliff on which the girl
lived with the eagle. When she had braided it long enough
to reach from the cliff to the shore she climbed down it to
her mother's camp. The eagle returned home, and finding her
gone he dropped the clouds he had brought, and broke them.
He then spread his wings and glided down to the camp. The
wind from his wings lifted the house. The girl's father said,
'You will be a good son-in-law if you glide down here slowly
and come very close.' The eagle did this, and the man took
up his bow and shot it, and it dropped down dead. The dogs
began to eat it and it was so large that they could climb inside."

That appeared to be the end. There must be gaps in the
memories of the Eskimo grandmothers who tell these stories.
Still, they are full of beautiful episodes, and if one could collect them from all the old women all over the arctic the vast
patchwork quilt would be completed — and one would have
a vision of creation as these direct, imaginative people saw it
long ago.

At half past three in the morning we were still pulling

salmon out of the net. Our fishing place lay under a heavy cloud, filled with rain. We could hardly make out the rock on the shore a few yards away. Once, as I came ashore and stepped from the kayak to an uneasily anchored ice pan, I was aware that I was wet to the bottoms of my feet and extremely cold. At almost the same moment Rick, who was examining the stomach contents of a fish, began to shiver and yawn.

We counted the fish. There were sixty-five, and we thought we were pretty good. But Father La Verge had told me that a few years ago they could take a thousand in a night with three or four nets. The arctic char, it seemed, was being fished out.

Pete and Panilu still dashed back and forth along the net. They apparently intended to stay there until every arctic char in Salmon River had made its pilgrimage. But Rick and I were in unspoken agreement — we had had enough. We called to Pete, who scarcely heard us, that we were leaving, and set out along the beach for the half-hour walk back to Pond Inlet.

The little settlement was for once sleeping and quiet. Even the dogs slept at the ends of their chains, some curled in a muddy heap, noses tucked in out of the rain, others stretched out, their big wolflike heads resting on their forepaws. A great white polar-bear skin hung on a back-yard clothesline, dripping with rain.

The only creatures awake at half past four in the morning were three little children seven or eight years old, playing on the beach. They were so intent that they did not look at us.

We were to have gone back to Bylot Island the next day,

but it was a day of inexorable rain. The ice had floated back and the water in front of the settlement was full of ugly ice debris, impassable either by boat or komatik. So I took a walk, did the round of visits and spent another hour at the organ, worshiping in my own way.

For dinner I fried a goose, which was the worst thing anyone has ever eaten. As it lay uncooked on the table, dark red and forbidding, I could see that it was going to be tough. So I fried each slice slowly for a long time, hoping that cooking would tenderize it. It did not. By suppertime it had the looks and consistency of *oogjoo* boot soles, and eating it, I felt like an Eskimo wife chewing her husband's shoes. Most of the population of Pond Inlet had heard about the goose or smelled it cooking and whites and natives crowded into the HBC kitchen, waiting for a handout. People chewed politely for several hours and we got rid of most of it. I maintained an embarrassed silence, hoping that everyone did not know that I was the cook.

After supper the peaceful hours wheeled by. "In summer the nights are long and bright," wrote the Greek explorer Pytheas in 300 B.C., of Thule. Here, in our own Thule, they never ended. Makpa came in at eleven for her nightly cup of tea and went out again, never glancing at the formidable pile of dishes in the sink. Probably she would be back around two in the morning to do the housework.

At midnight there was a small commotion in the kitchen. Oolayoo was there — a very old woman toward whom the others had deference. She had come at Pete's invitation, to tell me stories. Oolayoo had jet-black hair, as most Eskimos do, even the oldest. Gray hair on an Eskimo looks odd, as if dyed. Her wrinkled face was imperious and handsome, though she had only two visible teeth. (Eskimos' teeth, which used to be excellent on a straight diet of meat, have been ruined by the white man's starches and sugars.) She stood just within the living-room door, not looking at me, and murmured softly to Pete. She couldn't remember any stories, she told him. I went to her, shook hands and gave her a cigarette. She lit it, then immediately put it out and stuck it behind her ear. She had discovered that she remembered some stories and wanted to save my present for later.

Although she spoke in her native language I could follow most of the stories by her gestures and a few key words. Some Pete had told me and some I had read in his notebooks. Oolayoo's manner of telling was that of one who has told the stories hundreds of times. As with a mother who tells the same fairy tale to her children every evening the words had become embedded in her mind, and she repeated them with the unswerving faithfulness of a phonograph record. Her speaking had a growing hypnotic effect.

The first story she told was the only one I had heard which had anything approaching a moral.

"There was a man who entered the den of an *amagoot* [arctic wolf] and found only a female wolf. This wolf feared for the safety of the man, as there were many dens of the *ka-jait* [pack wolf] and hers was the only one of the arctic wolf. [Northern Baffin Island used to have two species of wolves, the *amagoot*, or solitary arctic wolf, and the *ka-jait*, a much smaller wolf which traveled in packs and was extremely ferocious and much feared by the natives.] She made the man hide under the sleeping skins and bade him take off his boots to dry. She hung the boots over the lamp. Before they had dried a *ka-jait* came in to talk, and when he had entered he said, 'There is the smell of man here. Where is there a man? Whose boots are those with tie strings?' The *amagoot* said, 'My husband wished for boots with drawstrings, so I made them for him.' This satisfied the *ka-jait*, so after a while he left. Later the husband of the *amagoot* came home and said, 'I smell man. Where is there a man?' His wife said, 'It is from this knife which I bought.' Her husband said, 'Put it away, or the others will start howling.' Later, when the *ka-jait* were asleep, the man came from hiding and the *amagoot* gave him a caribou skin she had hunted, in return for the knife. The man took the skin and returned home. When he came the rest of the men in the camp, seeing the caribou skin, wished to get some for themselves. The man told them of his adventure and they decided to go to the wolf and trade for skins. The man warned them, saying, 'There are many dens of the *ka-jait*. It was by luck only that I picked the one safe den of the *amagoot*.' One of the men said, 'He is trying to be the only one who has skins, and does not wish others to share his good fortune.' The men set off toward the dens in a large band. As they approached, a pack of wolves came toward them. They stopped and shouted, 'Buy our knives!' The wolves attacked the men and began to eat them. Two of the more agile men climbed onto a high rock out of reach of the wolves and shot at them with their bows and arrows. All the rest were devoured."

Oolayoo told story after story while we listened in wonder. The stories were spoken in a chanting monotone with the faintest suggestion of a rising inflection to indicate dramatic moments. These moments Oolayoo illustrated with stylized and simplified gestures like those of an Oriental dancer. She was almost stern in her telling, as if she were teaching. We

felt oddly transported as we listened to her and watched her
dignified, unexpressive face. We could smell the seal-oil lamps
of a thousand years ago, and see the silent, upturned faces of
Eskimo children long since dead, glowing in the dim ruddy
light.

When Oolayoo rose to leave, her lined, ancient, austere
face changed for an instant to sweetness as she smiled. But
she had not many smiles, this very old lady who had seen the
world when it was new. She nodded formally to us, spoke
a few low words to Pete and went away, leaving us all
feeling a little guilty, as if we were responsible for cowboy
songs and money and cotton print dresses and morning
prayers.

The house lapsed into quietness. Pete picked up a book,
Doug turned on the radio and closed his eyes, Bren disappeared into the office. I concentrated my every energy on
trying to roll a cigarette. The paper grew wet and torn and
the tobacco rolled into lumps with limp places between and
long tufts stuck out of both ends like untidy moustachios.
Pete watched me for ten minutes without a word. Then
he got up, laughing, and took it out of my hands.

"I'll never be any good in the north," I said. "I can't do
anything."

"You can open fruit-juice cans," said Pete.

Then he read a poem of Byron out loud, while the rain
beat on the roof and the ice on the sea disintegrated slowly.
The night was pale gray and full of fog. The earth revolves
more slowly near the pole. A man standing on the equator
whirls around at the rate of a thousand miles an hour. But
at Pond Inlet's latitude an ordinary bomber can keep up with

the sun. No wonder everything felt slower and easier here in the north. We were only going about two hundred miles an hour.

We heard the thump of feet and a concertina.

"There's a dance on," said Doug casually. "Want to go?" Suddenly we all jumped up, put on our jackets, pulled hoods over our heads and ran down to the HBC storehouse. There were only a few children dancing. The big room was empty of stores except for white fox and ermine skins hanging from the ceiling, gleaming softly. Makpa sat in a dark corner playing her fast, unmusical Irish jigs. One by one the older people drifted in and soon all Pond Inlet was there. Bren took my hand and pulled me into the circle. It didn't matter that I didn't know the dances. They consisted entirely of running in circles and swinging partners — English round and square dances learned from sailors off whaling ships a hundred years ago and by now reduced to their irreducible minimum. Pete started making the calls. Other men joined him, shouting lustily at each change, stamping their feet and leaping into the air. Round and round we went, girls one way, men the other. A little boy swung me — he came only to my waist. Next came a husky native who swung me off my feet and laughed as I lost my balance. And so around the circle and back to Bren, who swung better than any of them. He landed me on the floor in a heap. As I rubbed my bruised knee I reflected briefly that the only accident I could boast of in this difficult, rough northern world was bumping a knee on a dance floor. An Eskimo mother danced with a baby in her hood. He slept, his thumb in his mouth, while his mother whirled and thumped, and his head missed the wall by a hair each time she went around. Idlouk ran to the center and did a solo, kicking up his feet, mimicking and grimacing with great style. One after another the men took their turns in the center while the others laughed, clapped and shouted. The women seemed somewhat listless and they went through the motions of the dance with a minimum of effort, never smiling or shouting. Eskimo women in general lacked the spontaneous, uninhibited gaiety of the men — maybe from centuries of having too much to do.

The first dance lasted twenty minutes. The air grew thick, we were too hot, the shouting became wilder, the thumping heavier. Suddenly it ended. We all sat on the damp floor, breathed in the cool misty air, lit cigarettes. In a few minutes the concertina started again — this time Idlouk was playing it. Up again for another round. I could not see any difference between this dance and the first. More running, more swinging. We stayed about an hour and I think I must have run at least four miles. I limped back to the HBC house, drank quarts of water and fruit juice and lay on the sofa. Peace descended again. But the thumping and shouting went on all night, muffled in the fog.

We had a final visitor that night. At half past three in the morning an artist, Kiookjuk, came in carrying a piece of soapstone sculpture. Kiookjuk looked refined and melancholy; his forehead was wrinkled in a perpetual question. He handed the little statue to Pete. It was a carving of a man harpooning through an *agloo*. The figure was extraordinarily alive.

"Kiookjuk still uses a harpoon for most of his hunting," said Pete. "That's why he knows what it looks like. He only carves the things he knows.

"There is no real native art," he continued. "Once in a

while you find a natural artist like Kiookjuk. But before white men came none of them did anything like this. They used to carve designs on the ivory handles of their tools, and the women still show a sense of design in their embroidery. But so-called Eskimo art was invented by white men."

They had no native art, only the most rudimentary music, no literature except by word of mouth. Yet the Eskimos were not primitives. The world they had made for themselves was complicated, specialized and finely attuned. Among them were some of the most sophisticated people we had ever met. Kiookjuk's work of art was not the work of a cave man. It was delicately wrought and showed a truly intellectual sense of form.

Pete said something to Kiookjuk. The artist went into the kitchen and came back with another piece of sculpture. This was a mild, dignified, long-tusked walrus sitting on a mushroom-shaped pan of spring sea ice — just the sort of ice that we had crossed, painfully, on our way to Pond Inlet two days before. I gasped at Kiookjuk's instinctive, subtly formal artistry. The walrus sat just so: its arched, upright posture was perfectly in harmony with the shape of the ice. Yet it was absolutely real. At once I loved the smooth gray sculpture, the pompous, pathetic animal. Pete took it from Kiookjuk and handed it to me.

"I asked him to make it for you," he said, embarrassed.

They could not have given me a more beautiful present. I thanked them, and suddenly was full of tears. I turned away quickly, holding the north in my hands.

XVIII

"This Ice Is Good for Three
More Weeks"

THE next day we really did leave. It took us seven hours to
get around to it though.

Idlouk had told us to be ready at ten o'clock in the morning. But at three in the afternoon he still sat at the kitchen
table drinking tea. Outside there was a cold drizzle and clouds
were flying in, low and dark, from the ocean. I had been
ready to depart for five hours, and permitted myself the
luxury of impatience, though I took care not to show it. Politely I asked Idlouk when he thought we would be ready to
go. He smiled and made a graceful speech in his native language, which Pete translated. Idlouk had been ready to leave
since early that morning. He would have been happy to go,
in fact he wanted very much to get back to Bylot Island to
relieve the hunger of his family. But the weather was terrible
and he was afraid I would get wet.

"A woman," Pete translated, "is to be loved, and not to be
treated badly."

How could one be impatient with these people?

Somehow we managed to leave before supper. The rain had
stopped, but it was a forbidding afternoon of scudding black
clouds and a raw wind from the ocean. A flotilla of motor

boats set out from Pond Inlet to escort us home. As far as we could see Eclipse Sound was free of ice. We knew that there would still be ice in the center where the sound widened and the pull of the tide was feebler. But Idlouk was hopeful that one of the big leads would be open all the way through to our island. To be on the safe side, however, our fleet carried two komatiks and about thirty dogs. There might be much changing back and forth from boat to dog sled on this expedition over the uncertain sea ice of late spring.

Rick and I went in the big police motor launch, with Bren, who wanted a holiday. Several smaller boats contained Eskimos who were coming along for the ride. Idlouk's boat, its motor finally working, was among them, put-putting efficiently through the choppy waves. In addition to the sleds and dogs we carried supplies for Idlouk's family for the next few months, one live lemming, unhappy and shivering, and one dead, withered adolescent Lapland longspur. (The bird had been brought to Pete alive by an Eskimo girl but had died with a dreadful shudder about twenty minutes later. We were bringing the corpse home for Josselyn's collection.)

I watched Pond Inlet grow smaller as we slapped along in the rough breeze. It looked drab and insignificant — a row of plain little frame houses and a few tents straggling along a bare gray beach with a bare gray hill behind. The mountains were enormously threatening and the sea was an endless desert, and between them the settlement was a brave, small spirit.

I said a mental farewell: "Will I ever see you again, good, kind little town?"

It was even sadder to see the fishing place. I looked in vain as we passed it for the beauty I had found there before. The spot that had been enchanted in the golden twilight was now gray and flat and looked like any other part of the tundra. In the misty distance the lovely curve of white beach was flattened and dun-colored. No river showed, and no ruins. Only the big rock where we sheltered from the rain marked the spot. The whole night might have been a dream — the little river chattering over the rocks, the bird-haunted dwelling mounds, the fighting fish, the happy, careless people — all had vanished in the cold grayness of a later day.

Pond Inlet faded into the fog and I looked ahead at last. The sea was rough, but we bumped and splashed across it, not caring. There was no ice except an occasional small floating mushroom which the boat kicked lightly out of its path. We'll be home within three hours, Rick and I told each other. . . .

"Look there!" he said suddenly. Ahead was a thin line of white, and through binoculars we could see that the first boat, Idlouk's, had been unloaded and that dogs and luggage were spread all over solid ice. Our hearts sank — there was no lead. That meant that everything — dogs, sleds, luggage — would have to be taken off the boats. Our lighthearted escort flotilla would have to go back to Pond Inlet while we, heavy-laden, made our painful way by dog sled across the dangerous ice.

Through a narrow gap we entered a small harbor enclosed by high, jagged ice. Feverishly we unloaded the boats. The fierce wind was already closing the gap and in a few minutes the little fleet would be trapped. We barely had time for quick handshakes with Bren and the Eskimos. Two of the boats got away from the ice, but the third, the big police launch, was caught. Five hundred yards away we could see Bren and Panipookoochoo struggling against wind and ice. They pulled the boat onto a floating ice pan, shoved a miniature iceberg out of the way, heaved and tugged — and splashed safely into the water beyond. The sound of the motor died out and the boat disappeared in the murky distance toward Pond Inlet. We were left in the middle of the sea, feeling extraordinarily desolate.

Two komatiks were piled high. Idlouk's boat — the only one left to us in case we came to open water again — was on one of them, and Rick and I climbed disconsolately on top of the heap. The other komatik belonged to Kichualuk, Idlouk's son-in-law, a handsome, six-foot, blue-eyed Eskimo with a mustache. He had left Idlouk's camp a week earlier, taken his wife to her mother, Kidla, at our camp, and then had gone to Pond Inlet to trade skins, buy supplies and have a gossip. Little Panilu rode with Kichualuk this night. Giant and dwarf, they acted together with the trained perfection of circus performers.

With heavy hearts we started over the rough ice. We did not know what lay ahead of us, but we knew it would be long and desperately difficult. Even the dogs were depressed. Walking slowly, heads and tails down, they pulled their heavy loads without spirit. Bakshu, in harness again, hung back and trembled unceasingly.

We had not traveled for five minutes when a fearful sight met our eyes — drift ice, an endless river of it, moving out to sea. We could not see its opposite shore; it might be half a mile wide or five miles or fifteen miles. But to get to Bylot Island we had to cross it. We all got off the komatiks and simply stared. The Eskimos had no expression on their faces. For once they did not laugh.

"Let's swim," I said to Idlouk. He laughed then, and suddenly our hearts were high. We jumped onto the sleds and the dogs plunged into the icy water, one after another. The komatiks dipped in after them, sometimes reaching the next ice pan, sometimes burying their runners under its overhanging lip. The dogs floundered, slipped under the sleds, got tangled in their traces. A gap that was an easy span for Kichualuk's sled would be too wide by the time we got to it, and we would have to retrace our steps to find a nearer ice pan, or wait for one to come by on its way to the ocean. Fighting against the drift, we made little headway. After half an hour we looked back to the short stretch of solid ice where the boats had left us. It was not more than a hundred yards away and it seemed to be moving extraordinarily fast. But it was we who were moving — out to sea.

When I dared to leave the sled I leaped onto floating lumps of ice, took pictures and leaped back onto the komatik just before my ice islands sank. The camera would never be the same, I thought, but didn't care. Idlouk kept saying, "Only half a mile more." Sometimes he varied it with, "This ice is good for three more weeks." Rick kept saying, "Famous last words."

Rick had just said, "Famous last . . ." when our komatik lunged into a heavy pan and there was a frightening crunch of wood breaking. We were all knocked backwards and when I looked Rick had disappeared into the water off the end of the sled. He came up with his cigarette in his mouth, still alight.

"Wonder what the weather is in New York," he remarked.

We examined the sled fearfully. There was a deep crack in one sled runner and the iron underrunner swung loose, hanging on by only one screw at the front. But we could not stop. No ice pan would bear our weight for long, and even if it could have we dared not let ourselves drift further toward the ocean.

Gradually the ice pans were closer together and did not move so fast. Finally they did not move at all — we had crossed the terrible river. It had taken three hours. The dogs sank exhausted on a tiny ice island surrounded by open water. Our komatik lay on another little hilltop and in this icy, windy spot we had our first tea, huddled close together behind the boat on a caribou skin, our legs curled under us to keep them out of the water. We were not hungry, but we were cold, and the black, sweet, dirty tea was welcome. Panilu drank two cups of coffee and two cups of hot chocolate and then, for dessert, two cups of tea.

The old komatik had fallen to pieces. Idlouk, Kichualuk and Panilu fixed it without any carpentry tools. Idlouk pried pieces of board from a box with his bare hands. He fashioned new crosspieces from them, using his seal knife as a saw. Then he shot holes in the one solid runner with his thirty-thirty rifle, ran sealskin thongs through them and tied on the new crosspieces. Panilu pulled nails out of boxes using a caribou antler as a nail claw. Kichualuk made a support for the broken runner by piecing together box slats, and secured it to the runner with Panilu's rusty nails. The caribou antler was his hammer, but this tool was too light for him. He picked up his harpoon, held it high in his right hand — his blue eyes sparkling with laughter as he saw us watching him — and brought it down on the nails, one after the other, as if he were harpooning a seal. The end of the harpoon was hardly wider than a nailhead, but he did not miss.

In half an hour the splintered komatik was sturdy again.

An Eskimo can fix anything with anything — because he has to.

The komatik was loaded again and the dogs hitched. But we didn't start. Idlouk suddenly shouted, *"Killalooga!"* (narwhal). Five hundred yards away a grayish monster fifteen or twenty feet long heaved briefly out of a lead. Behind it was another and another — maybe a dozen of them — in a slow, pompous procession down the lead, the smooth dead-colored bodies (*nar* is ancient Scandinavian for "corpse") arching self-importantly out of the water like slow-motion porpoises. Sound was all around us, a strange, hissing, hollow blowing which filled the air and seemed to come from everywhere at once. Occasionally we could see a single twisted tusk projecting six or eight feet from an upper lip. (The purpose of the long pointed tusk, actually one of the animal's only two teeth, is not known, but the Eskimos think it is for fighting, as only the males have it, and its tip is always well worn. Narwhal tusks used to be sold in Europe as unicorn horns. Thin, carved and delicate, they have a decidedly fairy-tale appearance.)

The three Eskimos seized their guns and harpoons and raced off, Rick after them, splashing, falling, wading sometimes waist-deep. Four narwhals came up in front of them in one enlarged seal *agloo*. A shot sounded. The narwhals vanished, but Rick told me afterwards that one was killed. Before the Eskimos could get their harpoons into it to drag it out on the ice the body sank and was pulled away beneath the ice by a rapid undertow. Narwhals have to be shot almost point-blank so they can be harpooned immediately — otherwise they invariably sink. Usually they are hunted in open water from kayaks, the hunter using only a harpoon. The men watched and waited for an hour, but the ponderous parade had gone its way.

We had thought the drift ice was an ordeal. But the solid pressure ice, mountainous flotsam surrounded by wide moats of open water, was far worse. Most of the time we were off the sled; if we were on it we were hanging on desperately, bouncing and sliding. I cradled the camera and the soapstone walrus in my arms, shielding them from the frightful jouncing. In the bottom of the boat the lemming huddled in a corner of his cage, trembling miserably.

We would pull and push the sled to the top of a rough hill, where it paused, teetering sideways, then hurled downwards through space. Rick and I looked at each other, shuddered and crossed our fingers. Would it make the other side of the water? Or would there be the horrible, jolting crash as the runners buried themselves under the next undercut ice hill and the whole load slipped abruptly forward, straining and breaking the rotten crosspieces? Sometimes it made it — then we realized we had not been breathing. Usually it missed. We jumped off and tried to shift the loads back while Idlouk hacked at the ice with his seal knife to free the runners. Then we all tugged at the ruined, sagging sled, trying to get it up the next hill, while the dogs worked valorously. They were never whipped. On this trip the dogs were more heroic than we, and Idlouk knew it.

Every part of Idlouk's ancient komatik broke at one time or another, and we must have stopped ten times, taken all the loads off both sleds, turned them over, pulled nails and screws out of one and patched the other together again. Each time we stopped to fix something the men took off their boots, wrung several pints of water out of their heavy wool socks and put on dry ones. After a while there were no more dry ones and they rotated the wet ones. Young Panilu, observant and solicitous as his father, rubbed Rick's half-frozen feet to bring back the circulation.

The sky cleared and the sun came out, but the east wind blew hard and cold at our backs. The sun's rays were exactly level and the moon looked like a bright wisp of cloud directly above us. There was a thin golden mist at the base of the dark mountains, but Thule's peak rose dazzling white and deep black, gigantic above the fog. The ice was a wide sea of white waves, shadowed deeply on their southeast faces, brilliantly lit on their sunny sides.

It was beautiful, pure and dreadful — the earth as it was after it first hardened, and the cooling rains came, and there was no life but only snow and ice and water and black rocks. We did not belong here at all. But we *were* here, and we were very brave and full of spirit and laughter. There has never been anything as beautiful as this new earth, I kept thinking.

After a while I grew tired of feeling like the first person. As the earth turned and the sun moved along the ridge of mountains and slowly raised itself above them in the east I thought of lots of things, all very small. I painstakingly added up the number of hours I had spent on a komatik. At that time it came to about ninety. (By the time we were home it had reached an even hundred.) I wondered what we would have done with a dead narwhal and invented ways of turning it into a temporary komatik. I thought up a menu for the Annual Frost — soup of chile sauce, Worcestershire sauce, curry powder; raw fish; raw seal liver; one pilot biscuit for dessert. I thought of my bed — not my bed at home with inner springs but my warm, close, dark sleeping bag. I thought of it with almost unbearable longing. I went over the Eskimo words to "Oh! Susanna" until I could say them like a phonograph record. I started to compose a poem to Bakshu, the Worst Dog in the Northwest Territories. I thought about oatmeal, pictured it bubbling, slipping from the big spoon into the big porridge bowl, sliding down my throat. Usually I despise oatmeal. I thought of a story Pete had told about Jim Ford and two Eskimos. They were out in a big umiak with a motor. The motor died and they could not fix it. The ocean was rough, and the wind and current drove them toward an island with a cliff coming down to the sea. They knew there was no landing place along this part of the island, nothing but jagged rock — and that the waves would dash them to certain death. As they neared the deadly rocks Jim became more and more terrified.

"Can't we do anything?" he pleaded. "We're going to be killed." Jim was a tough man, but at the hour of death his toughness melted.

One Eskimo stood in the bow of the boat smoking a cigarette and watching the cliff impassively. "Don't you know you're going to die?" shouted Jim.

The Eskimo turned and smiled at him. "Of course I'm going to die," he said. "It's all right. My wife has family to take care of the children. And she is young; she will marry again. I have nothing to worry about." The other Eskimo, meanwhile, slept in the bottom of the boat.

As they entered the shadow of the cliff a miraculous crosscurrent kept them fifteen feet off the rocks, and they drifted all day until they reached the end of the cliffs and found a harbor.

I decided to stop thinking about that story.

At our sled-fixing stops we ate raw fish from our store of one hundred fifty arctic char. We sliced it away from the bones with our knives, peeled the skin off and ate it with our fingers. It was soft and chewy and had no taste at all. Once, as we rested for a few minutes on a caribou skin, Rick said, yawning, "Who would have thought, when we first met at the Bronx Zoo on that warm, sunny May day, that we would ever find ourselves sitting on a caribou skin on an ice pan at four o'clock in the morning?"

"In July," I added, chewing slowly on a piece of raw fish.

The Eskimos were never discouraged. They looked at the ruins of the sleds and laughed, and set to with their makeshift tools and their bent nails. After a while the wood was so rotten that they pushed nails in with their hands. They played leapfrog and wrestled on the ice and drank vast quantities of tea.

I was not discouraged either, but I was never any good at leapfrog. I walked and walked, jumping from one ice pan to another, trying to get the numbness out of my soaking feet. They prickled as the circulation began to come back, and I felt like the little mermaid with new feet, who thought she was walking on knives.

We came to an open lead, a narrow, twisting black ribbon of water heading uncertainly toward Bylot Island. Suddenly we were wakeful and excited again. We all unloaded Idlouk's komatik — for the last time, thank God, I thought — and pushed the boat into the water. The supplies and Rick and Idlouk and I were piled into it and the motor, after several discouraged sputters, started. Kichualuk, having no boat, put the broken komatik on top of his, which was not in much better condition, hitched Idlouk's dogs behind his own team and sailed away at great speed over the hummocks. The big man sat straight and still behind his big team, Panilu a small hump behind him. With an invisible twist of the wrist the great whip shot out and flicked a dog. Kichualuk looked aloof and godlike, an arctic giant who had all things under his control.

At last we were really sitting — no more bumps and jolts! I settled comfortably on a bag of flour, Rick poled with an oar and Idlouk tried with another oar to keep his motor away from the inward-shelving sides of the narrow lead. Ahead of us the lead closed. We got out and pulled the heavy boat over a short portage. In the water again the ice slanted shallowly toward the middle of the lead and the motor grated on it. Idlouk had to let the motor die, and we pushed ourselves along with hands and oars. Then the ice closed in again. We dragged the boat out. But it was about a hundred feet, mostly uphill, to the next open water, and the three of us could not move the boat another inch. Kichualuk and the komatiks were far away and we were stranded on a frozen desert.

"We're only half a mile from home," said Rick.

"We're going to die here," I said.

But Kichualuk was not so aloof as he looked. He turned his enormous team and galloped over the ice to us, the double sled weaving and bouncing like a small ship in heavy seas. He jumped lightly off the sled, pulled the great boat up over the ice as if it had been a ten-pound bag of sugar and slid it carefully into the water without a splash.

We looked ahead: the lead was narrow and ice bridges broke its course every few yards. But the boat journey had to be continued. There would be open water all along the Bylot Island shore. Besides, our loads were too heavy for one sled, and there was no further possibility of fixing the other one, a crooked, splintered mass of wood hanging over Kichualuk's sled like a dead body, sagging hopelessly at each end.

Eskimos never took long to come to decisions. Idlouk and his son-in-law conferred for half a minute. Everything, they then indicated, should be taken out of the boat. Idlouk and Rick would make their way somehow in the lightened craft and I would ride with Kichualuk. I followed the giant docilely, not a glimmer of will remaining. I would have followed him down a seal hole. But I came to a crack about four feet wide, stood still and simply looked at it, not speaking. Tears started out of my eyes and rolled silently over my face. Kichualuk turned around and came back, smiling and kind. He picked me up with one hand, lifted me over the crack and set me down as carefully as if I had been made of glass. He led me to the komatik and put a bearskin over my knees. As we sped over the ice he looked back frequently with his good, encouraging smile, his blue eyes full of warmth. The hard, aching core of weariness melted away like snow under the spring sun.

A wide lake of open water stretched several miles along the beach, where the Aktineq River had pushed into the sea, disintegrating the ice with its heavy current. Our camp was on the other side of the lake, and there was no place for a dog sled to cross.

Once again we unloaded everything. Rick and Idlouk

reached us, half poling, half dragging the boat. It was pushed into the lake and loaded again. I would be heaving sacks of flour around in my sleep for weeks, while boats changed to sleds and sleds to boats with exhausting rapidity.

Now the komatiks were temporarily abandoned. The Eskimos would later salvage the split wood and the rusted iron runners, which cost eighteen dollars a pair when new.

But we could not get away from the ice. The wind was almost of gale force and we were driven again and again into the rotten ice at the edge of the water. We paddled and poled furiously. After half an hour the boat was fifteen feet clear of the ledge. Then the motor wouldn't start! We drifted back and bumped into the ice again. That ice seemed almost human. It wanted to keep us.

The motor started. In ten minutes we were on the other side and Axel was helping us onto dry land.

It was twelve o'clock noon. We had been traveling nineteen hours and during all that time we had had no rest. We sat in the cook tent, talking and talking. Full sentences wouldn't come out, and we couldn't remember words. I had never known what it was to be tired before.

But the tiredness was nothing; a strange exaltation possessed us. We had done more than we *could* do, and the triumph of spirit was a light, pure and exciting as the cold fire of the nighttime arctic sun.

X I X
The End of Spring

SUMMER is a time of storms on Bylot Island, and all through
our last days the rain fell and the wind blew as the new season made its wild entrance. The tents flapped drearily. Rain
dripped through in a dozen places and streamed down the
walls inside. Water collected on the floor in dirty puddles.
Everything in the cook tent had been moved to the center,
and the foot lockers and crates we used as seats were piled so
high that there was no place to sit. Two people had to bail
constantly and basins were filled again with black water as
soon as they could be emptied. We were oppressed by the
entire wetness of everything, inside and out.

But the Eskimo family came to visit us in our soggy green-
ish darkness, always sympathetic and merry. Idlouk's family
had run out of food while its men were away and for two
days had had nothing to eat but tea and sugar. They had said
nothing of this, nor did they ask Mary for food, but were
prepared to wait stoically for the return of their hunters. By
chance Axel discovered their plight and brought them supplies. Kidla accepted with proud graciousness and the children, laughing, fell on the food like tigers.

Neither hunger nor discomfort appeared to distress them,
and we took heart from their philosophical calmness.

On the first evening came the newcomer Rebecca, Idlouk's

oldest daughter and wife of the blue-eyed giant Kichualuk. Rebecca hardly ever smiled, and her face was carven, like that of an Egyptian statue, with a look of eternal sadness. She had an ancient, dark beauty, the kind of beauty that graced an elaborate throne on the Nile three thousand years before Christ. She spoke not at all although she knew English perfectly; she had spent a year in England as nursemaid to a missionary's child. In spite of her association with missionaries Rebecca was the only woman we had seen who did not wear the usual tacky print dress. On her legs were the traditional silverjar trousers, full-cut and extremely elegant. She carried a caribou-bonneted baby in her hood, about six months old. Kidla's grandchild was older than Kidla's youngest daughter. Rebecca's husband sat beside her, dignified and shy. He had not the easy laughter of the others and they seldom played jokes on him. But his ready smile had extraordinary sweetness and warmth. He neither spoke nor understood English. But he shouldn't — it became him better to know only his own language. Kichualuk was a true Eskimo. His size, his shining health and his phenomenal strength, derived from white ancestors, did not make him different — they only made him better.

Conversation was halting until Idlouk, as was his wont when he saw that his charges were depressed, started doing tricks. He tried to juggle two stones while chanting an Eskimo nonsense rhyme, got completely mixed up, dropped the stones and let out a peal of laughter. He threw the stones to Kichualuk, and the tall man sat on the wet floor straight as steel, his blue eyes intent with concentration, juggling with one hand while he chanted rhythmically. Then he entertained us with some difficult feats of muscular control. We tried to emulate him and collapsed one by one, helpless with laughter. The tent began to look like a Martha Graham dancing class. The kamiks Kidla had made me were as pliable and close-fitting as ballet slippers and I found I could stand on the very tips of my toes and do a pirouette. I was childishly delighted to be able to amaze Kichualuk and even more so to hear him laugh when he tried the same thing. It was a happy evening.

But it was not a happy night. The rain continued and we slept under a waterfall. And what a misery to wake up to more wind and more rain! We lived in squalor all day, wringing things out and mopping things up. When not doing that we simply existed, and thought dimly and hopelessly, like lifetime prisoners, of the sun that must still be somewhere in the world.

During the day the lemming died. Rick had kept him in the only dry corner of his little tent along with a collection of dead spiders and beetles. The little rodent, our only live captive, had been treated like lemming royalty. He had moss and earth to burrow in and new green shoots and juicy roots to nibble on, and oatmeal for dessert. But he died. Nervous and delicate, lacking the mental resilience of humans, he had probably never gotten over the horrors of his delirious nineteen-hour journey across the ice. An autopsy showed no known cause of death. Josselyn made up the skin and then we had a beautiful, sad facsimile of a lemming. It was the last lemming we saw.

Late in the afternoon we tramped over the soggy tundra to a marshy lagoon. Two red-throated loons had created a large sloppy nest on its edge some weeks earlier. They were the wariest of all the arctic birds. No one could come within a quarter of a mile of the nest, and that part of our territory had been made taboo so they wouldn't be frightened away before the female could start laying. Now she had finally produced her clutch of two eggs, and Josselyn and Bill had set up a tiny tent as a blind about two hundred feet from the nest. The loons resented this strongly and it took them three days to get used to it. In order to watch them two people had to walk together to the blind. Then one went away while the other stayed hidden. The loons saw a monster approach, then they saw it go away again. Loons apparently cannot count.

Axel went into the blind first and took photographs. Then he hoisted a little flag which meant it was my turn. The blind was like a medieval torture chamber — you couldn't sit up and you couldn't lie down. I curved myself uncomfortably inside, kneeling in a bog, and peered through a three-inch slit. Quite close the loon glided effortlessly through the water toward her (or his — the parents are interchangeable while brooding, and resemble each other closely) muddy mound of a nest at the edge of the lagoon. Her body lay low in the water and her high-held head turned constantly from side to side. She circled warily a few times, then climbed awkwardly on the nest, looking top-heavy and off-balance. Loons are remarkable swimmers, divers and fliers, but they are not much good on land. Their legs are set way back toward the tail — the right place for swimming but wrong for walking. She arched her snakelike neck and turned the two eggs with her beak, to change the position of the embryos inside. (All birds do this — the embryo always floats to the top of the egg, and frequent turning prevents it from sticking.) She settled on them, sitting high and proud with her beak in the air.

314

Then she apparently saw someone approaching. Slowly she sank down, stretching her head and neck along the edge of the nest until she was nearly invisible, her brown back melting into the brown mud of the nest. When the intruder came close she gave a single flap of her wings and slid easily into the water without using her feet. She glided toward the blind with her beak headed skyward, looking like a dowager at a servants' ball. After a few seconds she took off, flying straight, fast and low out over the sea, uttering her strange hollow *"Quawk!"*

We left the blind and walked back through the rain and clouds to the old-squaw nest. One of the seven eggs was messily cracked and looked as if someone had sat on it. But when we bent close we saw that the squashed part was heaving as the wet baby inside struggled to free itself. We raced back to tell Josselyn that a duckling was hatching. But there was no hurry. The baby didn't manage to get itself out of its egg until about fifteen hours later. We saw it the next day, still wet, with eggshell clinging to its back, burying its ridiculously big black beak in the soft warm feathers of its nest against the rain and the biting wind. No doubt, if it could think, it was wishing itself back inside its cozy egg. It had no special markings but was just wet-colored, with some indefinite pale mottling around the face. Its brothers and sisters had not yet started on the long hard journey.

All over the soaked tundra were young longspurs, by now out of their nests and full of beans. We cornered and caught one, and brought it proudly back to Josselyn. But people had been bringing him baby longspurs for days now and he didn't want any more. "Put it back where it came from," he said. They were not much good at feeding themselves and would probably die away from their parents. But putting it back where it belonged was a problem, as one side of a tundra hill looked confusingly like another side of another hill. We wandered for an hour, trying to find the parents of our stolen baby. Finally we put it down near any old parents, hoping it would be adopted. We felt guilty — but it was fun catching them.

The following day the two loon eggs hatched and Josselyn took one of the babies for his collection. It was about the size of a duckling, dark gray from head to stubby tail, and the softest handful I have ever held. When Josselyn took the nestling the other baby crawled off the nest *inland*, toward the place where it knew instinctively lay safety — the tall reeds and the dark mud beneath them, baby-loon-colored. The little thing could not use its feet and had hobbled painfully on its stumps of wings while its parents circled nervously in the lagoon, scolding and advising. Baby loons can swim, but the first few days they are unsure in the water and need help. Sometimes one sees a mother loon carrying her nestlings on her back — but this one had not had time to get aboard.

While we were hovering over the captive baby loon Panilu shouted from the beach. "*Killalooga!*" We all raced down to the water's edge, and Idlouk launched his light kayak. His harpoon lay on the boat, its long sealskin thong attached to a whole sealskin blown up like a balloon. Two of the great mammals were arching out of the water just beyond the river mouth, playing heavily. They moved away from Idlouk but not fast. He kept his kayak close to the ice line, trying to prevent the narwhals from going out to sea and hoping to drive them in to shallow water where he could catch up with one and spear it. Usually two hunters take part in the chase, one driving the animal inshore, the other cutting off its escape. The nearest hunter drives his harpoon into the narwhal several times, until it is dead. If it gets away with the spear in it the attached sealskin bladder shows the hunter where it is and he will follow it until it tires. The hunters use the swift, quiet kayak in preference to a motorboat, as the animals confuse motor vibrations with the approach of killer whales and take shelter deep in the sea.

But even a ponderous narwhal can go faster than a single kayak. These two creatures evidently sensed danger. They splashed and cavorted, but they kept well out of Idlouk's way. The rain drove horizontally over the wild gray water and the wet gray beach, and Idlouk's kayak danced along the ice rim while the whales thumbed their noses at him. After an hour they went home.

Later that day the one remaining loon nestling died and Josselyn took the opportunity to collect the mother loon. The final loon, bereft, went scolding over the lagoons and inland ponds for hours afterward.

The day of the baby loons and the *killalooga* was our last on Bylot Island. The next day a plane would come to take us away. None of us could bring ourselves to pack. How could we leave now? Summer was just beginning, the time of open water and the hunting of narwhals and bearded seals in the inland waters and walruses and white whales along the wild ocean coast. And beyond summer, when the slow twilight came on and the icebergs sailed in from the ocean and the inlet froze over thinly — and beyond that, when Bylot Island was closed, silent, deeply frozen and ravens and snowy owls hunted for lemmings over the pale snow and the Eskimos followed their trap lines under the winter stars — all this was still a mystery to us. We had only seen the beginning.

The next morning we still had not packed. Axel and I went to the Eskimo tent to enjoy once more their gay hospitality. In front of it Kingmiachuck, the mother dog, was fiercely on guard. Kichualuk's dogs, unstaked, roamed hungrily over the campgrounds looking for scraps, and the new pups were considered particularly delectable scraps. The mother dog trusted no one and she lunged at us, snarling. We could not pass her. A small Eskimo child ran up, gave the dog a heartless kick and entered the tent. We went in on his coattails, somewhat embarrassed.

In one corner sat Idlouk, absorbed in his outboard motor, which lay in parts all around him. It had fallen into the water and he had to fix it all over again. Kidla was finishing a white fur-rimmed parka which we were to take back to Rosario in Boston. Eskimos in the far north use dog fur around their faces to repel moisture. Idlouk pointed to the yellowish fur on the new hood.

"Bakshu," he said seriously.

"No! Not the puppy."

"Bakshu," he said again, with a faint smile. I was too near to tears. Even Bakshu could set them off. But I looked outside and it was all right — the Worst Dog in the Northwest Territories was still alive. Idlouk laughed immoderately.

In the middle of laughter one of the boys shouted outside. We all ran out. There was a distant hum, the sound of doom. We scattered to our tents to stuff things into duffel bags. Then we sat down for the eternal waiting that was inex-

THE END OF SPRING

tricably associated with any operation in the north. The pilot had been looking for us, we guessed, and had not been able to find us in the fog. Anxiously we scanned the misty sky and laid out yellow tarps on the edge of the ice to mark the landing place. Our plane, a Catalina Flying Boat of the Mont Laurier line, was amphibious. At the mouth of the Aktineq it would have to land on open water as the remaining sea ice was rotten and the tundra too rough.

The camp looked like a deserted village after our hasty packing, the tents emptied and flapping open in the bitter wind. Mary and I puttered aimlessly about the kitchen tent, putting away a spoon here, a frying pan there. Suddenly we heard Bill's voice: "Air raid!"

There indeed was our plane, bright silver and red against the heavy sky, circling and swooping again and again. We shouted and waved; it almost touched our tents with its wings. The sight of the plane was extraordinary. All of a sudden the tundra looked brown and barren and lost. The plane seemed to be man landing for the first time on the moon.

Then it was gone into the mist, toward Pond Inlet. As we feverishly threw last things into boxes we told each other that it would probably be another five hours before the plane came back to us. The pilot was by now sitting in Pete's kitchen having three dozen cups of tea.

But an hour later it was back again. That must be a tough pilot. How had he avoided those three dozen cups of tea? The plane landed easily on the water. Four of Idlouk's children watched it land, standing at the edge of the beach. They looked awfully little.

The plane performed some aimless-looking gymnastics, evidently trying (and failing) to get up on land. Then it anchored. In the small piece of open water it looked as flimsy and impotent as a baby carriage. Behind it was the great white ice sea, before it were the frowning, tremendous arctic mountains, above it wild black clouds. We were frightened at the toy that was going to take us out of this very big icy world.

Rick and Idlouk went to it in the outboard, bucking a fierce wind. They brought the crew back with them. These were nervous men, in a hurry. We must leave that instant, the fog was closing in, the weather was bad, the water was full of ice pans, everything about the north was unpleasant and dangerous. But we couldn't. We were too much in the habit of not being in a hurry and we went right on getting supper. Airily we dismissed the dangers — somehow it would work out and if not, then Idlouk would fix it.

But in the middle of supper the airmen suddenly rushed to their plane. Two huge, slow, inexorable ice pans were closing in on it. The pilot couldn't get his motor started. There were a horrifying few minutes, then miraculously it caught and the plane grated its way out of the trap, losing its anchor. (But it had another.)

We were not carefree any longer. The tents were struck in a hurry and the men carried immense loads on their backs in a steady stream from camp to shore. Idlouk ferried back and forth between the beach and the plane, his little boat piled high, icy water splashing over the sides.

The Eskimo family came down to the shore in the driving rain to see us off. Kidla had dressed herself in her beautiful winter costume of caribou, vivid brown and white, the skins fitted together in an artful pattern. She had the stump of a cigarette in her hand and her vivacious face was full of smiles.

The baby Susanna peeped forth from the large brown hood, her face incongruously small and white. We shook hands and said good-by as if we were coming back next week.

I sat in the wet boat, not looking back. Before me was our iceberg. It was pretty sick. A big piece had fallen out of the middle (perhaps that was the place Ned had cracked with his ice ax), leaving a dirty brown hole. The jagged, fortresslike part was almost level with the sea ice and the proud, soaring peak sagged tiredly to one side like the hump of an old camel. But it would not give up — it was just going to melt away ignominiously and let itself die in bed like an old woman.

Axel and Josselyn and I were the first aboard. I sat resolutely in a dark corner, away from the window, trying not to think or see. But it was unnecessary to be so stoical. We were still under the spell of the north — we didn't get away for sixteen hours. Al Allard, the pilot, came aboard and announced that the fog was too dense over the dangerous mountain barrier of northern Baffin Island. He had to fly by sight alone and he didn't know the country and he wasn't going anywhere that night.

We three spent the night in the plane with the crew, while the others stayed onshore in the one tent left standing. Axel and I settled ourselves in a tiny space on the metal floor of the plane and Josselyn sat in a chair. He sat there all night. Around midnight Axel asked him if he didn't want to come and curl up with us on the nice flat floor.

"I want to sit in a chair," said Josselyn. "I haven't sat in a chair for six weeks and I want to sit in one for a long, long time."

The three airmen took two-hour watches, worrying about

ice pans. The rough water slapped against the thin metal hull of the plane and it sounded as if someone were throwing rocks at us. It was such an entirely uncomfortable night that we almost forgot to be unhappy.

We breakfasted early on sardines and raisins. About noon the others drifted out of the tent onshore and for half an hour they said good-by to the Eskimos. Finally all were on board, and Idlouk and Panilu were pushing off in their outboard for the last time. Idlouk had his best parka on, with his Coronation medal pinned on his breast. He stood at the back of the boat while I stood in the open doorway of the plane's belly, and we took pictures of each other. Then the boat drifted away. My last view was of Idlouk trying to start his motor while Panilu rowed desperately against the wind. The boy was singing, and over the roaring of the gale and the splashing of the water I could hear shreds of the Norwegian sea chantey.

In a moment Idlouk's white tent was a tiny, inconspicuous dot on the big tundra. Our beautiful island was spread beneath us. The great Aktineq River tumbled through a narrow gorge at its source in the forbidding, deep-seamed gray expanse of the glacier, and widened majestically between its low banks as it approached the huge white sea. Thule and Castle Gables thrust their black rocks in the air toward us. The tundra was all one color and would look like a desert to any eyes but ours. . . .

I can feel it under my feet, bouncy and full of life. Wherever I walk birds spring up in front of me, fly high in the air and glide slowly to earth, singing with heartbreaking sweetness. There are clusters of flowers, yellow and white and purple, and many-colored mosses and new green grass, and patches of snow and old ice twisted and tortured and full of holes, and bees flying into and out of lemming holes. And the low sun deepens the colors of the alive tundra, red, brown, gold and green. The chill, thin air feels like very early morning in very early spring. It is an enchanted island.

In a few minutes the fog enclosed it. A word had been said, a hand moved, and our island was gone.

Index

Index

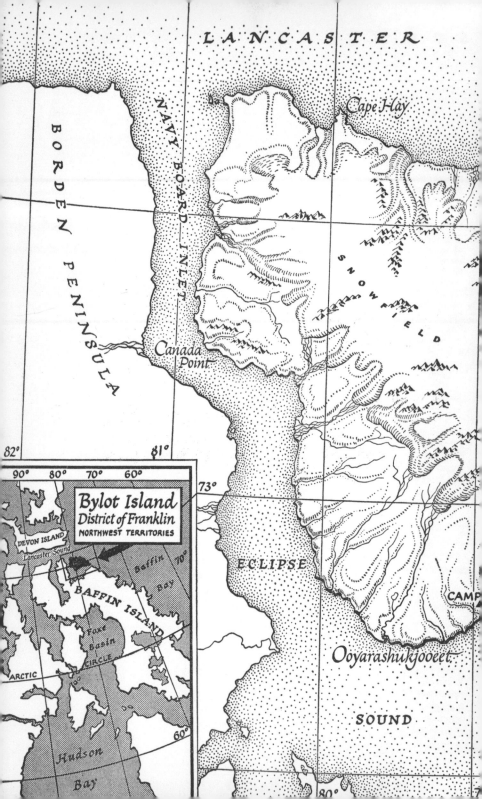

LANCASTER

Cape Hay

NAVY BOARD INLET

BORDEN PENINSULA

SNOW FIELD

Canada
Point

82° 81°

90° 80° 70° 60°

Bylot Island
District of Franklin
NORTHWEST TERRITORIES

DEVON ISLAND
Lancaster Sound

73°

Baffin
Bay

70°

ECLIPSE

BAFFIN ISLAND

CAMP

Foxe
Basin
CIRCLE

ARCTIC

60°

Ooyarashukjooeet

Hudson
Bay

SOUND

80°

SOUND

Bylot Island

BAFFIN

BAY

73

SNOWFIELD

Mt.
Thule

Sermilik Glacier

The
Castle
Gables

Button Point

Jlookishak

POND INLET

Pond Inlet

BAFFIN

Salmon

River

ISLAND

78°

77°

76°

Sam'l H.Bryan